MARTIN BUBER

Also by Aubrey Hodes

DIALOGUE WITH ISHMAEL

MARTIN
BUBER

An Intimate Portrait

AUBREY HODES

THE VIKING PRESS

New York

Acknowledgment is gratefully made to the following for permission to quote from the sources indicated:

Davar Ltd.: From an article by Samuel Hugo Bergman, December 19, 1961.

Ha'Aretz: From "Notes on Martin Buber" by Baruch Kurzweil, June 18, 1965. From September 17, 1965 issue (Yehoshua Brand).

Harper & Row, Publishers, Inc.: From Pointing the Way by Martin Buber. Copyright © 1957 by Harper & Row, Publishers, Inc. From Eclipse of God by Martin Buber (Harper & Row, Publishers, Inc., 1952). From The Knowledge of Man by Martin Buber (Harper & Row, Publishers, Inc., 1966). Reprinted by permission of the publishers.

Holt, Rinehart and Winston, Inc.: From "My Road to Hasidism" by Martin Buber from Memoirs of My People, selected and edited by Leo W. Schwarz. Copyright 1943 by Leo W. Schwarz. Copyright © 1971 by Ruth Newman Schwarz. Reprinted by permission of Holt, Rinehart and Winston, Inc.

Rubin Mass, Publisher: From Two Letters to Gandhi by Martin Buber.

Maariv: From an interview with Rafael Bashan, January 27, 1961.

The Macmillan Company and Routledge & Kegan Paul Ltd.: From Between Man and Man by Martin Buber. Copyright © 1965 by Martin Buber. Reprinted by permission.

Routledge & Kegan Paul Ltd.: From The Way of Man by Martin Buber.

Schocken Books Inc.: From Israel and the World by Martin Buber. Copyright © 1966 by Schocken Books Inc.; reprinted by permission of Schocken Books Inc. From The Way of Response: Martin Buber, edited by Nahum N. Glatzer. Copyright © 1966 by Schocken Books Inc.; reprinted by permission of Schocken Books Inc.

The Zionist Library, Jerusalem: From Am v'Olam (People and World) by Martin Buber.

To
Professor Ernst Simon
and other fighters
for Hebrew humanism
in Israel

"You shall not withhold yourself.

"You, imprisoned in the shells in which society, state, church, school, economy, public opinion, and your own pride have stuck you, indirect one among indirect ones, break through your shells, become direct; man, have contact with men!"

—MARTIN BUBER, in "What Is to Be Done?" 1919

Acknowledgments

I wish to thank all those who have helped me with this book:

Professor Ernst Simon, the literary executor of Buber's estate, who gave me access to his papers and invaluable moral support; Rafael Buber, for allowing me to reproduce material about his father; Mrs. Margot Cohn, Director of the Buber Archives at the Hebrew National and University Library in Jerusalem, for her patience and cooperation; Ze'ev and Barbara Goldschmidt, who made me welcome in Buber's home and encouraged me to write this book; Landshövding Bo Hammarskjöld, for granting me permission to publish the correspondence between his brother and Buber; Mr. Ernst Blumenthal, for the original Swedish text and authorized English translation of Dag Hammarskjöld's letter to the Swedish Academy in June 1959, recommending Buber for the Nobel Peace Prize; Mrs. Rhena Eckert-Schweitzer, who gave me special permission to publish Buber's correspondence with her father; the estate of Bertrand Russell, for permission to publish letters from Russell to Buber and myself; the late Bishop James A. Pike, who wrote a memoir about Buber specially for this volume; Dr. John A. T. Robinson, for allowing me to quote from his unpublished Ph.D. thesis; Aaron Asher, for listening so perceptively when I first told him about this book, and for commissioning it; Alan Williams and Barbara Burn, of Viking, for the devotion with which they saw the manuscript through to publication; Robert O. Ballou, my faithful editor and warmhearted friend; the editors of *New Outlook* in Tel Aviv, and particularly Simha Flapan and Shmuel B'ari; David Meiron and Merle Kessler, of the *New Outlook* office in London; Rhoda, Gabriel, and Tamar for their love and understanding.

Also: the late Shmuel Yosef Agnon; Nelson Algren; Saul Bellow; Anthony Wedgwood Benn; Professor Norman Bentwich; Professor Samuel Hugo Bergman; Professor William Hamilton; Roy Oliver; Senator Jacob Javits; H. J. Blackham, former Director of the British Humanist Association; George Ivan Smith, Director of the United Nations Information Centre in London; Dr. Henry P. van Dusen; Maurice Friedman; Malcolm Diamond; Professor Daniel A. Fineman, of Tel Aviv University; Professor Shalom J. Kahn, of the Hebrew University, Jerusalem; Jacob Sonntag, editor of the *Jewish Quarterly*, London; Dr. Simon Shereshevsky, editor of the *Ichud* journal *Ner*.

And: Rafael Bashan; Alfred Bernheim; Ruth Bondi; Aharon Cohen; James Marshall; Anton Nyerges; Walter Schwarz; Avraham Shapira; Suzanne Spencer; Dr. Robert Weltsch.

Aubrey Hodes
London, February 1971

Contents

MARTIN BUBER

The Asylum

In 1953 I was living on a kibbutz in the hills of Nazareth. A close relative whom I loved deeply was in the schizophrenic ward of a Jerusalem mental hospital, and twice a week I made the painful pilgrimage to see her.

On those days I got up at five to bump down the hill with the milk truck, sitting on top of the icy cans. Then with a bus full of other half-awake kibbutzniks to Haifa; the long, slogging journey to Jerusalem; and a brief, sometimes stormy, sometimes silent and chilling session with my relative, who emerged from her ward wearing a white sack that closed off her whole shape and being from me, leaving only the angry, despairing eyes and cropped institution hair.

We sat on a bench in the visitors' room with other sad couples, or walked in the pale sun on the gravel of the courtyard, until we had nothing else to say, or too much.

Some days she was too ill and could not or would not see me. I do not know which was worse, seeing her or not seeing her. But always afterward I stumbled into the world outside gasping for air, fighting off the aura of evil which seemed to cling to me, as if contact with the world of the mad could infect one with an unseen virus.

The mental home was in Talbieh, overlooking Mount Zion: a

quiet suburb of square stone villas lined with pepper trees. After leaving I often walked along those streets in a daze, or sat staring across the Valley of Hinnom to the dead white walls which shut the Old City in as the walls of the asylum shut in my relative.

It took several hours before I could face úp to the body-jerking ride homeward, with its alternate twitchy drowsings and awakenings, and at the end of it the two-mile walk up the mountain path toward the huts and telephone poles of the kibbutz that appeared suddenly like a mirage.

One day I took a different way—not toward Mount Zion, but away from it. I remember being confused. She had been violent that day, and a male nurse had taken her away. I felt empty, drained of hope for her. People looked at me as they went by with their normal parcels of shopping. I came across a small park with a rose garden and sat in it until I stopped shaking. Then I asked someone the way to the bus stop.

I turned left as I had been told to do, into a green street. A garden drew me, with two tall trees, a cypress and a palm. Something led me to walk over to it and to stand looking at the tranquil, shuttered house with the metal nameplate:

M A R T I N   B U B E R

I can remember now the trembling which came over me as I said this name to myself. But it was not a trembling of awe— that came later. It was a trembling of peace, as if that small metal plate possessed some quality of healing by virtue of the name engraved upon it.

I had heard of Buber. Some friends who knew of the spiritual ferment I was undergoing had said, "You should talk to Buber." I had read a letter from him to Gandhi about the Jewish claim to the Land of Israel, and some of his Hasidic legends. But I did not yet know him, in the strange way, both intimate and remote, that one knows a beloved writer. I did not then associate his name with a living, breathing person writing and thinking in that quiet house. All I knew was that standing outside his house that gray stone day I drew a mysterious strength from his presence within.

I do not know how long I stood there. But when I left I was calm. After that I took to sitting on a bench near the house after each visit to my relative. This place seemed in the world and yet not wholly of it. The secret knowledge that I was going to sit in its shelter sustained me through the agony of these visits, which deepened as my relative moved helplessly toward a crisis.

I began reading anything of Buber's I could lay my hands on: *Moses, Paths in Utopia,* an address on education. But I was disappointed. His writings seemed austere and forbidding. They did not beckon me to seek direct contact with him. For a while I even stopped my semiweekly vigils outside his house, embarrassed by what I began to feel was a juvenile form of hero worship without any intellectual basis and rooted only in my own despair.

Then one wintry day I went into a Haifa bookshop. The bookseller recognized me and said, "Here's a new book by Buber. Just came in." He handed me a thin volume called *The Way of Man.* I opened it at random and began reading. The words flashed toward me as the words of the Baal Shem Tov, the founder of Hasidism, had flashed toward Buber himself fifty years earlier:

> No encounter with a being or a thing in the course of our life lacks a hidden significance. . . . The highest culture of the soul remains basically arid and barren unless, day by day, waters of life pour forth into the soul from those little encounters to which we give their due.[1]

I read the whole of that wise little book standing in the ice-cold corner of the bookshop, while the owner glowered at me. But it was not reading so much as listening. There was no paper between us. As I read I heard the murmur of a deep, warm voice that pierced me with its compassion. It was a luminous moment, a quantum leap of insight and enrichment.

From then on I had a burning desire to meet Buber, to talk to him face to face. Friends had said to me, "Buber sees many young people who need guidance. Just write to him." But now that I had discovered him, the trembling of awe held me back. The very insight which drew me to him frightened me. Would he see more deeply into me than I had myself? What could I conceal from him? It seemed preferable, less demanding, to meet him in a book, close but emotionally detached, a source of consolation that could be turned off with a gesture of the hand.

But a day came when I could wait no longer. I found my relative in a worse state than I had ever seen her. I couldn't reach her—couldn't give her the support she needed. This failure weighed on both of us. I left the asylum in a condition nearly as bad as her own.

At the end of Buber's street was a small grocery shop. I dragged myself there and dialed Buber's number.

There was a click at the other end, and I heard the virile, gentle voice I later came to know so well say, "Buber."

I told him stumblingly that I was a young kibbutznik who was facing many personal problems and was confused and filled with doubt. (I used the Hebrew word *ye'ush*—despair.) I had read some of his writings, and thought it would help if I could talk with him.

There was a pause. Then Buber asked, "Where are you now?"

"In Jerusalem." I could not tell him I was only thirty yards from his house.

"Hmm . . . Well, why don't you come here now? I'm free, if you want to come immediately."

I told him I would come right away and put the phone down. Now that our initial encounter was inevitable, I wanted it at once. But I could not appear on his doorstep without a reasonable interval of time. I walked to the end of Lovers of Zion Street, starting to shrink now from our meeting. Then at last I turned back to the house, past the nameplate, up the green path. I rang the bell eagerly and afraid.

The door opened and he stood there, shorter than I had imagined him, in a brown suit. He did not smile, but welcomed me gravely, holding his hand out in a courteous, rather old-fashioned way. His fingers were small and delicate. But the touch was firm.

He led me through the front door into his study and closed the door behind us. I sat down before a heavy wooden writing desk, and he sat facing me, leaning forward slightly, as if ready to listen. Neither of us spoke. I raised my head and looked into his eyes, which were gray, proud, secure, tender, near. We sat like that for a moment.

Then I began talking, at first fumbling in my still clumsy Hebrew, then more openly as I felt his silent response, his eyes fixed on me, melting my resistance. I told him about the kibbutz, my relative, the visits to the mental home in Talbieh; about sitting on the bench in front of his house; about *The Way of Man* and how the words had come toward me clothed in his voice which, I said suddenly, surprised at myself, I had recognized in the bookshop before I had heard it on the phone.

Buber listened with intense concentration, leaning forward when I groped for the right word in Hebrew. Several times I gave the word in English, and he supplied the Hebrew equivalent—but suggesting it, rather than forcing the word upon me. Every now and then he nodded his head. I remember that he did this vigorously when I said I felt my relative's illness was starting to follow almost physical laws, rather than those of a mental breakdown.

He waited until I had finished speaking. Then he began talking in his slow, precise Hebrew with its Germanic inflection. I cannot remember all that he said that first time, and in quoting his spoken words (here and throughout this book) I am doing so from memory. But I know that he spoke of my involvement with my relative's illness as one of the crucial human encounters he had referred to in *The Way of Man*. Her illness, he said, had a hidden significance for my own life. Only I could discover the meaning it held for me. But in order to do so I had to check my unconscious view of her as a person who was being drained of her human shape and becoming a thing, an object. I had to penetrate through the skin of her sickness to the basic unchanged humanity, enter into her world—but with understanding, not with pity, concerning myself directly with her recovery. And in doing so I might be able to discover the deeper meaning of my existence, and my capacity for love. Otherwise, I would not be able to reach her, and I would not be able to unlock the riddle of my responsibility toward her.

For I had a responsibility, he said. Love was responsibility for the loved person by the one who loved. Only by accepting this responsibility could I affirm my real self, my authentic personality. The situation called upon me to make a concrete commitment, to realize my responsibility in action—to see her as a single unique distressed individual, not just as one of a depersonalized throng of mental patients.

But, he said, only I could decide whether to make that commitment. I should listen to the voice of the situation and question myself. Then I would know how to act.

At that time I had not yet read *I and Thou*, and I had not penetrated deeply enough into Buber's thought to know that he was applying his views on dialogue to my predicament. He offered no easy solution, no gift-wrapped grace. His words were immediate, intimate, demanding. He challenged and drew to the surface my latent desire to serve, to give to others. But he showed me that my love for humanity was too diffuse, and that it had to be focused in a way which would spring from my own particular form of giving. He spoke to my condition, as the Quakers say, and from that day on I was his.

Meeting and Living

At the time of this first meeting I was twenty-five and Buber was seventy-five. But this was not any barrier to our understanding. I began coming to see him, at first after visiting my relative, then, when she became well enough to leave the mental home, making the long journey to Jerusalem just for the sake of the hour or two with him in his study. We maintained this close relationship until his death in 1965, at the age of eighty-seven.

To me he was a revelation. Other writers and thinkers had answered some of the questions I had asked. But Buber answered the questions I had not asked. He had the unique gift of seeing through the protective cloak of evasion to the hidden core of my anxiety—an X ray of the heart which astonished and enthralled me at every new encounter with it. Looking across the worn oak desk at this quiet, scholarly-looking man in his old-fashioned tie and waistcoat, apparently sheltered from the world by age and a wall of books, I wondered how and where he had acquired this ability to pierce through the surface of a personality to the center, to pinpoint what I had hardly guessed at in myself, much less formulated clearly.

In one of these early talks I asked him how he had discovered this gift of understanding in himself.

There was a pause. Then he answered, "It came to me through

a devastating experience during World War I, when I was in my late thirties. A young man came to see me, as you have come to see me. We sat talking as we are now. But I failed him. And this forced me to ask myself, why did you fail him? I have written about this, and how it caused a decisive change in my thinking which has remained until today."

When I left that evening Buber gave me a copy of *Between Man and Man*. Riding home in the bus I read the passage he had marked, called "A Conversion":

> What happened was no more than that one forenoon, after a morning of "religious" enthusiasm, I had a visit from an unknown young man, without being there in spirit. I certainly did not fail to let the meeting be friendly, I did not treat him any more remissly than all his contemporaries who were in the habit of seeking me out about this time of day as an oracle that is ready to listen to reason. I conversed attentively and openly with him—only I omitted to guess the questions which he did not put. Later, not long after, I learned from one of his friends—he himself was no longer alive—the essential content of these questions; I learned that he had come to me not casually, but borne by destiny, not for a chat but for a decision.
>
> He had come to me, he had come in this hour. What do we expect when we are in despair and yet go to a man? Surely a presence by means of which we are told that nevertheless there is meaning.[1]

After reading this something was still not clear to me. I asked Buber at our next meeting, "What happened to the young man?"

Buber closed his eyes for a moment, as if in pain. Then he said quietly, "He went. And shortly afterward he took his own life.

"Do you see what that means? He came to consult me in the hour of his deepest need. He came to ask me whether he should choose life or death. I talked to him openly. I was sympathetic. I tried to answer his questions. But I answered only the questions he had asked me. And so I failed to see through to the man behind the questions.

"And why did I fail?

"Because that morning, before his visit, I had been filled with religious enthusiasm, a mystical ecstasy, in which I felt myself in tune with eternity and the life beyond. Then this young man came to see me. It was an everyday event, an event of judgment. And it 'converted' me because it showed me that there could be no division between the life here and the life beyond."

> Since then [Buber wrote in *Between Man and Man*], I have given up the "religious" which is nothing but the exception, extraction, exaltation, ecstasy; or it has given me up. I possess nothing but the everyday out of which I am never taken. . . . I know no fulness but each mortal hour's fulness of claim and responsibility. Though far from being equal to it, yet I know that in the claim I am claimed and may respond in responsibility, and know who speaks and demands a response.[2]

"If," he said to me another day, "I am able to guess now the question you wish to ask me but have not put into words, it is perhaps because of what my young friend who is dead taught me—that dialogue is possible if the people who are genuinely trying to converse listen not only to what is said but also to what is felt without having been expressed in words. For me this is what I mean by religion—not removing yourself into another world, but responding to the call that comes into your everyday life. Above all, listening to both the silent and the spoken voices when one man speaks to another, so that together they can remove the barrier between two human beings."

And he did try to listen and respond to the whole of another with the whole of himself. A conversation with Buber was as far removed as possible from ordinary social talking or chat. It was a mutual and conscious attempt to communicate not only words but feelings, attitudes, anxieties—the inner self of one to that of the other. And as this was the purpose, he was impatient of anything which he felt interfered with or got in the way of this potential dialogue.

This impatience extended to all forms of mechanical communication or recording, whether electronic or the more ordinary pencil or pen. I remember clearly what happened during our second or third meeting, when he said something I thought summed up my confusion precisely. Without turning my head away I wrote the phrase down in the notebook lying on my right knee.

Buber stopped in the middle of a word, and opened his eyes wide, as if astonished.

"What are you doing?" he asked.

"Writing down something you said that struck me."

He gave me a look which was not angry but kindly, benevolent almost, and said, "If you wish to remember what I say, why then do you not listen to the words themselves as I say them to you? Then you will surely remember their meaning. Whereas if you write them down to read afterward you will concentrate on the writing down and not on what I have said. The important thing is to understand what we are saying to one another, for then you will always remember it. Is that right or not?"

I saw what he meant, and never tried again to write his words down in front of him. And I never saw Buber allow anyone to take notes while he spoke, except one or two journalists whom he trusted.

If Buber disliked pens and pencils, he had a positive antipathy to tape recorders. He considered them not a mechanical aid to conversation, but a definite hindrance. They set up barriers, instead of helping to eliminate them. "For," he said, "if two people are trying to talk with one another directly, honestly, and this electrical device is placed between them, to record what they say, they will no longer be talking to one another but to the machine. And the vital human response will be lost. They will not say the same things to one another that they would have said if the machine had not been taking it all down. So the machine not only sets up a wall between them, it also distorts what they actually say."

This opposition to the common journalistic aids often puzzled visitors, especially professional newspapermen.

One day a well-known journalist came to see him. Buber

watched closely as the reporter set out his notebooks, his camera, and his tape recorder and switched the machine on.

Buber looked at him with a mixture of irritation and tolerant forgiveness.

"I hope you were not thinking of putting that on while we talked," he said.

"Well, I thought it would be more accurate—"

"But all we are going to do is to talk to one another. Is that right? Then we shall see whether we say anything worth putting down. But to talk to one another we do not need an electrical companion, do we? Come, let us try without it."

The journalist stared at Buber in astonishment. But he switched the tape recorder off. It was, I suppose, a small victory for wisdom over technology—one of many Buber won over the men from the mass media who invaded his world from time to time.

He shunned publicity also, as he did tape recorders, feeling that either ruined any possibility of real dialogue, particularly on delicate political and religious questions.

"In 1952 I was in the United States," he told me one day. "An important man, who headed a large foundation, invited me to meet him. He wanted to hear my opinion about a project the foundation was considering. He said, 'We are thinking of inviting thirty or forty people from various countries to the United States for several months. All we want is that they should talk with one another, should talk about the present condition of the human race.' He asked me whether I would take part.

"I said, 'What you are saying is wonderful. I have dreamed of this for years. I am ready to take part. But on one condition— there must be no journalists present.'

"He looked at me in astonishment. 'This is impossible!' he cried. I said, 'By all means let everything said at the meetings be tape recorded and kept. I agree to this. But if journalists are present who will not take part in the talks, who will be witnesses, not participants, and if everything is to be published almost at once—there will be no point in the meetings.'

"Of course he did not agree to this. And the meetings never

took place." Buber shook his head at the memory of this. "You know," he said, "the really sad thing is that he could not understand what I meant."

All my conversations with Buber began in the same way. He would greet me at the door and lead me into his study. Neither of us spent much time on the usual social preliminaries. Our minds were already on the coming talk. After we sat down there was always a silence—not a tense silence, uneasy as between two people who were not sure of each other, but a silence of expectation. This was not consciously agreed between us. It was a flow of peace and trust forming a prelude to speech. The silence was the silence of communication. As Buber explained, "Speech can renounce words. It can renounce all the media of sense and sound, and it is still speech."

A Hasidic tale he loved told of Rabbi Menahem Mendel of Vorki, one of the later Hasidic masters, who once spent an entire night in the company of his *hasidim*, or disciples. No one spoke, but all were filled with deep reverence and experienced great elation during this silence, which was so profound that one could hear the fly on the wall.[3]

When we did begin talking there was never any fixed or rigid pattern. Sometimes he asked me if there was anything specific I wished to ask him. If there was not, we might discuss something that had happened in Israel that week—a book that had appeared or a political development, invariably something touching on Israel's relations with the Arabs. But often Buber himself would suggest a topic for discussion. It might be the need to evolve a kind of Judaism which would respond to life in our times, or the relation between the man of action and the man of contemplation in a true democracy. But whatever our discussion was, I always left with a recommendation from Buber to read a relevant passage in his own writings.

This was one of the most valuable things about our relationship. He directed me to the basic concepts of his own thought and told me where these were most lucidly explained. I went home and studied the passage. The next time I came we discussed it and I could ask him about any points which were not clear to me. In this way I studied together with him *I and Thou, Between Man and Man,* and other major works of his. I do not think I would have had the courage to approach them without Buber's own direct and personal guidance. But he was so kind and helpful, so genuinely anxious that one should understand the idea behind the words, that these awe-inspiring volumes, which had once loomed up before me like massive slabs covered with a language I could not decipher, opened up and became part of my own private world, gained and won forever.

When he said something he leaned back in his chair, relaxed, coming straight to the focal point of the idea. But when I replied or suggested some new idea he moved forward in his chair, concentrating on every syllable, encouraging me with his eyes, those wonderful eyes which were so penetrating, piercing, and yet so warm, friendly, and good.

I have a picture of Buber on my writing desk which shows his eyes like this, with the touch of sadness which shot through them often and stayed longer toward the end of his life, and particularly after his wife died. There is a painting by Rembrandt in the National Gallery in London which shows an old rabbi, one of the Jews Rembrandt must have known in Amsterdam, whose lined face has the tragic serenity of a man who has looked into the truth and come out whole and still believing. There is no bitterness in this brown and gray portrait, only an open readiness to be a friend of the world, to embrace life as it is, the sublime and the low together.

I am living in London now, and often when I'm near the National Gallery I go in to see this painting and think, if Rembrandt could have painted Buber, this is how he would have done it.

As I came to know Buber, I was continually surprised to find how concrete his thought was, how rooted in the real world. Anyone who thinks of him as an abstract mystic has either not read him or has not understood what he read. And no one who met Buber even briefly could fail to see that here was no shuttered recluse. What was so remarkable was the way he combined brilliant intellectual mastery with an intuitive insight which struck through the armor of words to the tender, vulnerable core beneath. He was able to do this because he had harmonized thought and action, word and deed, into an integrated experience of living. And he expressed this experience in his personality, which was direct, honest, immediately genuine.

Because word and deed were as one in him, he was able to concentrate with an intensity he brought to bear on everything he did. This power of concentration, focused like the rays of the sun through a burning glass, was one of the many enduring things I learned from him. He taught me to live in what he called the given moment—the moment in time through which we were passing. We could allow it to float by emptily, or we could fill it with meaning. But we could do this only if we lived intensely in the moment through which we were passing and did not use it for halfhearted actions or speech.

Whatever Buber did was done intensely. This does not mean that he was dour and earnest. He laughed often. But when he laughed he laughed intensely. When he drank a cup of tea he drank and enjoyed it intensely. To see him read a letter that had just arrived in the post was an education: the eyes, the mind, the memory, the entire acute person responding to the new situation, to the stimulus of the unexpected question.

Some people found this intensity exhausting. They were afraid of it. Some hinted broadly that it was a pose. I did not feel any of these things. And I knew that Buber's intense projection of himself was totally unselfconscious and sincere. When I sat opposite him, trying to put a fugitive idea into words of everyday speech, and felt his eyes on me, burning and searching, I responded with a similar intensity, saying things I had not consciously thought out and had not realized were buried so close beneath the surface. It was Buber's concentration on what I was about to say, his commitment to my not-yet-spoken words, which made them come alive.

Because of this natural intensity in his nature, he disliked anything superficial. I learned this at our second meeting. In Jerusalem, before going to his house, I had bought a copy of his book *Israel and Palestine*, about the Zionist idea and the link between the Jewish people and its homeland. At the end of our talk I held the book out to him and asked him to autograph it.

Buber took the book rather gingerly and asked me, "Have you read it?"

"No," I replied. "I bought it this afternoon."

"Well, don't you agree that it would be more important to see what I say in it? Writing my name in it is not a talisman, you know. You still have to read the book and understand it yourself."

But he saw my crestfallen face, and must have decided he had been too hard on me, for he signed the book in Hebrew: Mordechai Martin Buber. I have it still. But I never again asked him to autograph anything for me.

Something similar happened to Anthony Wedgwood Benn, former Minister of Technology in the British Government. He was in Israel in 1963, to take part in a seminar on the possibility of establishing peace between Israel and the Arab states. At the end of the seminar I took Benn and some of the other overseas visitors to meet Buber, who had not been well enough to come down to Tel Aviv for the seminar.

In a letter written to me later, Benn recalled:

Before I went to Buber's house, I had been given a beautiful photograph of him and I asked him at the end whether he would be so kind as to put his signature on it. He declined, saying that it was not his habit to sign photographs. I told him that I felt equally honored to have a photograph which he had declined to sign, since this was clearly a more characteristic memento of him than one which I had persuaded him, against his better judgment, to sign.

The thing I remember most about Buber was the very quiet way in which he received us and his habit of giving his entire attention to the person to whom he was speaking. I remember

you telling me that he made a practice of not offering his
guests any refreshment, as it destroyed the nature of the dialogue that would otherwise take place.

I also remember that one woman from New York made a
suggestion to him about some educational work that might be
undertaken in a kibbutz. "Are you prepared to do this work
yourself?" he asked her. She said that she was not thinking of
doing it herself but thought that it might be a good idea if it
was done. In the kindest possible way he explained that he did
not think that ideas were worth pursuing unless the people
who advocated them were prepared to put them into practice
themselves. Though I'm sure he didn't intend it as a rebuke, it
was a very testing comment and it made one feel that he was
interested more in people than in ideas and wanted to know
how far people were prepared to sacrifice themselves in order
to make real the ideas which, otherwise, it would be so easy to
throw off in conversation in the expectation that others would
take them up.[4]

With great perception Benn here grasped one of the outstanding things about Martin Buber, who, more interested in people
than in ideas, always looked for the depth of another's readiness
to realize his ideals in action.

"I believe in people," he said to me. "If I trust someone, we
can work together to make our ideas concrete. But ideas cannot
change anything themselves. They have to be shown to be true.
And only people, living human beings, can do that."

What counted for Buber was the sincerity and impulse behind
one's actions, which could often be more meaningful than the
objective quality of the action itself. Early on in our acquaint-
ance I brought him a poem I had written. It sprang from the re-
vulsion I had felt at the Kibya incident in October 1953, when Israeli units carried out a reprisal action against a Jordanian village
and killed sixty men, women, and children. I asked him if I could
dedicate the poem to him.

"Read it to me," Buber said.

When I had done so he smiled.

"I know nothing at all about poetry—especially modern poetry," he said. "But I understand why you wrote it, and what you want to say. Yes, you may dedicate it to me."

In an essay written in 1947, "Books and Men," he wrote:

> If I had been asked in my early youth whether I preferred to have dealings only with men or only with books, my answer would certainly have been in favor of books. In later years this has become less and less the case.

For, he explained, the world with all its imperfections means more to us than an ideal of perfection. "And although purely delightful books even now come my way more often than purely delightful men, the many bad experiences with men have nourished the meadow of my life as the noblest book could not do, and the good experiences have made the earth into a garden for me."

He revered books—"those that I really read"—too much to be able to love them. But men were "the brown bread on whose crust I break my teeth, a bread of which I can never have enough. . . . Aye, these tousle-heads and good-for-nothings, how I love them!" He felt that in any man there was more to love than to revere. "I find in him something of this world, that is simply there as the spirit never can be there." He needed the human world, the "mixture of prattle and silence" which is dialogue with men.

> Here is an infallible test [he wrote]. Imagine yourself in a situation where you are alone, wholly alone on earth, and you are offered one of the two, books or men. I often hear men prizing their solitude, but that is only because there are still men somewhere on earth, even though in the far distance. I knew nothing of books when I came forth from the womb of my mother, and I shall die without books, with another human hand in my own. I do, indeed, close my door at times and surrender myself to a book, but only because I can open the door again and see a human being looking at me.[5]

It was this delight in human exchange, in the "mixture of prattle and silence," which I found so refreshing about Buber. In the intimacy of his study he came alive far more vividly than in his books. The hours I spent with him there are preserved in the amber of my memory so clearly that I can close my eyes and see every detail of the room: the antique map of Jeruṣalem, the Piranesi etching of the Piazza Navona in Rome, a drawing of thorns from the Judean hills by the Israeli artist Leopold Krakauer, the brown high-backed sofa with its soft blanket where he rested in the afternoon, the books on art and philosophy in the glass-fronted shelves, the Hebrew and German Bibles which were always within his reach, the glowing oil stove in winter, and, across the worn oak writing desk from me, above the pile of manuscripts, letters, and proofs, Buber's face, so alert and receptive, so rockfast and free, so open to the presence of his companion.

Apart from these meetings, he phoned me quite often, or I called him in Jerusalem. A phone call from Buber was an eerie experience until you became used to it. An Israeli journalist, Ruth Bondi, says, "It was as if the phone rang and it was Paradise, with Elijah the Prophet on the line."

The first time my wife, Rhoda, answered the phone and heard Buber at the other end, she was taken aback and could not answer. "As if," she said, "it was the voice of Plato or Spinoza coming over the wires, into our house." But then I took her to meet Buber and he was so dignified yet friendly, "like an aristocrat from the court of Franz Josef," she said, that he put her at ease and she overcame her shyness of him.

When I dialed 3051, his number in Jerusalem, I knew that he would answer it himself and that I would hear his gentle but decisive voice announcing without any fuss or preliminaries, "Buber!" He disliked having his secretary or any of his friends answer the phone for him. This was part of his direct nature.

And he resisted all our attempts to replace the old-fashioned black telephone on his writing desk. It was one of those models one sees today only in museums of science and technology, with an upright and a conical receiver and a quaint, angular shape. Bent over it, concentrating on the voice of the caller, and nodding or shaking his head according to whether he agreed or disagreed with what the other said, Buber looked like a daguerreotype of Alexander Graham Bell listening to his assistant's voice coming through from the other end of his invention.

"All real living is meeting," Buber wrote. Meeting him was for me living, or rather a coming alive, a waking into clear, diamond-hard perception of the universe without sentimentality or intellectual prejudice. I have written this book so that others who have known him only from his writings can feel a little of what it was like to encounter Martin Buber, and how this meeting with him, this total and cataclysmic experience, changed the entire course of my life.

Answering for Ourselves

Buber's superb essay "The Question to the Single One" bears the motto, "Responsibility is the navel-string of creation. — P.B." [1] P.B. was his wife, Paula, a highly intelligent woman who wrote novels in German under the pseudonym Georg Munk. The statement summarized the basic element in Buber's teachings about society.

The key word for him was "responsibility," responsibility of the individual for his life and his actions. He asserted firmly that responsibility was closely bound up with human truth—a truth that could be displayed only in action. For "man finds the truth to be true only when he makes it true," [2] when he confirms it himself. The vital word here is "himself." We have to answer for and from ourselves. We can of course shrink from this or pass the ultimate decision on to someone else. But then, Buber warns, we will sacrifice the solution to the riddle of our existence; for, unless we decide with the whole of our beings what we are to do or not to do, and assume responsibility for it, we become sterile in soul.

He explained in the essay "Dialogue" in *Between Man and Man*, which has a section on the meaning of responsibility, what he meant by this. "Genuine responsibility," he wrote, "exists only where there is real responding." But to what should we respond?

To what happens to one, to what is to be seen and heard and felt. Each concrete hour allotted to the person, with its content drawn from the world and from destiny, is speech for the man who is attentive.[3]

This attentive man faces creation as it occurs. He listens to the sounds of his life, to the events of the personal everyday things that happen to him. (This is what Buber meant when, in conversation with me, he spoke about "the poetry of the everyday.") We are addressed, spoken to, by these sounds and events, the speech directed at us. The question is whether we will respond to them or ignore these signs of creation.

Sometimes we try to evade commiting ourselves to these signs. We "wrap silence about us," [4] or we simply step aside, although in both cases we carry away a wound that is not easily forgotten. Yet it can happen, Buber says, that we do the opposite:

We venture to respond, stammering perhaps—the soul is but rarely able to attain to surer articulation—but it is an honest stammering.[5]

When this happens, when we accept the challenge, we enter into the situation which has come into our lives in a way we could not have foreseen. And this situation flows into our lives. "Only then, true to the moment, do we experience a life that is something other than a sum of moments." [6] The concept of responsibility is brought out of the academic "province of specialized ethics," [7] where it swings free in the air, and becomes rooted in the everyday. What happens then is described by Buber in a magnificent passage:

A newly-created concrete reality has been laid in our arms; we answer for it. A dog has looked at you, you answer for its glance, a child has clutched your hand, you answer for its touch, a host of men move about you, you answer for their need.[8]

Buber's ethic of responsibility implies a response to every life situation. This response should spring from the depths of our personality and be spontaneous, unprogramed, and entered into fully. He rejects any mechanical, preconceived code of behavior. He was completely against any dogma or system imposed upon the individual. Indeed, he spoke of "the intoxication of ritual" and "the madness of dogma." He appreciated the "objective compactness" of dogma, but saw in it the once-for-all which resists the unforeseeable moment of the situation. And because a dogma states as absolute truth a conclusion in advance of any given situation, it stifles the individual response which has in it the power of creating a dialogue with life.

He was conscious that one of the ways men avoid facing a situation unprepared is to erect around themselves a fence of dogma or "certainty." Then, when a situation arises, a man does not have to decide anything but merely retreats behind the fence around him and follows the rules imposed upon him. He does not ask, "What do I think?" He asks, "What does the committee think? What did the party say?" (or the rabbi, the priest, the newspaper columnist, the television pundit). They answer for him and he accepts their answer unquestioningly and evades the need to make a decision.

In *Daniel*, written in 1913, ten years before *I and Thou* was first published, Buber distinguished between two attitudes to human experience. In the first stage, "orientation," a man tries to find a system in the universe around him, a pattern that he can apply to a solution of the problems of his existence. He seeks a formula, a governing rule. And he thinks this will make him free. But the formula imprisons him. He lives with only one part of his being, surrendering the quest and insecurity which alone can make him truly free.

Some men never emerge from this primal stage of development. They remain trapped all their lives by the values, ideas, doctrines they accepted in their youth, never daring to move from this safe anchor. Others, however, break loose and seek the inner meaning of life by exploring their individual experiences. This process, which Buber calls "realization," strives to attain greater awareness and understanding. It is subjective, creative, intensely personal.

The liberated man discovers his direction. He lives in the moment in time through which he is passing. His life has meaning. And, paradoxically, his withdrawal into an individual searching for truth places him in a relation to the community more harmonious than that of the man who passively accepts the norm from force of habit.

In his previously quoted statement, "All real living is meeting," [9] Buber summed up all his teaching, as Hillel and Jesus summed up the Torah (or, as Jesus put it, "the Law and the Prophets"), in a sentence. Meeting in Buber's sense means opening yourself, not hiding behind a rigid code or ritual. It means relating to other people and nature with the whole of your being. This is what Buber calls the I-Thou relation. It implies a genuine encounter, a reciprocal relationship which puts the I in tune with life.

The I-It relation, on the other hand, is not a genuine meeting. The expression implies treating the other person or thing as an object, to be used or thought of only as a thing, not as a subject on the same level as oneself.

The subjective importance of answering for ourselves can often be greater than the objective value of our reply. To put this another way, the greatest value of the response is in the fact that it is being made as a real expression of the self, that making it will deepen our realization and our sense of I-Thou. Buber was fond of making this point by quoting the Hasidic legend about Rabbi Zusya, who said shortly before his death, "In the world to come I shall not be asked: 'Why were you not Moses?' I shall be asked: 'Why were you not Zusya?'" [10]

We cannot all be Martin Luther Kings or Einsteins or Bubers. But each, in Buber's conception, can contribute something in his own particular way to human truth. In order to do this, however, each must first find out who he is. Only when he knows this can he discover the way he needs to respond. As Rabbi Bunam said, "When a man has made peace within himself, he will be able to make peace in the whole world." [11]

In *The Way of Man* Buber remarks that there is a conflict between three principles in man's being and life: the principle of thought, the principle of speech, and the principle of action:

> The origin of all conflict between me and my fellow-men is that I do not say what I mean, and that I do not do what I say. For this confuses and poisons, again and again and in increasing measure, the situation between myself and the other man.[12]

A man must realize that these conflicts between himself and others are nothing but the results of conflicts in his own soul. And the only way out of this, Buber urges, is through the crucial realization: "Everything depends on myself. I will straighten myself out."[13]

Responsibility toward the world with which you want to establish a relationship of I-Thou, of meeting, begins with inner awareness of your deeper self and responsibility to yourself. If you transform yourself, you can transform that part of the world which surrounds you.

Buber sums this up with a parable, told by Rabbi Hanokh:

> There was once a man who was very stupid. When he got up in the morning it was so hard for him to find his clothes that at night he almost hesitated to go to bed for thinking of the trouble he would have on waking. One evening he finally made a great effort, took paper and pencil and as he undressed noted down exactly where he put everything he had on. The next morning, very well pleased with himself, he took the slip of paper in his hand and read: "cap"—there it was, he set it on his head; "pants"—there they lay, he got into them; and so it went until he was fully dressed. "That's all very well, but now where am I myself?" he asked in great consternation. He looked and looked, but it was a vain search; he could not find himself. "And that," Rabbi Hanokh said, "is how it is with us."[14]

The Need to Say No

This emphasis on personal responsibility led Buber to insist on the importance of individual protest. There are times when a man must say "yes," he told me, and times when he must say "no." And if he is convinced that he must say "no," then he should say it, even if he is the only dissenter in his society or country.

Buber saw this readiness to be nonconformist as an integral part of a genuine democracy. Those who were prepared to obey their individual consciences and to say "no," even when everyone else was saying "yes," were the yeast of a free society. Their numbers were not important; they could not hope to attain a majority, nor indeed should they strive to do so. But if the number of people who genuinely, responsibly said "no" fell beneath the number demanded by the crisis which posed the question, that society would be in danger of losing its freedom.

"Do you remember Abraham's argument with God in Genesis over Sodom?" Buber asked me one day when we were discussing the nature of protest. "God had decided to destroy Sodom because it was a wicked city. But Abraham said to him, 'If there are fifty righteous men in Sodom, surely you should not destroy them too, together with the sinners?' And God said, 'If I find in Sodom fifty righteous within the city, then I will spare all the place for their sakes.' Abraham kept lowering the number until

he got God to agree that if there were only ten righteous men in
the city, he would not destroy it.

"And so it is today. A handful of just and honest men can prevent a society from becoming corrupt, if they speak out and say,
'No!' In the end, of course, there were not even ten righteous
men in Sodom to oppose the evil around them, and so the city
was destroyed."

I remember an instance of personal conscience at work which
aroused Buber's admiration. This occurred during the Kafr Kassem shooting, a notorious incident which took place on the eve of
the 1956 Sinai campaign. On October 28 of that year forty-seven
Arab villagers, citizens of Israel, returning home after the day's
work in their fields, were shot down in cold blood by Israeli border policemen. While they were out in the fields a curfew had
been imposed because of the war with Egypt which was to
begin the next day. The Arabs did not know about the curfew.
At the briefing session before the incident, the Israeli officer in
charge had been asked what was to be done about any villagers
who returned from the fields after curfew time. He replied, "May
Allah have mercy on their souls." This officer later gave the
order to fire which cost the lives of men, women, and children
who were unaware of any change in the normal routine of the
village.

Buber felt strongly about this flagrant case of inhumanity. I
proposed the erection of a monument to the forty-seven dead, to
be paid for by funds collected among Arabs and Jews. Buber was
abroad when we discussed this, but wrote to me from his vaca-
tion home at Castello Rubin, in Merano, Italy, to express his
wholehearted support. The plan was to set up this memorial in
the village of Kafr Kassem on the first anniversary of the massacre. But the authorities refused permission, and the project had to
be abandoned. Several officers and men were eventually tried for
the murders and sentenced, only to be released when the furor
died down.

Yet at Kafr Kassem there was one officer who told his men not to shoot. The villagers did not know about the curfew, he declared, and so he would not open fire upon innocent people.

This officer, Buber exclaimed, was a true democrat. He listened to the voice of the truth within him and applied it to the situation which confronted him. He did not respond like a robot, but retained his humanity and refused to carry out an order he knew could not possibly be justified. If each person in an army or a democracy would act so courageously, antisocial actions such as the Kafr Kassem catastrophe could not take place.

Buber was a political realist. He knew that individual actions such as the officer's refusal to shoot could not become official policy. He saw these actions and all passionate protest as a corrective, as a means of moderating the policies of the majority and rendering them more tolerant and less rigid. "I am not a perfectionist," he used to say. "I do not seek a utopia. But I think we can improve the nature of democracy here in Israel and elsewhere."

Every political party, he said, was composed of two main groups: the majority, which sought power and was concerned with momentary advantage and tactics, and the minority, which was devoted to long-range values and cherished a vision of the future. The danger was that the majority of members in a mass party would completely lose sight of moral and human values. When this happened, it was the task of the minority to provide an ideological corrective. If it could do this, it could be a very important influence in the life of the party and the state. And this ideological corrective must be backed up by such essential acts of civil disobedience as the officer's refusal to shoot.

This officer, Buber added, was not a pacifist. He took part in war and would not refuse to shoot in the height of a battle. But he knew that to fire at unarmed innocent villagers would be murder, and so he refused to cooperate.

We should seek to develop this almost instinctive response to inhuman orders so that members of a democracy would refuse to carry them out. This can only be done by educating the citizens to awareness. They should learn to give the state not only their taxes, but also their time and thought in a constant scrutiny of the leaders of the party and the state, and their decisions and actions.

The task of the intellectual and the spiritual man is to supply the necessary corrective. To do this he must have no direct interest in the holding of power. He should not seek to rule. But he should draw intelligent conclusions from his awareness of social problems and present them forcefully and courageously to the statesmen who carry out policy.

Buber did not believe in mass demonstrations. He disliked slogans and thought them an artificial oversimplification of complex issues. I could not imagine him sitting down in front of a government office, as Bertrand Russell did in 1961 in protest against British nuclear armament. Some people in the Israeli peace movement criticized him for this "elitist" approach and urged him to carry protest out into the streets. But, quite apart from the special nature of Israeli society as an exceptionally lively democracy, this was simply not his way.

The aim, he always insisted, was to restore to the life of the state a sense of the eternal, of long-range objectives, of goals which could be realized only by generations to come. There was a tension between the political expediency of the hour and the values we had to transmit to the future. He felt this tension, as though it were an electric force. It sparked the struggle of conscience within him. And only those of us who were close to him knew how he wrestled with his conscience before taking a stand which often left him isolated even in his own minority camp.

In the speech he made when receiving the Bialik Prize for Jewish Thought in December 1961, he dealt with this human spiritual tension.

"We must not float above the situation contained in this hour," he said, "and we must not drown in its noise and tumult. . . . In everything I have said at certain times about the problems and tasks of those times, I have never lost sight of the horizon of the eternal, from which the light shone into the midst of the present."

The basic evil of our time, he told the gathering in Bialik's house in Tel Aviv, was the separation between our awareness that the eternal values were still valid and our desire to obtain a temporary advantage, whether this was real or imaginary. This "catastrophic split in our consciousness" had to be overcome. The question was whether we were ready to try to solve the problems of the hour through what the absolute commanded us to do.

"Our life will not be genuine," he warned, "if we do not follow the dictates of the spirit." But these spiritual imperatives should not be followed abstractly. They had to be applied concretely, practically, without dogmatism, to the changing situation, which made different demands at different times. "If we listen intently to the voice of the present situation," he believed with all his heart, "we shall hear what we are charged with doing." [1]

This attempt to reactivate the eternal, to bring back the awareness of the absolute which he felt we had lost in our century, was linked with his concept of God as the Eternal Thou, in which the I-Thou found its highest expression. "Every particular Thou is a glimpse through to the Eternal Thou," [2] he wrote. In other words, every I-Thou—every loving relationship with man and the world—opens the window to the ultimate Thou. God has to be approached through an I-Thou relationship with people, animals, trees, even—as he said in his 1909 book *Ecstasy and Confession*—a heap of stones. Without these life-enhancing encounters, real relationship with God could not be achieved on earth. Similarly a real relationship with other human beings could be attained only if the link between the I and the Eternal Thou is also present. Three elements need to exist in this harmonious interplay between the individual and the universe: the self, an "other" (which may be a person, a nonhuman animal or even a tree), and the Eternal Thou. And when a man has learned to say

Thou, he becomes an I. When he has matured enough to meet his fellow men, to enter into a dialogue with others and with absolute values, then, and only then, can his authentic personality emerge. When he embraces the life of dialogue in his everyday actions, he comes out of the crowd, his face takes on a shape, he speaks with a distinctive voice, he becomes himself.

It is the task of every man to realize his own unique potential, to say "yes" and to say "no" according to his convictions, sometimes plunging into the maelstrom of the world with his whole being, sometimes withdrawing into "an inner-worldly 'monastery,' " [3] but always engaged in the constant discovery of himself in relation to mankind and the world. This is more important than to repeat something done by another man, even if the example has been set by the greatest in history.

To drive this point home Buber used to tell the story of the wise Rabbi Bunam, who said in old age, when he had already grown blind:

"I should not like to change places with our father Abraham! What good would it do God if Abraham became like blind Bunam, and blind Bunam became like Abraham? Rather than have this happen, I think I shall try to become a little more myself." [4]

The Buddha said, "We should live like the lotus blossom. It grows out of the water, but its petals are not wet."

I was struck by this saying and related it to Buber.

He smiled at me and said, "This is what I have been trying to explain all my life."

The Test

The fall of 1956 was a difficult time in Israel. The *fedayeen* raids were at their height. Scarcely a day passed without a driver of a tractor being shot on the border or a civilian ambushed on a main road a few miles from Tel Aviv. There was a sense of foreboding in the air, a quiet dread. The death of a stranger in a lonely field in the Negev brought us the oppressive scent of our common danger and mortality.

One late September day I came to see Buber. I had never seen him so grave, so concerned about the threat of war. His face was lined with worry, and his voice low and earnest. The autumn sun streamed in through the half-open shutters like pale honey, while Buber spoke about his concept of the existential test. By this, he said, he meant a crucial experience that tried not only a person's momentary response to a given challenge, but also the entire structure of values and beliefs upon which his life was based.

It was the essence of this self-confrontation, he said, that it could not be prepared for in advance. It could not be anticipated, and the situation which would contain it could not be predicted. It could occur and be over in a flash, or last an agony of time. But it could always be recognized—perhaps only much later —as a genuine life-evaluating test because of the implications it held for one's total existence, not merely for the life of that passing moment in time.

Whether one passed or failed this test, he said—and one always knew the true result, could not conceal the outcome from oneself, although others might not even know that the test had taken place—one's life would never be the same afterward. It could reveal unsuspected reservoirs of strength and courage which could change the direction of a life. Or it could uncover a vacuum of hypocrisy and evil within a superficially smooth and successful exterior.

"Think of Herzl during the Dreyfus trial," he said. "Or Saul, when he became Paul. Then, on the other hand, the Germans under Hitler. Then you will know what I mean.

"A nation can undergo this test as well. In this case every individual in the nation can scarcely escape a personal test which mirrors the trial of the community. I feel that Israel is about to face an existential test of the kind I have described." He looked out of the window and we were silent for a while. Then he said, "And each of us will be tested then, each in his own way.

"I was thinking this morning," he continued, "of Ben-Gurion. I think I can understand the inner struggle he is going through and the burden he carries. I can sense his loneliness at this decisive moment. If only he could talk to me, really talk! If only he could share the burden! But things have not developed between us the way I hoped they would when Israel was established. He is only four hundred yards from here. But there is a chasm between us. And it will grow deeper because of what he wants to do."

As he walked with me to the door to say good-by he seemed gloomy and withdrawn, a mourner. But as we shook hands he looked at me and his face brightened. "I was not entirely right," he said. "It is true that we cannot tell exactly what form the test will take. And so we cannot prepare specifically for it. But even an awareness that some kind of test is coming is a preparation."

This was a month before the Sinai campaign. Walking past a drugstore at night where bandages were being loaded into an army truck, Rhoda and I heard the news that Israel had invaded Egypt. When we came back to the house there was a note on the door telling me to report to a meeting place on the southern coast. On it the messenger had scribbled, "See you in Suez." I packed a kit bag and left to join my unit. It was Monday, October 29.

We spent that night in a eucalyptus grove outside Beersheba. I had trained as a medical orderly and was attached to the hospital corps under a doctor who knew I had volunteered for medical service because I would not carry a gun. We spent the whole of that week practicing stretcher-bearer drill, listening to messianic speeches by Ben-Gurion, and worrying about Egyptian bombs landing on the white-plastered cubes of thin cement in Tel Aviv's new suburbs. Several men were stung by scorpions. A truck driver who had survived Dachau ran amok and we had to give him a shot of morphine to stop his screaming. One day we were suddenly packed into a troop carrier and driven for four hours to an airfield, where we waited for three hours and were just as abruptly driven back to the eucalyptus grove. No one told us why.

On Friday morning we were awakened at three o'clock to attack Gaza. As we drove toward the town mosques and minarets seemed to float out of the mist. One prong of our force attacked the airfield, while another skirted the refugee camp and cut off the escape route by sea.

I found myself crawling on my hands and knees behind a platoon moving toward one of the hangars, dragging out the men who suddenly threw their hands in the air and fell down jerking and twitching. Some of them tried to cling to me and I had to hit them to get free and rush to other soldiers who needed me more. When a man who was clutching my shirt and begging me not to leave him died in my arms it was almost a relief.

By noon it was all over. Gaza had fallen, and the town's military commander, wearing dark glasses, drove past us to a prisoner-of-war camp. We were ordered to move southward along the Mediterranean. Our food supplies had been left behind in the general Egyptian collapse. So we filled our arms with bunches of fresh dates from a warehouse in Deir el-Ballakh and ate them in the truck traveling through the dunes. They were coarse, heavy with dark-brown sap, and delicious. We munched them the whole of that day and night until our corned beef and biscuits arrived from Beersheba.

At Khan Yunis a group of *fedayeen* put up a sporadic resistance. The road into the town was mined, and the tank leading our convoy exploded and burst into flames before anyone could get to it. We had to scrape the crew off the inside of the tank like *pâté* out of a tin. Traffic was stopped while a company of men went into the town to find the *fedayeen* and smoke them out. Two hours later we moved into Khan Yunis and took up quarters in an abandoned school.

In Gaza we had picked up an elegant German-made ambulance. Now it was parked in front of the school, in the shade of some sand-blasted olive trees. The doctor told me to get some supplies out and treat anyone who needed it, as there'd be no more fighting that day. Some men came along for routine care of wounds and scratches. Most of the unit stretched out wherever they could find a flickering spot of yellow shade and went to sleep.

I was standing in front of the ambulance sorting out bottles and bandages when I saw a man in front of a prickly-pear hedge about twenty yards away. He was about sixty, fat and partly bald, in a filthy white shirt and torn khaki trousers, a civilian Arab. He took one hesitant, groping step from the hedge toward me, rolling his brown-stained eyes in terror, ready to draw back if I lifted my hand. Another step, and I saw that one arm hung in front of him with blood seeping out through the piece of cheap colored cloth tied around it.

Now he was coming slowly, like a crippled crab, toward the ambulance. Suddenly he made a desperate rush toward me and flung himself full length on the wooden bench in the shade of the olive trees.

I looked at his arm. It had been broken, probably when we shelled the town, and it was starting to suppurate and smell in the midday heat.

He turned his eyes up to me as a puppy might have and held

out his arm, which was trembling quietly. I remember that the only word he said was *enta*, "you." He said this several times, like a child learning grammar, looking at me to see what I was going to do. Then he seemed to have decided that he could do nothing more; it was in my hands; fate would decide what happened to him; he could not care any more. He closed his eyes and lay on the bench shaking and sweating.

I took off the dirty red and white cloth and dressed the cracked arm. It was a bad fracture, but with care it would heal in a few weeks. I put a splint on and padded it with a clean bandage, while he groaned and murmured short little bursts of words every time it hurt. Perhaps he was praying.

While I was doing all this I did not think of him as an Arab, as someone belonging to the town and country we had occupied. To me he was simply a man with a broken arm: and I had to set it. I did this as well as I could—probably rather clumsily. There was nothing noble or heroic about the act itself. The heat, the sticky red glue on the skin, his cotton-white face and staccato chanting made it a human occasion forced on both of us by need, pain, and accident.

As I was finishing the bandaging, two young soldiers from my unit, Moroccan boys of eighteen or nineteen, came past carrying Sten guns and drunk with victory. One of them noticed the old Arab lying on the bench and said something to his mate. They laughed and came over. Then they saw I was working on his arm.

"What're you doing?" the bolder one asked.

"What you see. His arm's broken."

The young Moroccan sneered. "And you're fixing it! I'll show you what to do with Arabs!" He took the old man by the collar and began pulling him to his feet.

I forced his hand away firmly. "This is a first-aid station," I said, trying to keep calm and to sound official. "I'm in charge here. Please go away."

He looked at me, more surprised than annoyed. It seemed to dawn on him slowly that for some reason I objected to his taking the Arab away and shooting him in the dunes. This puzzled him, and as he couldn't understand it he spat at me like a cat. "We want to have some fun with him! What's that to you?"

"Yes," the other one shouted, "what's the difference? Is he your father or something? Give him to us!"

I moved in front of the old man as the two came toward him. He was dazed with pain and fright, his pink lips pumping together without any sound coming out. I pushed his limp heavy body into the ambulance and closed the door.

The two Moroccans yelped at the sudden way he had gone.

"Give him to us!" the older one snarled. "Else we'll fix you instead!"

I stood in front of the ambulance and said nothing.

The older, taller one cocked his rifle and looked at the younger curly-haired one uncertainly. They muttered something in Arabic, glaring at me with black eyes filled with hatred and frustrated greed to kill.

Finally they rushed off. I sat down on the bench feeling quite calm and still inside, not afraid at all. Inside the ambulance I could hear the Arab shuffling around. He was moaning again, in the short bursts of wailing I had heard in mosques. I closed my eyes and let the sun flow over my chest and arms.

In a few minutes they were back with their sergeant—a short, coiled-up, tense man, born somewhere in Europe, I thought—Austria perhaps.

He began quietly. "I hear you have a prisoner here."

"He is a civilian."

"Let me see him."

"No. He is old and wounded and not involved in the war."

"I want to question him."

"How do I know you won't hand him over to them?"

He shook his head impatiently and changed his tactics, becoming tougher, steelier. "Look, these men here have done a good job. They've been fighting and won a big battle. Now they feel like a bit of sport. He's an old man, you say. And wounded. So what do you care? Why're you sticking your neck out? The

boys want to let off steam. Okay. Why not? Anyway, how do
you know he isn't with the *fedayeen*? Khan Yunis is full of them.
So come on now, bring him out."

"No," I said quietly. "This is a first-aid station, and I'm in
charge here. Besides, since when do we shoot unarmed civilians?"

"Bring him out, I tell you. That's an order!"

"I won't."

He turned red and spluttered. "Move away from the ambulance. Else you'll get a bullet in your head!"

I couldn't move. Something inside me had taken over, like an
internal clock. But I knew he was not going to shoot me. He had
lost. The Moroccan boys looked dejected.

"All right," he shouted. "You've asked for it. Now there'll be a
court-martial. And you'll pay for this."

He motioned to the two boys and they went off arguing
among themselves.

When they had gone I opened the door of the ambulance and
helped the Arab out. His body shook and slithered with panic.
He looked older than when he had gone in. I motioned with my
head toward the prickly-pear hedge he had come from, and he
disappeared, shuffling across the sand. The last I saw of him was
the gash in his dirty cotton shirt as he moved behind the hedge.

In the afternoon the doctor came back and I went off duty till
the next morning. I wandered down to the edge of the sand
dunes, past the looted shops and the police station punched full
of holes like a slab of cheese. In a clump of fig trees water was
trickling from a broken pipe. I sat down and leaned against the
rough, friendly bark.

So that was what Buber had been talking about. The old Arab
had been the bringer of the test. He had come into my life, with
his broken arm, his wailing from the Koran, his fright and sweat,
and had gone out again. I did not know his name. I had not spoken a single word to him. I would never know what happened to
him—whether his arm healed in time or whether it became deformed and useless. But I knew now that if I had let them kill
him; had opened the door of the ambulance or allowed them to

push past me and open it; had said to myself, why should you concern yourself with another Arab being shot when so many have been killed already, civilians and soldiers? had tried to pretend that another bullet in the dunes added to thousands could not alter anything, could not change what had already been done and would still be done in the name of security and defense, and that in any case an order was an order, and I had not asked this enemy to come shuffling toward me with his broken arm, moaning in a language I could not understand—then, I knew now, something would have shriveled within me, something which was present and stronger now would have died not only for the frozen isolated moment in the dunes but also for the rest of my life. For those minutes in front of the ambulance I had been responsible for this stranger. I had been involved with his life as if it had been my own. If I had failed him I would have failed myself. The unexpected, unlikely messenger from Khan Yunis had forced me to realize my abstract principles in action—or abandon them. I had been pinned against a concrete either-or; and I had come through.

Of course, there was no court-martial. The next day the company commander issued an order banning all looting and the unauthorized killing of Arab civilians or combatants. We were transferred to a former Egyptian army base in the Sinai Desert and spent a month there hauling oil drums and moving out captured food supplies until we were evacuated and went back home.

As soon as I could I went to see Buber at his home in Jerusalem. We talked about the war, about its implications for Israel's role in the region, about the future of the refugees in the Gaza Strip. Then I told him about the incident in Khan Yunis—about the Moroccan boys and the sergeant, about the Arab who had been sent in my path, about the moments in the dunes when reason and conscience had crystallized beyond thought to a step forward away from the ambulance or a step back.

Buber listened intently, focusing on every word. When I described the two young Moroccans bursting onto the scene he closed his eyes in pain.

I came to the end and stopped. Telling it was harder than living through it had been. I wondered about the old Arab and if he'd got away.

Buber leaned forward and gave me a long, intense look. In it I saw pride, love, trust. I had never heard his voice so tender. "You have passed your test," he said.

Childhood: The Horse

Martin Buber was born in Vienna on February 8, 1878. His parents were middle-class Jews, not particularly religious or intellectual, although his father seems to have been an unconventional and freethinking man of great vigor.

When he was three years old his parents separated and he went to live with his grandparents. Toward the end of his life Buber spoke and wrote about this upheaval in his life, which had a decisive influence on the direction of his thinking.

To me he spoke about this only once. I had been telling him about a kindergarten for Jewish and Arab children in Acre, set up by our friends the Quakers. This led us to talk about the growth of perception in children and the age at which they become aware of such things as prejudice and conflict.

"I can remember very clearly," he said, "the moment at which I became aware that life was not always idyllic but was sometimes tragic. When I was three years old my parents' marriage broke up and I was taken to the house of my father's parents, in Lemberg. At that time Lemberg was the capital of Galicia, the crown province of the Austro-Hungarian Empire. Today, of course, it is called Lvov, and is in the Soviet Union.

"My grandparents were good to me. But neither of them said a word about my mother and when I could hope to see her again. And I was too timid to ask.

"In the house in Lemberg there was a large courtyard surrounded by a wooden loft, so that you could look down into it. I can remember very clearly standing there one day with the daughter of one of the neighbors, who used to look after me. We were leaning over the balcony railing, looking into the yard. She was much older than I was, and I suppose I must have felt I could ask her about my mother, although I was afraid to ask my grandparents.

"I can still hear her voice as she said, in a matter-of-fact way, 'No, your mother is not coming back any more.' I remember becoming silent. There was nothing more for me to say. But I felt that what she said was true, and the truth made me sad.

"I wanted to see my mother. And the impossibility of this gave me an infinite sense of deprivation and loss. Do you understand? Something had broken down. When I was thirteen I even coined a private word for it, which had this meaning, a-meeting-that-had-gone-wrong.

"And now I will tell you something strange. When I was thirty-three I saw my mother again, for the first time in thirty years, and at once this private word flashed through my mind, and I remembered the moment on the wooden balcony overlooking the courtyard. Whatever I have learned in the course of my life about the meaning of meeting and dialogue between people springs from that moment when I was four." [1]

Buber's grandfather, Solomon Buber, was a famous Hebrew scholar who published several critical editions of the Midrash, a classic Jewish exegesis on the Scriptures. The atmosphere in the home was one of piety and learning, with a strong emphasis on Jewish tradition. Solomon Buber gave his grandson a good all-round education, including the study of the Bible and the Talmud. But the grandfather and his wife, Adela, considered European languages also essential. They were the new kind of learned Jews who were at home in the works of Kant and Goethe as well as in the Torah and the Midrash. So young Martin read not only the classical Jewish writings, but also the prose and poetry of Heine, Schiller, and other German authors, and studied French.

He received private lessons at home and did not go to school until he was ten.

Both his grandparents exerted a strong influence on him. Solomon took him for walks in the woods around Lemberg and helped him to gain an appreciation of the peace and sanctity of nature, as well as a love for books. Adela was a remarkable woman who ran the family grain business so that her husband could be free to study. She was intelligent and self-taught and spoke excellent German, which she passed on to young Martin.

Despite the orthodox atmosphere of his grandparents' home, however, young Martin began to have doubts about formal Judaism as he approached his *bar mitzvah*. When he was twelve he began rebelling against the concept of a vengeful God. The story of Saul losing the right to his kingdom because he did not kill Agag, king of the Amalekites, appalled him.

"The scene in which Agag approached Samuel and was 'hewed in pieces before the Lord' filled me with fear and trembling every time I read it," he said. "Even many years later, when I had to translate this passage into German, I found it difficult to put down these words from the Scriptures. I could not believe in a God who punished Saul because he had refused to kill his opponent."

The rigid ritual of the synagogue also worried the boy. At his *bar mitzvah* ceremony he delivered a talk on Schiller, instead of the usual dissertation on a passage from the Bible. Soon afterward he gave up saying daily prayers, although he continued studying the Bible and Talmud with great intensity.

When Buber was fourteen his father remarried and moved to Lemberg. Martin went to stay with him, in a house which was close to the Parliament. From the balcony he could look down into the square in front of the Parliament, he recalled.

"One day I heard shouts. I looked down and saw Polish students beating Jews. It was the first time I had seen violence like this against Jews, in a public place in the center of the city. It frightened me. And I remember wondering, why do they hate us so much?"

Buber's father had become interested in agriculture and managed his parents' farm, which became famous all over Eastern Galicia for its progressive methods and the way the workers were treated. The boy often accompanied his father in visits to the farm and to the peasants who lived on the estate. He was struck by the way his father approached the animals, "almost as if they were people," he said. "The workers too were always spoken to in a direct, honest way. This was something I learned from my father which books had not taught me and which I have always remembered."

From the age of nine Martin spent the summers on the family farm. And there he had another luminous moment of insight which took him a step further along the road to his mature philosophy of dialogue. He has described this incident in *Between Man and Man*:

When I was eleven years of age, spending the summer on my grandparents' estate, I used, as often as I could do it unobserved, to steal into the stable and gently stroke the neck of my darling, a broad dapple-gray horse. It was not a casual delight but a great, certainly friendly, but also deeply stirring happening. If I am to explain it now, beginning from the still very fresh memory of my hand, I must say that what I experienced in touch with the animal was the Other, the immense otherness of the Other, which, however, did not remain strange like the otherness of the ox and the ram, but rather let me draw near and touch it. When I stroked the mighty mane, sometimes marvellously smooth-combed, at other times just as astonishingly wild, and felt the life beneath my hand, it was as though the element of vitality itself bordered on my skin, something that was not I, was certainly not akin to me, palpably the other, not just another, really the Other itself; and yet it let me approach, confided itself to me, placed itself elementally in the relation of *Thou* and *Thou* with me. The horse, even when I had not begun by pouring oats for him into the manger, very gently raised his massive head, ears flicking, then snorted quietly, as a conspirator gives a signal meant to be recognizable only by his fellow-conspirator; and I was approved.

But once—I do not know what came over the child, at any rate it was childlike enough—it struck me about the stroking, what fun it gave me, and suddenly I became conscious of my hand. The game went on as before, but something had changed, it was no longer the same thing. And the next day, after giving him a rich feed, when I stroked my friend's head he did not raise his head. A few years later, when I thought back to the incident, I no longer supposed that the animal had noticed my defection. But at the time I had considered myself judged.[2]

The Way to Hasidism

Life in Lemberg was secure and well-rooted, in a familiar Jewish environment and with the strong presence of Solomon Buber always nearby. But when he was seventeen Buber left for the University of Vienna, to study philosophy and the history of art. Here, he wrote later, he plunged headlong into the turbulence of the period:

> Until I was twenty, and to a lesser degree even afterward, my spirit was in constant and multiple flux. Tension and release followed each other, determined by manifold influences, forever assuming new forms, but remaining without a pivot and without cumulative substance.[1]

After Vienna came the Universities of Berlin, Zurich, and Leipzig. During all these student years Buber lived in the *olam ha-tohu*, the world of spiritual confusion, of learning and study without any clear direction. His curriculum included no Jewish studies, and he was drifting away from the formal Judaism of his childhood without finding anything else enduring enough to take its place.

At all these great universities his interests were secular and remote from any leaning toward religion. He was fascinated by the life of these cities outside the walls of the universities. In Vienna he often stood in line for hours outside the Burgtheater; and, if he was lucky enough to get tickets for the highest rows in the gallery, sat enthralled by the dramatic struggle on the stage and the speech of the actors. In Leipzig he went to the Church of St. Thomas, where Bach had been cantor, and there, he said, he heard Bach's music played and sung as Bach himself would have wanted.

It was in Leipzig too, in 1900, that he was caught up by Zionism, the new doctrine of which Theodor Herzl was the striking, magnetic prophet. For the twenty-two-year-old Buber Zionism meant "the revival of coherence, equilibrium and replacement in the community." [2] It gave him "the salvation of a racial bond" [3] and a Jewish cause he could believe in. The next year, while still only twenty-three, he became editor of *Die Welt*, the official Zionist organ. One of the writers for this journal was the Roman Catholic Paula Winkler, who later married Buber and was converted to Judaism.

But basic differences soon emerged between Herzl's approach to Zionism and Buber's. Herzl was concerned with political objectives. He sought a national solution for the Jewish people in Palestine, and thought this would bring about a renaissance. Buber, on the other hand, shared Achad Ha'am's view of a cultural and spiritual Zionism. He considered the renewal of true Jewish existence and spiritual regeneration more vital than political nationalism limited to the territorial goal.

The rift was too fundamental to overcome. Buber, who was never an organization man, became disillusioned with the political infighting of the Zionist movement. At the age of twenty-six, he decided to refrain from writing and lecturing and to live in solitude seeking a new direction which had a deeper meaning than that indicated by the purely political.

As he explained, Zionism brought him back to Judaism and allowed him to reappraise it. But this was only the first step:

National confession alone does not change the Jew; he may remain as impoverished spiritually—if not quite as unsupported—with it as without. For some people, however, national confession is not sufficient unto itself, but a soaring upward. It is not a haven, but a passage to the open sea. Such people are led to transformation, and so it happened with me.[4]

Formal orthodox Judaism had disappointed Buber. Zionism had, to his mind, concentrated on the end rather than the means. Now he was again to seek a vital trend within Judaism which he could accept intellectually and emotionally and to which he could devote his brilliant but free-flowing personality. And, as happened so often in Buber's life, and as happens to people who refuse the comfort of dogma but follow their own truth wherever it leads them, the next step was in a totally unexpected direction: toward Hasidism, the movement of joyous mysticism which had developed in eighteenth-century Poland.

Buber's interest in Hasidism was kindled during his childhood summers on the family farm in Bukovina. Occasionally his father took him to the neighboring town of Sadagora, the seat of a dynasty of *zaddikim*, or "righteous men"—that is, of Hasidic master rabbis. There he watched the *hasidim* swaying and chanting in ecstasy around the man they followed because of his spiritual perfection.

Sadagora was "a dirty little town"; the rabbi's ornate palace repelled the boy; the Hasidic house of prayer and its worshipers in a trance were strange to him:

> But when I watched the Rabbi stride through the rows of supplicants, I understood what a leader was; when I saw the *hasidim* dance with the *Torah*, the Scroll of the Law, I knew what a community was.[5]

Buber watched all this with the eyes of a child—but an unusually perceptive and thoughtful child. And he made comparisons. He compared the *zaddik* with the district chief, "whose power rested on habitual coercion," [6] and, on the other hand, with the rabbi in the more conventional synagogue in Lemberg, who was certainly a righteous and God-fearing man but was nevertheless "the employee of a worship-directorate," [7] the agent of an organization. Here among the *hasidim* in Sadagora Buber found something else: "the living germ of humanity, true community and true guidance." [8]

Out of this perception as a child—"not through ideas," as he noted, "but through pictures and emotions"—came the awareness that "common veneration and common joy are the foundations of real human communion." [9]

The world, he learned then, is for the *zaddik*, the just and perfect man. And only the just and righteous man can be the true savior of the spirit.

The Hebrew word *hesed* means "loving-kindness." So a *hasid* is a man who meets the world with loving-kindness, affirming the reality about him, hallowing it and so transforming it and himself.

Later, during his adolescence, this early perception dimmed and began to slip into the unconscious. He spent his summers elsewhere and started to forget these Hasidic memories of his childhood. But after several years he returned to a newly acquired estate of his father's, near Czortkow, which was the seat of a collateral line of the same dynasty of *zaddikim* as those he had met at Sadagora.

This time Buber reacted differently to his direct contact with the *hasidim*. "In the interim," he wrote later, "I had been seized by the mental ferment which frequently characterizes the decisive years of youth, awakening the creative functions of the intellect, but bringing to an end the natural vision and perception of childhood." [10]

He found himself intellectually estranged from the *hasidim*, removed from their world and even looking down at them, "from the heights of a rational man." [11]

But although his impressions this time were less powerful and distinct, and although he was not moved as he had been before in Sadagora, he did hear for the first time the name of Besht—the initial letters of Baal Shem Tov, "Master of the Good Name," as Rabbi Israel ben Eliezer, the founder of Hasidism, was called.

Buber's visit to Czortkow was almost forgotten in the years that followed, the years of study in what he called "the world of confusion," [12] the years of involvement in the early days of the Zionist movement. But in 1904, shortly after Herzl's death, Buber came across a small book called the *Zevaat Ribesh*, the teaching and testament of the Baal Shem Tov. Buber himself recalled, in his memoir "My Road to Hasidism," how these words shone before him on the page:

> He apprehended the character of ardor in its entirety. He rose from his sleep in a passion, for he was sanctified, he had become a different person, according to the characteristics of the Holy One, blessed be He, when He created the world." [13]

In that moment, suddenly overwhelmed, Buber had a revelation in which, as he put it, he "experienced the Hasidic soul." He described this revelation movingly:

> Something indigenously Jewish rose in me, blossoming, in the darkness of exile, to a new conscious expression. I perceived the very resemblance of man to God, as deed, as an act of becoming, as a duty.[14]

Then he remembered Sadagora and Czortkow, his childhood experience of the *zaddik* and his followers. The memories of their community of joy reawoke in him and lighted his way. "I comprehended the idea of the perfect man," he recalled. "And I perceived my responsibility in proclaiming it to the world." [15]

He withdrew into one of the most rewarding periods of his life, a time of meditation and private study. He began searching out whatever he could find of the scattered Hasidic lore. Most of these tales had been handed down over the generations by disciples of the great rabbis. Some of this literature had disappeared. Some was recollected only in oral form and had to be written down. Buber sank into all of it, discovering a new world of thought and symbolic imagination, "one secret domain after another" [16] during the five years he spent living among the *hasidim* in Galicia.

Zionism had allowed him to re-establish contact with Judaism. But this renewed contact had not been profound enough. "I became acquainted with Judaism before I actually comprehended it," he wrote, in summing up this feeling. The next step was therefore "the will to cognizance"—the deeper study of what it meant to be a Jew, part of this unique community. But by "cognizance" Buber did not mean accumulating a mass of anthropological, historical, and social data, important though this might be. This was never his way. He was not a systematic academic scholar. His approach was intuitive rather than methodical. Always he looked for the wellsprings, the living sap rising in a man or a movement. Now he sought "the immediate recognition, the eye-to-eye recognition, of national character in its creative documentation." [17]

And in the Hasidic tales he found the creative folk expression of Jewish life at its most earthy, pure, and sublime.

At last he had found a creative current within Judaism to which he could respond. The message of Hasidism was exemplified in the marvelous story by the Yiddish writer Isaac Loeb Peretz, *If Not Higher*. A rabbi disappears from the synagogue for a few hours every Day of Atonement. One of his followers suspects that he is secretly meeting the Almighty, and follows him. He watches as the rabbi puts on coarse peasant clothes and cares for an invalid woman in a cottage, cleaning out her room and preparing food for her. The follower goes back to the synagogue. And when he is asked, "Did the rabbi ascend to heaven?" he replies, "If not higher."

It was this emphasis on joyful service, on reaching God through love for man, which so overwhelmed Buber. In the Hasidic tales an illiterate shepherd boy cannot read the prayers, and the only way he can show what is in his heart is to play his flute in the synagogue. And this music, the Baal Shem Tov tells the congregation, will reach heaven before our prayers.

A gloomy and sad guest from the Land of Israel, who is mourning for the destruction of Jerusalem, is told, "Beloved of the Lord, you who await the rebuilding of Zion, be joyful and happy!"

Rabbi Zusya travels from village to village collecting money to ransom prisoners. He comes to an inn where he finds a large cage in which are many kinds of birds. "Are these not prisoners?" he asks himself. "And should they not be ransomed?" And Zusya opens the cage and lets them go free.

The *hasidim* accepted the world with gladness. Today we would say they said yes to life—all of life, the high and the low, the sublime moments and the times of despair, the feasting and the poverty. They saw that there was nothing inherently evil in food, the love of man and woman, dancing, the flesh altogether. What counted was what man made of these things that had been given to him by God. In Buberian terms, a man's relationship with liquor, sex, and other worldly things could be *I-It*—using it without meeting it—or *I-Thou*—entering into it as a whole person in tune with life and the world.

There is a divine spark in every human being, the *hasidim* taught. But these sparks are isolated by shells—the *klippot*—which enclose each person as armor would. Only by living an authentic life and hallowing the world can a man cast off these shells and break their confining embrace.

The way of doing this is through *kavannah* and *hitlahavut*—two key Hasidic concepts. I know no better definitions of them than those Buber himself gave me when I asked him how I should explain them to some non-Jewish friends.

"*Kavannah*," he said, "is the direction of the heart. It is the concentration of your will, focused toward the highest Thou, toward God, if you wish. *Hitlahavut* is fervor, enthusiasm, responding with all one's heart and soul. It is a total commitment to the particular *kavannah* you wish to hallow at that time."

Hasidism gives the precept "love your neighbor as yourself" a new meaning. We should do this not because it is a commandment from God, but because through it and in it we meet God. In his brilliant address on Henri Bergson and Simone Weil, given to the Jewish Theological Seminary in New York in November 1951, Buber summed up this interpretation:

> You think I am far away from you; but in your love for your neighbor you will find me—not in his love for you but in yours for him.[18]

The Hasidic message, Buber declared in the same address, is, "You yourself must begin":

> Existence will remain meaningless for you if you yourself do not penetrate into it with active love and if you do not in this way discover its meaning for yourself. Everything is waiting to be hallowed by you; it is waiting for this meaning to be disclosed and to be realized by you. . . . Meet the world with the fullness of your being and you shall meet God. If you wish to believe, love! [19]

Fired by the Hasidic tales he was able to collect in the remote villages of Eastern Poland, Buber began translating them into German. But when he saw the first of these, *Sippurei Ma'asiyot*, the tales of Rabbi Nachman of Bratzlav, in print, Buber was disheartened. He had translated them exactly as they had been written. But the purity and clarity of the original tales had been lost, and the content distorted by interpolations added over the years by the rabbi's pupils.

He saw that he would have to adopt a different approach. "The stories would have to be told out of my own being," he wrote, "just as the painter absorbs the lines of his model in himself and creates the picture out of the formative memory." [20]

He began retelling the tales, "modestly and clumsily" [21] at first, as he said later. He tried to reproduce the sound of the tales as Rabbi Nachman had first told them to his pupils before his death in 1810. Now the stories began coming alive, partly as fairy tales, partly as symbolic parables, always rich, with a thread of fantasy and almost Oriental imagery.

Buber experienced "a sense of union with the spirit of Nachman." [22] He had found the way to attain true fidelity to the words of the rabbi, even greater fidelity than that of the version handed down by Nachman's disciples.

Other books followed: *The Legend of the Baal-Shem*, *The Great Maggid*, *The Hidden Light*, and gradually, over the years, the entire treasure trove of the Hasidic stories and legends which is now famous as *Tales of the Hasidim*.

The world Buber presented to the German and Western reader was, he said, one of legendary reality. He considered Hasidism the one great attempt in the history of the Diaspora—the Jewish dispersion and exile from Palestine—"to found a true and just community based on religious principles." This attempt failed, he felt, partly because it was too oriented toward life in Eastern Europe. "Its connections with Palestine were only sporadic and not influenced by the desire for national liberation." [23]

Every revolution becomes a dogma. As Buber would say, every Thou becomes, sadly, an It. This is the "exalted melancholy of our fate." [24] And although Hasidism, which rebelled two hundred years ago against formal, mechanical synagogue worship, has lost its original impetus toward community and has become ritualized, stagnant, and ossified, nothing can touch Buber's immense imaginative anthology of its great era. It remains one of his supreme achievements, the work in which he gave the world of the West a poetic and religious literature which would otherwise have been lost and become the exclusive property of a minority Jewish cult.

It was one of the numerous ironies of Buber's life that he— the greatest interpreter of Hasidism to the Jewish people and the civilization of the West—was not considered a *hasid* by today's *zaddikim* and their disciples. Buber did not attend prayers in synagogue and rejected the prescribed rituals. So he could not have been at home in any of the dozens of Hasidic *stiebels*, or courts of the rabbis, within a mile or two of his house in Jerusalem. But for me and many others he remains a *zaddik*, and one of the greatest.

The Narrow Ridge

"I do not accept any absolute formulas for living," Buber said to me one day. "No preconceived code can see ahead to everything that can happen in a man's life. As we live, we grow, and our beliefs change. They must change. So I think we should live with this constant discovery. We should be open to this adventure in heightened awareness of living. We should stake our whole existence on our willingness to explore and experience."

What he advocated was a "holy insecurity." This insecurity, this openness to life and to the world, should be total and apply to religious and philosophical beliefs and the way one approaches everyday existence. In a famous debate with religious dogmatists in 1919, he declared:

> O you secure and safe ones, you who hide yourselves behind the ramparts of the law so that you will not have to look into God's abyss! Yes, you have secure ground under your feet, while we hang suspended looking out over the endless deeps. But we would not change our dizzy insecurity and poverty for your security and abundance.[1]

One of Buber's favorite symbols for his position was "the narrow ridge." In the essay "What Is Man?" he explained that by using this phrase he wanted to say that I did not rest on the broad upland of a system that includes a series of sure statements about the absolute, but on a narrow rocky ridge between the gulfs where there is no sureness of expressible knowledge but the certainty of meeting what remains undisclosed.[2]

"The narrow ridge is the place where I and Thou meet," he added. When I asked him to clarify this symbolism for me, he replied, "This is not just the golden mean of the Greek ideal. No, it takes more daring than that! If you like, you can think of the narrow ridge as a region within yourself where you cannot be touched. Because there you have found yourself: and so you are not vulnerable.

"I have already said that every Thou in our life is doomed to become an It, a thing. The man or woman whom we love, whom we seek to fulfill totally, becomes a given imperfect person with a known nature and quality. A young medical student dreams passionately of curing suffering humanity. Then he becomes a doctor in a crowded hospital, with pressure, with not enough time to devote to every patient. And the suffering humans become objects. They recede to the world of the It. This is the tragedy of being human. And in order to avoid losing the I-Thou we must make our stand on the narrow ridge, as a company of soldiers takes up its position on an embattled hill and says, 'From here we shall not retreat!'

"And, as you have asked me for a clearer definition, I will say, the narrow ridge is the meeting place of the We. This is where man can meet man in community. And only men who are capable of truly saying 'Thou' to one another can truly say 'We' with one another. If each guards the narrow ridge within himself and keeps it intact, this meeting can take place."

In a later conversation he explained that mankind in our time was being polarized between the two extremes of individualism and collectivism. He found serious fault with both these dogmatic attitudes. "Individualism understands only a part of man," he said, "but collectivism understands man only as a part. Neither embraces man as a whole, as a unity."

Individualism sees man only in relation to himself. But collectivism does not see *man* at all, it sees only "society." With
the former man's face is distorted, with the latter it is masked.[3]

He understood perfectly well the reasons for this either-or
choice facing mankind in the twentieth century. It was caused by

the union of cosmic and social homelessness, dread of the universe and dread of life, resulting in an existential constitution of
solitude such as has probably never existed before to the same
extent. The human person feels himself to be a man exposed by
nature—as an unwanted child is exposed—and at the same
time a person isolated in the midst of the tumultuous human
world.[4]

The first reaction of the spirit to this new and disturbing situation is modern individualism; the second is modern collectivism.
Because man is solitary, he faces despair, and to save himself from
this despair he "resorts to the expedient of glorifying it."

But when this inevitably founders, "the human being tries to
escape his destiny of solitude by becoming completely embedded
in one of the massive modern group formations." But here too
there is a built-in illusion. In a collective there is no joining of
man with man: "the 'whole,' with its claim on the wholeness of
every man, aims logically and successfully at reducing, neutraliz-
ing, devaluating, and desecrating every bond with living beings."
Here man's isolation is not so much overcome as overpowered
and numbed. And—Buber's most fundamental objection—
"modern collectivism is the last barrier raised by man against a
meeting with himself." [5]

When both these illusory ways of organizing human society
break down, what Buber calls "the possible and inevitable meeting of man with himself" [6] can at last take place. The individual
must come face to face with his fellow man. For the fundamental
fact of human existence is neither the individual as such nor the
aggregate as such, but "man with man." [7] When one human
being turns to another as another, as a particular and specific person to be addressed, and tries to communicate with him through

language or silence, something takes place between them which is not found elsewhere in nature.

Buber called this meeting between men the sphere of "between." And it is here in the "between" that he saw hope for a third alternative between individualism and collectivism: the path of community, of small groups of people who recognize one another in the crowd and come together in a genuine encounter for the sake of all mankind, not only for that of their particular group, country, or race.

The narrow ridge was the territory of "between," as Buber saw it. And it was characteristic of his genius that he himself lived all his life in the "between," on the narrow ridge, as consistently as any member of the human community he hoped would develop as a third alternative to world chaos.

Buber had great courage. It might seem strange in a world that associates courage with war or at least with acts of physical daring: but I think Buber was the bravest person I have ever met.

When I think of Buber I remember most powerfully the fortitude which sprang from his secure vitality; his optimism and spiritual stamina, without sourness or despair; the cheerful perspective of a long view; what Paul Tillich called, in an almost Buberian phrase, "the courage to be."

During the last decade of Buber's life I witnessed many examples of this indomitable side of his personality. Two incidents in particular, which took place when he was well into his eighties, made an unforgettable impression on me.

The first was in 1961, vhen attempts were being made to form a World Peace Brigade. Buber had agreed to become one of this group's sponsors, together with Bertrand Russell, Martin Luther King, and other distinguished people associated with the concept of nonviolence.

The man behind this new movement was an idealistic, unusual figure—Anthony Brooke, a descendant of an Englishman named James Brooke, who became Rajah of Sarawak in 1841 and whose family had ruled this North Borneo territory ever since. In 1946 Sarawak was ceded to Britain as a Crown colony by the ruler, also a descendant of James Brooke. Anthony Brooke, a nephew of the ruler, opposed adherence to the British Common-wealth on the grounds that this was illegal and unconstitutional and that no plebiscite had been held. But the Sarawak nationalists were defeated, the agreement went through, and Brooke went into exile vowing to devote himself and his sizable fortune to the struggle against colonialism and for world peace.

Brooke conceived the idea of an unarmed brigade of volunteers for peace, who would be sent to areas of conflict to help refugees and the wounded and would also endeavor to bring the combat-ants together, using Gandhian techniques of passive resistance and persuasion.

His right-hand man was the Reverend Michael Scott, a Protes-tant clergyman who had been expelled from South Africa and was one of the foremost anti-apartheid lobbyists at the United Nations. He was particularly renowned for his struggle on behalf of the indigenous African inhabitants of South-West Africa, which had been illegally taken over by South Africa.

Brooke and Scott informed Buber that the founding conference of the World Peace Brigade would be held in the resort town of Burmana, in Lebanon, at the end of December. They asked Buber if he would be able to attend and to make the journey to Leba-non from Israel.

This immediately raised some interesting possibilities. Buber's name was well known in Lebanon. His books were displayed in bookstores there, and students at the American University of Bei-rut could take a course in his philosophy.

Further, the Lebanese authorities knew that Buber, an Israeli citizen, was one of the principal sponsors of the proposed World Peace Brigade. Yet the Foreign Minister, Saif Salem, had agreed that the conference should be held in Lebanon. This suggested that Buber could become the first Israeli citizen to travel openly and by invitation to an international conference held in an Arab country.

In his reply to Brooke and Michael Scott, Buber made it clear that the first meeting of the new organization should be held only in a country which was prepared to admit every single one of the sponsors, without discrimination.

So already he had fixed in his mind the idea of going. And during one of my calls upon him at that time he brought up the subject himself. Buber had a way of becoming suddenly mysterious and lowering his voice when he had something confidential to discuss. Now, too, he leaned toward me and asked, "Well, do you think I should go to Lebanon?"

I answered with another question: "Do you think you'll be given a visa?"

At this his expression changed. He sat up in his chair, almost clenched his fist, and said with great emphasis, "I'll tell you. If I can get my visa, not only should I go—but I *must* go. Because this would establish a very important principle: that travel across frontiers is possible for men who are seeking to make peace. And if I am refused a visa simply because I have an Israeli passport, I will demand that the conference be transferred from Lebanon to somewhere else where I will be admitted.

"No, the real problem for me in connection with this journey is not political, but medical."

He was silent for a moment. Then he said, "I asked my doctor about this the other day. And he told me, Out of the question. No more exhausting journeys. But perhaps if I have the visa and I explain to him how important it is he would let me go just this once. [With a wry smile.] My last journey abroad."

There we left it. But about a week later Buber phoned, quite late at night. He had his enigmatic, almost conspiratorial voice. "Do you remember the journey we were speaking about? Well, I will not be able to go. I have not been feeling too well this week. And my doctor says I must not think of it. So . . ."

What made this incident memorable for me was Buber's eagerness at the age of eighty-three to embark on this unpredictable trip if there was the slightest chance his presence could contribute to the beginning of an Israeli-Arab dialogue. And it revealed to me an aspect of his personality of which I had not been aware, that of the visionary who was not afraid to think imaginatively and act boldly and alone. Suddenly some things I had not fully absorbed from his teachings fell into place.

The second example of Buber's courage which I want to describe here was his testimony at the trial of Aharon Cohen, the well-known writer on Israeli-Arab affairs.

Cohen, who was a member of the Mapam (left-wing Labor Zionist) kibbutz of Sha'ar Ha'amakim, had published two authoritative books on the history and sociology of the Arab world. For years he had been working on his magnum opus—an analysis of the Zionist movement's relationship with the indigenous Arabs of Palestine and the neighboring lands, from the late nineteenth century to the present day. As was to be expected from his known views on this subject, he was strongly critical of the official point of view, and in particular of Prime Minister David Ben-Gurion's attitude toward the Arabs.

In 1958, while this book was being prepared for publication, Cohen was arrested on a charge of giving information to a foreign agent. What had happened was that he wished to obtain copies of Russian-language periodicals on the Middle East, dating back to before the revolution. It was proved at the trial that these were not available in the Hebrew University and National Library. So Cohen got in touch with the Russian Scientific Mission in Jerusalem, which helped him to obtain these sources for his research. During their meetings they asked him for his views on Israel's Middle East policies—views which Cohen had constantly expressed clearly and emphatically in public.

The Russians also asked Cohen about Mapam's attitude toward the Ben-Gurion coalition Government, of which it was then a part. And here Cohen made a foolish but human error. He was a member of Mapam's left wing and unpopular with the party's hierarchy, which considered that he overemphasized Marxist theory. So when his Russian contacts came to visit him at his kibbutz he wrote down their names in a kind of personal code. This was done primarily to conceal their visits not from the Government or the Secret Service—no one who knew Cohen could possibly think that he would pass on military or security secrets, even if he knew any—but from the leaders of Mapam, who liked to conduct all talks with Russian circles themselves.

Unfortunately the law in Israel was particularly stringent and, many thought, Draconian on this point. Anyone meeting "a foreign agent" could be called upon to explain why he had done so; and if the explanation did not satisfy the court, he was deemed to have passed information even if there was no evidence to this effect.

The definition of "a foreign agent" was also unclear. It could be a diplomat, a journalist, or a businessman from abroad, so that an Israeli citizen who met the correspondent of the *New York Times* casually at a cocktail party and chatted with him for half an hour was in theory liable to be asked to explain what he had been talking about.

Aharon Cohen became the first victim of this reactionary law. His arrest shocked Mapam and the kibbutz movement, and his trial became a *cause célèbre*. Cohen himself believed he had been arrested in order to stop the publication of his book. The fact is that some of the material he intended to publish was impounded to be used at the trial, which was held only after an excruciating delay of three and a half years, in 1962.

Buber knew Cohen well and had worked with him in efforts to bring Jews and Arabs together. In fact Buber wrote the preface to the third volume in the trilogy, *Israel and the Arab World*. Describing it as "an extremely important scientific work," Buber noted that it was as objective as possible and presented "tried and well-founded facts which, even if they are assembled with a certain concept in mind, are undeniably true and enable the reader to learn what actually happened and to draw his own conclusions."

Buber added, "Only someone who grew with these events and from his experiences could have written this book. Aharon Cohen grew with his experience, and in effect he continued faithfully what others had begun. A book like this can only be written with an inner fervor and a love of the cause. For history is written not in order to recall the past and also not for the future, but essentially for the present, so that the members of the present generation can learn its lesson."

When the trial opened in Haifa, Buber told Cohen he was ready to testify on his behalf. He was absolutely determined to do this, and ignored all medical and other considerations. Buber, who was then eighty-four, knew the long journey from Jerusalem to Haifa and his courtroom appearance would be an ordeal. But he believed Cohen was innocent and that the peace movement in Israel should stand by him all the way. By choosing to testify he threw the weight of his moral authority into the scales.

The Haifa District Court was crowded when Buber made his appearance as the first witness for the defense. He began by noting that he had known Cohen since 1941, when they had been among the first members of the League for Jewish-Arab Rapprochement, together with Henrietta Szold and Dr. Judah L. Magnes.

"These people," Buber testified, "were not of the kind commonly called idealists, in other words, people who believe what they believe and do not perceive the reality around them. All the people who founded the League for Jewish-Arab Rapprochement saw very clearly the reality of the situation and out of this reality came to the conclusion that there was only one way for the people of Israel to enjoy a great future in its country—to enter this region actively and dynamically, so that there would be not only a close relation between those living in the Middle East, but also cooperation, in order that this part of the world might begin a new era in its history."

Aharon Cohen had represented Hashomer Hatzair, Mapam's kibbutz movement, on the League's Executive Committee. At the end of 1941 he became secretary of the League, and Buber recalled that he met him frequently, particularly after Cohen had visited Syria and Lebanon in the fall of 1942. When the Anglo-American Commission of Inquiry visited Palestine in 1946 the League's spokesmen before it were Professor Ernst Simon, then chairman, and Aharon Cohen.

"Since my youth," Buber continued at the trial, "I have been studying human beings, and my entire philosophical thinking is based on a knowledge of their nature. Knowing human nature means knowing people, and this is the only way to learn something about mankind as a whole. I mention this in order to show that I have some experience in knowing people, and I was extremely impressed by Aharon Cohen."

At this point the prosecutor, District Attorney Y. Bahaloul, objected to Buber's remarks on the ground that they were abstract and not relevant to the trial.

But after the defense attorney, Advocate Toister, had intervened, Justice S. Kassan allowed Buber to continue, and he explained, "I am not talking about abstract things. I consider myself an expert in these matters. What we are discussing is not abstract or vague in the slightest.

"Whenever I met Aharon Cohen I always had the impression that he was extremely sincere—and this impression has remained with me till this day. When we say a man is sincere we mean basically that he says what he thinks—that is, his thoughts and his speech are identical and form a complete unity. This does not mean he utters the objective truth. Objective truth is not granted to mortals. But he says what he thinks. His mouth speaks what he thinks."

Justice Kassan: "In other words, his heart and his mouth are one."

Buber: "Yes. For me this is the main thing."

After making this statement Buber was cross-examined by both attorneys and answered questions from Justice Kassan, President of the Court, and the other two judges. For nearly three hours he remained there, replying patiently to all the queries leveled at him, his voice clear and unhurried, explaining in an almost fatherly way his conviction that a man such as Cohen could not possibly have acted deceitfully in the way the prosecution claimed he had.

He recalled how Cohen's factual knowledge of the Arab world

had impressed Dr. Chaim Weizmann, who had asked Buber, "Who is that young fellow?"

"My own profession," Buber volunteered at one point, "is philosophical anthropology, and I consider Aharon Cohen's books on the Middle East a contribution toward this science. I found in these books facts that I knew, but I also found facts that enlarged my knowledge."

In the middle of the cross-examination a fascinating discussion took place between Buber and Justice Kassan about the former's collections of Hasidic legends and whether they could be compared to Cohen's research on Jewish-Arab relations. Buber outlined his method of composition and explained that there was no real basis for comparison, as Hasidism dealt with religious faith and man's relation to the absolute, whereas Cohen's writings dealt with scientific and observable facts.

The end of Buber's testimony came when Justice A. Friedman asked him whether it was not possible that Cohen would tell the truth about certain matters but not about other matters, and whether, if he had done this, Buber would have noticed it. To which Buber replied, "I consider that I have some understanding of people, and so I declare that what Aharon Cohen says he thinks. He can make a mistake. But he says what he thinks. I have always found this to be true of him . . . and I cannot recollect a single thing which would contradict this."

Although other people also testified to Cohen's good character, the verdict went against him. Justice Kassan and later the Supreme Court, to which Cohen appealed, stated that they did not believe he had given any information to the foreign agents he had met. But, as they did not find his explanation of these contacts convincing, they were bound under the law to sentence him to prison. Eventually Cohen served nearly three years in jail before being pardoned by President Ben-Zvi.

Buber's courage—the kind of genial optimism which made him want to go to Lebanon and led him to give evidence in favor of Cohen—found its way into his writings and inspired many people who never met him in person. Professor Ernst Simon has noted what one of the bravest German fighters against Hitler, Friedrich Hielschen, wrote in his autobiography. Hielschen was a high German official who had access to the Ghetto of Lodz, from which he was able to save a number of Jews. When the Gestapo finally caught him he was tortured to make him reveal the names of his helpers. Hielschen made up his mind not to disclose any names even under the worst torture. In order to keep up his morale, he recited some of Buber's Hasidic tales to himself. As Hielschen himself noted after the war, the "vigor of love and comfort" stored in them helped him endure the torture. "Buber was not present in the flesh during this dialogue," Simon comments, "but he was there." [8]

We who were close to him in Jerusalem during the last years of his life witnessed his courage during the controversy over his stand on the Eichmann trial, when he was already over eighty. We saw his tolerance and patience during bitter personal attacks on him and marveled at it. We could see how hurt he could be, but he absorbed the hurt and transcended it, never answering bitterness with bitterness, remaining calm even when we, his friends and disciples, were indignant.

This quality of fortitude was noted by many who came into contact with him in Germany and in his Jerusalem period. In *Martin Buber: The Life of Dialogue*, Maurice Friedman quotes a striking testimony by the socialist thinker Dr. Heinz-Joachim Heydorn. Heydorn pointed out that what makes Buber's life great is more than his output of books or his speeches:

> Outside of Albert Schweitzer I know no one who has realized in himself a similar great and genuine deep identity of truth and life. . . . This little, old man with the penetrating, incorruptible eyes has already begun to project into the brokenness of our time like a legendary figure; he is a living proof of what this life is capable of when it wills to fulfill itself fearlessly and only in responsibility. . . . Buber has accomplished

what one can only say of a very few: he has reached the limits of his own being . . . and through this has made the universal transparent.

And the American Jewish scholar, Nahum N. Glatzer, has written:

When I first met Buber, his appearance told me that this was how the prophets of old must have looked. Later the image of the prophet gave way to a more human likeness. I discovered his fondness for good food, and his quick, folksy language, so different from his literary style.

However, the prophetic and the earthy Buber are deeply interrelated; are, in fact, one. His philosophy calls for a man who combines the intellectual and the concrete, the "religious" and the "secular"; a man who responds to a given situation with his undivided personality. For the world of man is a responding world; by responding we truly live.[9]

Because Buber walked the narrow ridge in a state of holy insecurity, which some men have called grace, other free spirits responded to him with admiration and respect. The writer Max Brod, the friend of Kafka, who first met Buber in Prague at the turn of the century, proposed quite seriously that he should be appointed Foreign Minister of Israel. If anyone could find a way to make peace in the Middle East, Brod said, Buber could.[10]

Saul Bellow met Buber in Jerusalem in 1959 and was greatly impressed. "He was *something*," Bellow told me. "Unforgettable." Other American Jewish writers found their way to Buber's writings. A study of his influence on such diverse figures as Norman Mailer and Allen Ginsberg would yield some surprising results. On the other hand, some prominent American Jewish intellectuals were amazed when I mentioned Buber's only novel, *For the Sake of Heaven*, and confessed they had no idea he had written any fiction.

Twenty years after the publication of *I and Thou* in 1923, the English thinker J. H. Oldham wrote:

I question whether any book has been published in the present century the message of which, if it were understood, would have such far-reaching consequences for the life of our time.[11]

The key words here perhaps are "if it were understood." Too many people who could open themselves to Buber's uncompromising message are in awe of him and have not penetrated his admittedly difficult prose style. Others know only *I and Thou* among all his books and have not discovered his wonderfully poetic lyricism or his illuminating essays on such "un-Buberian" subjects as theater, psychiatry, and anthropology.

For myself, having grown to love the man and his spiritual integrity the more deeply I entered his world, I recall what he said in *The Prophetic Faith* about the true prophet, "this quivering magnet needle, pointing the way to God." [12]

Ever since the time of Samuel, the Hebrew prophet has replaced the priest with a prophetic guidance, "instituting free announcements in place of the oracle fettered by sanctuary tradition." [13] This prophet is altogether bound by the present moment, whose potential he is to realize. Men cannot hear from him what they wish to hear:

> They can only hear what they shall hear, that is what is designed in this hour and set before them, that they may let drop into it their "yes" and "no," their decisions and their refusals to decide, the molten metal of their hour, and supply God with the material for his work.[14]

Whenever I come again upon this passage, I think to myself: If ever there was a "quivering magnet needle" in our time, it was Martin Buber. And, like all the great Hebrew prophets, he spoke not only to the Jewish people but, through them, to all mankind.

Hebrew Humanism

At one of our earliest meetings Buber said to me, "I would like to convert you to Judaism."

I was startled by this, and mumbled, "I don't know what you mean."

Buber smiled and said, "When I say Judaism I mean the kind of Judaism I believe in, which I call Hebrew humanism."

This was the first time I had heard him use this term. And in his usual informal way of teaching, when I went home that night he gave me his essay "Hebrew Humanism," published in 1942, and said, "Perhaps you would like to read it and then when you come next time we can discuss it."

In this essay Buber explains that the term sprang from the Italian Renaissance idea of affirming man and the community of man, and the belief that peoples as well as individuals could be reborn. When in 1913 he and a group of friends discussed founding a Jewish school of advanced studies—the genesis of the Hebrew University—he defined the spirit behind the idea as Hebrew humanism. Later, when Hitler came into power in Germany and Buber was faced with "the task of strengthening the spirituality of our youth to bear up against his nonspirituality," he called the speech in which he developed his program "Biblical Humanism," in order to make the first half of the dual concept still clearer.

After he had settled in Palestine and came to clarify his ideas in the essay "Hebrew Humanism," he defined the second half of the concept as *humanitas*. By this he meant the content of true humanism, which would not be merely an intellectual movement but "one which will encompass all of life's reality." [1]

Clearly there was a similarity between European and Hebrew humanism. But the term "Hebrew" was inserted to prevent the mistaken assumption that Buber was concerned with "some sort of vague humanity at large." And the use of the alternative term "Biblical" indicated that

> in this task of ours, the Bible, the great document of our antiquity, must be assigned the decisive role which in European humanism was played by the writings of classical antiquity.[2]

The Jewish people and more specifically the Jews living in Israel should, he insisted, seek to reach a farther goal than that of European humanism. It was not enough to transform our inner lives. We had to aim at nothing less than the transformation of our life as a whole: "The process of transforming our inner lives must be expressed in the transformation of our outer life, of the life of the individual as well as that of the community." And there was a mutual influence at work: "The change in the external arrangements of our life must be reflected in and renew our inner life time and again." [3]

For what the Bible has to teach us, and what no other voice in the world can teach us with such clarity and force, is

> that there is truth and there are lies, and that human life cannot persist or have meaning save in the decision on behalf of truth and against lies; that there is right and wrong, and that the salvation of man depends on choosing what is right and rejecting what is wrong; and that it spells the destruction of our existence to divide our life up into areas where the discrimination between truth and lies, right and wrong holds, and others where it does not hold, so that in private life, for example, we feel obligated to be truthful, but can permit ourselves lies in public, or that we act justly in man-to-man relationships, but can and even should practice injustice in national relationships.[4]

The Biblical *humanitas* which speaks to us from the Book today is the unity of human life under the inspiration of eternal values. It is true that because of our human shortcomings we cannot attain perfect justice in the abstract, and we are sometimes compelled to accept wrongful acts in order to preserve our community. But what matters, Buber says, is

> that in every hour of decision we are aware of our responsibility and summon our conscience to weigh exactly how much is necessary to preserve the community, and accept just so much and no more.[5]

Biblical *humanitas* is "this trembling of the magnetic needle which points the direction notwithstanding."[6] God—Buber's "Eternal Thou"—cannot be confined to a separate and isolated section of life labeled "religion." The ethical commandments given to the Jews by the Bible cannot be forgotten when we enter the world of politics or society or the state. The man who wants to follow the path of our Hebrew Biblical humanism will resist

> patriotic bombast which clouds the gulf between the demand of life and the desire of the will-to-power. He resists the whisperings of false popularity which is the opposite of true service to the people. He is not taken in by the hoax of modern national egoism, according to which everything which can be of benefit to one's people must be true and right.[7]

This was, of course, the source of the epic clash between Buber and Ben-Gurion, the first Prime Minister of Israel. A fascinating book could be written about the relationship between these two men, who continued the Biblical disputes between the prophets and the rulers. The trouble with Israel, cynics said, is that Ben-Gurion dabbles in philosophy and Buber dabbles in politics. But their confrontation touched on the very core of Israel's existence and national direction. And the echoes of their dispute remind us irresistibly of the debate between the intellectuals and antiwar protesters in the United States on the one hand, and the Johnson and Nixon Administrations on the other. There are the same overtones of visionary idealism versus official opportunism, of dynamic dreamers against cynical ground-based clerks. And Buber speaks not only for his minority circle within the Zionist movement but for all men of the pure flame when he calls for a decision in favor of "national humanism" and against "national egoism." [8]

Some Jewish nationalists, he points out, regard Israel as a nation like any other nation and consider survival a sufficient aim in itself. This is a shallow nationalism, which does not set the nation a task that will be over and above its normal everyday existence. But this is not enough for any nation, and especially not for the Jewish people, "for just as an individual who wishes merely to preserve and assert himself leads an unjustified and meaningless existence, so a nation with no other aim deserves to pass away." [9]

What Buber hoped for in the State of Israel was "a renewed people, a renewed religion, and the renewed unity of both." [10]

During my early meetings with him we spoke about the revival of Jewish national life and the need to express the Jewish ethos in our relationships with our non-Jewish neighbors in the Middle East. But it was only later, when we became more intimate and comfortable with one another, that he talked about his attitude toward orthodox Judaism.

Buber's entire philosophy was based on individual responsibility and a refusal to take shelter behind group dogmas and beliefs. So it is not surprising that he disliked organized Judaism and in particular its rigid approach to ritual.

"I am in favor of every religion in its beginning," he said. "Then it is fresh and spontaneous, filled with love and joy. If only it would stay that way! But then it becomes codified and organized. It becomes a mechanical repetition of a formula which has lost its original meaning. Look what happened to the *hasidim*! And nothing can hide the face of God from young people as organized religion does."

He felt strongly that Jewish religious leaders should move in the direction of the necessary changes brought about by Israel's rebirth. "We have radically altered the circumstances of our lives," he said to me. "We have our own state, for the first time in nineteen centuries. And yet no Chief Rabbi of Israel has found the courage to say, 'Come, let us acknowledge this revolutionary alteration of our situation and institute the reforms which must flow from it.' We need someone who would do for Judaism what Pope John XXIII has done for the Catholic Church." (This was during the Second Vatican Council.) "Perhaps we need a *Sanhedrin*: an assembly of religious leaders from all over the world. A kind of World Jewish Council, which would bring the laws up to date and would discuss such vital issues as war and poverty, on which our organized religion is almost silent.

"But if a religion is to stay fresh and spontaneous, the only way is for it to change itself constantly, to renew itself in each generation, from the inside. Else it will harden and die, even though it might not be aware of its approaching death."

What he sought was human truth, not otherworldliness. Man cannot approach the Divine by reaching out beyond the human, he insisted. He can only approach the Eternal by *becoming* human in the highest sense of the word.

So for Buber the world of religion was the world of the between: the sphere of relationships between men on this earth. Ritual and the performance of routine commandments were far less important to him than social action. Judaism should come out of the synagogue and meet God in the midst of human experience, in the cities and refugeee camps of our time. He dreamed of small communities of Jews who would translate their religious consciousness into loving action. Only then could the individual Jew realize the essence of his inherited Jewishness—not by obeying any externally imposed discipline, but by fulfilling his own inner meaning and becoming what he found potentially present within himself.

Although he had this clear vision of the form a renewed Judaism should take, he belonged to no religious group or synagogue.

There was no rabbi or community in Israel that tried consciously to follow his lead. Then in 1961 fate put me in touch with a group of people who wanted to set up a reformed and revitalized synagogue in Kfar Shmaryahu, a quiet suburban village six miles north of Tel Aviv.

In the fall of that year Rhoda and I moved from Tel Aviv to Herzlia Pituach, a few minutes walk from the Mediterranean, where our little cottage was set among pinewoods growing out of the sand dunes. There we joined several people—mainly English-speaking immigrants and Israeli-born *sabras*—in a new community formed with a definite purpose.

We wanted to break away from the rigid kind of religious service usually observed in Israel, which was an importation from Europe in the days before the birth of the State, and find a form of worship which sprang from the conditions of life in our own independent country.

It was absurd, we felt, to recite prayers about the longing for the Holy Land, composed centuries ago in Poland or Germany, or to beat our breasts about the suffering of exile when we were actually living in the land itself. Jewish life in our time had, we felt, some joy to place beside the sadness.

So we brought an Israeli-style *halil*, or recorder, into the synagogue, and an accordion, and played folk songs. We read aloud the story of the revolt in the Warsaw Ghetto. But we also read poems by Avraham Shlonsky and Natan Alterman, writers drunk with the beauty of our landscape, to express our astonished feeling of renewal. We joined hands and danced in the synagogue to the music of popular Israeli tunes such as *Hava Nagila* and did the *hora* holding the Scrolls of the Law.

Also, we said, we would adapt our communal affirmation of Judaism to the familiar pattern of life in the second half of the twentieth century. Cars were not godless objects which broke the law about making fire on the Sabbath, but simply a means of transport which enabled people to enjoy their day of rest more fully. And in an age when marriage was a democracy and husbands and wives equal partners we thought it ridiculous to segregate women upstairs and not allow them to play their full role in worship.

So the members of our congregation drove up to the synagogue on Sabbath mornings and entered and sat together as a family. Women were called to the Law and stood side by side with men during the service. Afterward, on a spring or summer day, people drove off—not furtively from a parking lot in a side street, but from the synagogue's own car park—for a day picnicking in the forests of Mount Carmel or by the seaside, with their outdoor equipment in the back of the car. We saw nothing wrong or un-Jewish in this, and found the combination of morning worship and open-air recreation a harmonious way of expressing our sense of fulfillment as Israeli Jews, in a country where there is only one real day of rest a week.

Now, of course, this relaxed, contemporary approach to Jewish existence is common in the United States, through the Progressive Judaism movement and its Reform Temples. But in Israel in 1961 it was greeted by orthodox circles as something close to heresy—an attitude which still persists at the time of this writing. Our pragmatic views were all branded as "Christian" and condemned with hysterical vehemence. Our rabbi was not recognized by the Chief Rabbinate and could not therefore marry or bury members of his own congregation.

Two of the founders of our group were the writer Meyer Levin, and his wife, Tereska Torres. As a young man Meyer had written a book based on Hasidic legends, and he was devoted to Buber as I was.

In the summer of 1962, when our little group became more cohesive, Meyer and two other residents of the village of Kfar Shmaryahu applied for permission to use the village hall for the High Holiday season.

Most members of the Kfar Shmaryahu Council, which ran the affairs of the village, supported the orthodox synagogue, which was then the only one in the area. They refused permission to use the village hall for our Reform-style services.

Meyer and his two friends applied to the Supreme Court for an injunction against the Kfar Shmaryahu Council. They argued that they were taxpayers who wished to use the village hall for a public function. They were prepared to pay the usual fee for the use of the hall, which was available for the evenings they wanted it. But the hall had been denied to them purely because they wished to pray in a way different from that favored by the majority of the Council. The issue was simply whether a Jew living in the independent sovereign State of Israel was entitled to worship freely as he wished.

And on the eve of Succot, the Festival of Tabernacles, the Court handed down a historic decision upholding the right of every Jewish resident of Israel to pray according to the dictates of his conscience and ordering the Kfar Shmaryahu Council to give us the use of the hall.

The news of the decision came through shortly before noon, a few hours before Succot began. Meyer, his co-plaintiffs, the rabbi, and all the members of the congregation who could manage it rushed to the village hall and began building the traditional *succa* (a symbolic decorated hut, commemorating the wandering of the Jews). Men left their offices and went off to the woods to find branches and greenery. There was an ambience of joy and fervor which filled everyone working against time to get the *succa* ready for the evening service. All of us felt that this was what community meant; what freedom could be like; what Judaism was all about. Meyer and the rabbi, stringing bunches of grapes from the roof, looked like Essenes. Our religious ecstasy flowed all that day and filled the green prayer room that evening with a harmony and brotherhood forming our new congregation in one great surge of understanding and love.

The next time I saw Buber in Jerusalem I told him about this experience and the awareness we had all had of communion and rebirth. He was deeply interested, and, as he usually did when something caught his imagination, asked many questions: How many members did we have? How many of these were English-speaking? How many *sabras*? Were women prominent in roles

other than seeing to the decorations? Had we discussed the shape
of the future community? What would happen if someone
wanted to get married or died and the rabbi could not act for
him? Would we let someone join the community if he could not
pay the membership fee?

Then, after I explained that we ourselves did not know the answers to these questions—it had all happened so suddenly and
we would have to explore the issues as we went along—Buber
leaned back in his chair and said, "Important things sometimes
happen like this, in a spiritual explosion. And when a whole community feels it, it can lay the foundation for that community to
exist, to live its own life. Of course, some people will drift away
once the initial excitement is over and the real existence of your
community begins. But you seem to have a dedicated group of
men and women who want to make something new. And if you
can build on this and extend the nucleus, you might do something important for Jewish life in this country.

"One of the questions is the role of prayer in a community.
You know that I myself do not believe at all in prayer as the
objective, as an end in itself. Prayer is a prelude. Study, meditation, fasting, if anyone thinks it necessary for him to fast, are the
preparations. But then must come action. Spiritual energy must
overflow into social action. Otherwise prayer becomes intro-
verted, narcissistic, sufficient in itself.

"If you want to avoid this, I think you would be wise to start
from the beginning with tasks outside the ritual and ceremonial.
Try to reach new circles—sabra youth, disillusioned with se-
vere unbending Judaism; recent settlers in the immigrant camps;
Oriental Jews. From what you have told me your members are
wealthy and living in a middle-class suburb.

"You must be careful not to become narrow and exclusive.
Try to bring in people from other sections of society, even if
they cannot pay membership fees. They have other things to
contribute. For the same reason you should avoid having services
in English. Some of your American and South African members
will no doubt want this because it will be easier for them.

"But you should resist the temptation. A Reform movement in Israel cannot be the same as a Reform Temple in America. It must be for the whole nation, not only for some English-speaking Jews. Give lessons to those members who do not yet speak Hebrew. The community could do this. But the principle should be Hebrew inside the synagogue and at meetings."

I passed Buber's advice on to our members, who appreciated it. And from that time on, at his own request, I kept him in touch with the development of our community and the spiritual direction it was taking.

This direction was, as Buber had suggested, strongly toward social action and involvement in the life of Israel outside our synagogue nucleus. Our first rabbi, Jerry Unger, had left the year after that triumphal Succot celebration. He was replaced by Moshe Zager, a graduate of the Hebrew Union College in Cincinnati.

Moshe and I became close friends and spent a lot of time talking about what our congregation could do in our immediate environment to assist areas of neglect or indifference. One day we went for a walk down to the sea, past the ruined Crusader castle of Arsuf, talking about the next stage in our program. We went through the *ma'abara* (immigrants' transit camp) of Nof Yam, a dirty, untidy heap of tin and asbestos huts dropped onto the hot sand, with no trees, only barricades of prickly pears left from the former Arab village. And I remember clearly how on that day our eyes were opened to the meaning of this everyday sight, and we saw not only the possibilities in the *ma'abara* but also our obvious duty and obligation.

Here was a small colony of recently arrived settlers from North Africa and Eastern Europe, living in near-hovels only two or three minutes' walk from the neat villas, the clipped lawns, the pompous luxury hotels, of Herzlia Pituach.

This was the beginning of efforts to set up a nursery school and kindergarten in the *ma'abara* which involved us all for months and which eventually prompted the local authorities to take over this responsibility themselves.

But although the work in the *ma'abara* was a new departure for us, what I remember most vividly from this period, and what Buber thought most significant, was our link with the members of the Bnei Israel community in their struggle for recognition.

The Bnei Israel were Jews from Bombay in India. Many of them had immigrated to Israel and lived in Lod and other towns near Tel Aviv. Most of them were orthodox and followed all the traditional Jewish customs, with several quaint additions of their own, for example in the dishes they served at the Passover Seder.

But although they were so devout and apparently conformist, the Bnei Israel were not accepted fully as Jews by the Chief Rabbinate. They were short and dark and looked exactly like everybody's image of an Indian. Orthodox circles in Jerusalem darkly suspected intermarriage. So when a Bnei Israel boy wanted to marry a girl outside that community, he was asked to produce proof that his parents and grandparents had been Jewish, and not ordinary Indians of the Hindu or Moslem faith.

Moshe and I learned about this for the first time, in common with our fellow Israelis, when several Bnei Israel youths who had been refused permission to marry Jewish girls asked the Government to send them back to India.

The Chief Rabbinate's insistence on "Jewish racial purity" appalled us. It smacked of the Nuremberg Laws and of the prying back unto the second and third generation.

Moshe and I went out to Lod to meet some of the Bnei Israel who were pressing the authorities to recognize them as Jews or to let them return to India. We were impressed by their sincerity and passion, and could not disagree with the alternatives they posed to the Israeli government.

For their part, they said to us, "We are like your community in Kfar Shmaryahu. You too are in conflict with the rabbis in Jerusalem. You cannot worship as you please. We are in the same boat. And so we would like to cooperate with you. Then we can fight together for our rights as Jews in the State of Israel."

We agreed to do what we could to help them in their struggle for recognition. As a first step it was decided that, because we were centered in Kfar Shmaryahu and they were in Lod, we would come out to them one or two evenings a week, and they would attend festivals and other special occasions at our synagogue.

When we met in their tiny assembly hall in Lod there was usually a short service, and then they split up into various groups, some learning the Bible and others Hebrew. The atmosphere was earnest and fervent, almost evangelical. Sometimes they visited us and we prayed together. Our visitors soon tired of our sedate German or Russian tunes and burst into strange-sounding Indian chants which first startled, then captivated us and swept us along in their naïve rhythm until we were all hoarse and felt tremendously affectionate toward one another.

So when the Bnei Israel finally lost patience and decided to hold a sitdown strike in Jerusalem, it was natural that we would help people who by now were our friends. They squatted outside the Jewish Agency in Jerusalem and declared that they would stay there in Gandhian nonviolence until their demands were met.

We helped them with blankets, clothing, and food. We sat with them on the stony ground outside the Jewish Agency, and helped with the care of the children and babies who squatted uncomprehendingly with their parents. I found it moving to sit the whole day under an awning sheltering us from the hot sun and to feel the despair of these simple people and their agony once they had come to the Promised Land and found they were not accepted as the Jews they had always been in India.

After two or three days, when the authorities made no move, several of the more rebellious younger Bnei Israel began a hunger strike. They carried this on for several days, after which the Israeli Government initiated a compromise solution which satisfied the Indian Jews' demands and ended the sit-in. The Chief Rabbinate agreed to accept a statement by a Bnei Israel bridegroom that he was a Jew, without examining his background.

Buber followed the Bnei Israel struggle closely. The open strip of ground where families camped out in makeshift tents and blankets was only a short walk from his house. And I remember that one day, after spending several hours with the squatters, I strolled over to his place and related some of my impressions.

In his opinion, the fact that the Bnei Israel won their civil liberty only after a public protest pointed the way for other religious groups which did not receive equal treatment under Israeli law.

"I would not be surprised," he said, "if in the long run you members of a Progressive or Reform community will have to do something similar in order to ensure your own rights." The problem as a whole will only be solved, he added, when there is civil marriage and divorce in Israel as an alternative to the religious ceremony.

As time went on the Kfar Shmaryahu Reform bridgehead began to stabilize and then to expand. Around the original solid nucleus gathered others who sensed that, fifteen years after Israel's birth, something was lacking in the country's spiritual makeup and sought to restore it. We began experimenting with new forms of communal worship and expression—midnight study groups which went on until three or four in the morning and left us exhausted but exalted; prayers in the open air. And we went deeper into questions of Jewish identity and how our renewed contact with the Holy Land should affect the outward symbols of our faith, after so many centuries of introspective seclusion.

During the exploration of this seminal problem I invited Buber down to talk with us. It was the summer of 1964, and Rosh Hashana was drawing near. I asked him whether he could visit us at the festival and meet our members for a discussion on the forms Jewish expression should take now we had our national independence.

But Buber was already not well enough to undertake the journey to the coast. He said he would have liked to see what we were doing and to celebrate the holiday with us. However, his doctor would not even let him leave his house in Jerusalem, much less make a journey and return of some eighty miles.

"But I would like you to take a message to your members," he said.

He thought for a moment, half-closing his gray eyes.

Then he said, "Please tell them they are doing something very important in Jewish religious life. This is the kind of pioneering we need now: spiritual pioneering. Perhaps if the *hitlahavut* of the original *hasidim* could be brought into contact with the soil of this land something new and lasting might result. This is my hope for your community on Rosh Hashana."

If ever a man was "no prophet in his own city" (the literal form of the Biblical proverb) Buber was that man. Yehoshua Brand put his finger on the central paradox in Buber's life when he wrote:

Buber was an enigma even in his lifetime. On the one hand he was surrounded by admiration and affection, especially in Germany and Western Europe, where people considered him an original thinker, a new Jewish prophet. He was respected not only by the leaders and philosophers of these countries, who hearkened to his words and even made the pilgrimage to Jerusalem to see him, but also by the masses, the young people who sought him out. But on the other hand here in Israel he was surrounded by a wall of indifference and we hardly listened to him, not at the famous Biblical symposiums and not on other occasions, and our young people knew scarcely anything about him.

What was the reason for this strange attitude towards Buber? We are familiar with the tortured path which is sometimes the lot of an original spirit. He is pushed to one side by those who have seized the positions of influence, for whom mediocrity is their standard and routine plodding their main virtue. He is mocked and isolated, and sometimes they bring about the decay of his creative powers. But if this man attains recognition among the wise men of other nations and is acclaimed by them—he is doubly scorned for this!

Perhaps the mutual contempt displayed in all spheres of our lives in the Diaspora, and also in Israel, is responsible for eliminating from our hearts all feelings of honor and respect for human greatness. If we do not succeed in correcting this serious fault, we will not be able to produce truly great men.[11]

Buber's lifelong friend and disciple, Professor Shmuel Hugo Bergman, had a different explanation for Buber's lonely position. Although Buber had lived in Jerusalem since 1938, Bergman noted, there was a barrier between him and the rest of the Yishuv, the modern Jewish community of Palestine, "as if he was a foreign element in our midst and was not entirely one of us." One of the most decisive reasons for this alienation, Bergman felt, was

the fact that Buber's name is famous all over the world and he is perhaps the only one among us who has such a great international reputation. He is better known and more famous in the United States, Britain and Germany than in Israel. In its attitude to its great son the *Yishuv* is like the hen in the fable, who sat on a goose egg, hatched it out and then did not know what to do with the result.

In the range and extent of his writings Buber surpasses the dimensions of a small community. We, the Jews who live in Israel, are like one large family, with our common celebrations of joyous occasions and our many family squabbles. We are one house. And, as the Czech proverb says: "What you cook at home you have to eat at home." Here at home Buber is one of us, someone we know. But at the same time he belongs to the whole world. Do we really need Hammarskjöld to come here from the United Nations and to tell us who Buber is and what he means to him? Don't we all know that Buber lives in Talbieh in Jerusalem, in Lovers of Zion Street, and that he is one of us? This detracts a little from the homeliness and the family feeling of our little community. It is certainly, I think, one of the reasons for Buber's so-called "alienation" in our midst.[12]

Whatever the reasons for this isolation, the fact is that Buber was loved and adored by his small familiar circle but bitterly criticized or at best ignored by most of the population of Israel. Dr. Baruch Kurzweil, a prominent literary critic, expressed a prevailing view when he attacked Buber's "unbounded self-confidence, which is the mark of narcissism."

Kurzweil complained that people were drawn to Buber because they saw him as

> a man of the spirit, a rare wise man filled with self-calm, self-confidence and the love of life, a good man, whose words were well-spoken, quiet, and full of optimism and hope. And so the miserable people, the divided souls, eaten up by doubt, sought Buber's company. A wise man who loved himself and life so much was sure to love them as well. And with great compassion and sympathetic patience, mingled with complete indifference, Buber received all those who came to him. He took them all under the wing of his infinitely broad ego. . . .[13]

A strange picture of Buber—even though he did have his Olympian side. But no one who had any close contact with him would recognize the self-centered poseur of Kurzweil's description. This and similar hostile broadsides invariably sprang from prejudice and conservative opposition to his views on Jewish religious ritual and such political questions as Israeli-Arab relations and the Jewish attitude to Germany.

The widely differing appraisals of his position in contemporary Jewish life emerged strikingly from tributes paid to him by several prominent American rabbis.

At the Kingsbridge Heights Jewish Center in the Bronx, Rabbi Israel Miller, President of the Rabbinical Council of America, credited Buber with "opening up the multi-colored world of Hasidism to Western culture and to the non-Jewish community."

Yet, the rabbi felt, Buber's theology could not be universally accepted by orthodox Jews:

> Though his thinking reflected exceptional religious sensibility and a deep sense of spiritual perception, and provided useful insights into the relationship of man and his Maker and man and his fellow man, it failed to realize the central role of *Halacha* [religious law] in Jewish life, both at the practical and philosophical level.

Rabbi Miller stated that "Buber tried to divorce the religious experience from its positive Halachic context," and overlooked the importance of "this divine imperative in Jewish life." Without the normative element in the religious experience, the rabbi said, no faith community can thrive, and particularly not the Jewish community:

> To equate religious awareness with a subjective inner experience is contrary to the very essence of Judaism.

As would be expected, Reform preachers took a more positive attitude toward Buber's life and teachings.

Rabbi William F. Rosenblum, rabbi emeritus of Temple Israel of New York, declared that the measure of a philosopher's greatness is the impact he makes on universal thought.

"In this respect," he said, "Martin Buber will take his place with such great Jews as Maimonides and Spinoza, who influenced not alone their own people in their lifetimes and not alone the non-Jewish world of their era, but Christian thought in general."

Rabbi Rosenblum remarked that Buber put Hasidism in modern dress:

> He gave the *hasid* a new image, a Jew no longer dressed in a *kaftan* and wearing *payot* [earlocks], but a Jew and a neighbor like any other, whose identifying mark was that he made his religion more a matter of the heart and head than of the mind alone.

And in a perceptive address Rabbi Joseph Sternberg told Temple Ansche Chesed:

> The postwar world was plunged into profound philosophic and experiential perplexity, both individual and collective.
> Armed with technological weaponry, equipped with scientific advances, engaged in automatic activity, man stood in danger of losing his soul. Martin Buber came to find it for him.[14]

The debate between Buber's supporters and his detractors will continue—because the worldwide trend away from formalism and toward spontaneity and freshness of spiritual discovery is having repercussions within all movements inside Judaism. Buber was not only part of this trend but, we can now see more clearly, one of its supreme originators.

"In all my speeches and essays during the last sixty years," he said to me, "I have never described Judaism as something which should be known for its own sake, but always as something which shows us the way. It is important to study our heritage and literature, to read the wisdom of our great teachers, perhaps even to pray, if someone finds it helps him to pray. But none of these things should be an end in themselves. Judaism is sterile unless it tells us how to act. If we try to listen to its real voice, it can give us what we have lost: the link between our everyday lives and the absolute."

The Zionist movement and the longing for a Jewish state were focused on the relation between Jews and their surroundings. Buber put the question in a different way, with a change of emphasis. What does it mean when a man says, "I am a Jew"? What does it imply for his own life, for his integrity and conscience? How should he fulfill the inner meaning of the Jewishness he has inherited?

Buber uncompromisingly rejected all practices that did not spring from the depth of the personality, and for him this meant replacing the mechanical repetition of inbuilt, structured *mitzvot*, or religious commandments, with the unstructured and challenging vision of Hebrew humanism.

To fulfill this vision man must become man in the truest sense of the word, "wholehearted" as he was created to be, responding to God's demands of truth and righteousness. But it is not enough that here and there a man ascends "from the biological law of power, which the nations glorify in their wishful thinking, to the sphere of truth and righteousness." This transformation must happen in the life of the entire people, "thus providing an order of life for a future mankind, for all the peoples combined into one people."[15]

Biblical man, Buber says, is man facing this demand:

He accepts it or rejects it. He fulfils it as best he can or he rebels against it. He violates it and then repents. He fends it off, and surrenders. But there is one thing he does not do: He does not pretend that it does not exist or that its claim is limited.[16]

And when a man incorporates this demand for righteousness, "absorbs it with his very flesh and blood," [17] and lives by it not because it is an externally imposed code, but because it springs from within his inviolate, indestructible core of conscience— then this man is a Hebrew humanist. And through his life the original ethical impulse of the Bible would speak clearly to all Jews and to all men, as Buber did in his life. I do not think this vision is any less topical or challenging than the demands of orthodox organized Jewry.

Facing the Middle East

Buber was convinced that Arab-Israeli relations were first and foremost an internal Jewish problem. One of his closest associates in his efforts to improve them, Professor Ernst Simon, has pointed out that

> Buber considers our attitude to the neighboring people not only Israel's major foreign policy problem, but also an indivisible part of the Jewish question and of Judaism itself, precisely as anti-Semitism is a Christian question, a touchstone of this religion's moral validity.[1]

Buber believed that the Jews who were returning to the land of their forefathers should behave toward the people already living in this land according to the precepts of the Old Testament. He drew a sharp distinction between Israel and what he called "Zion." Israel was the physical and geographical fact, the autonomous strip of territory which would offer the scattered Jewish people a focal point and conditions of normal national life. But this country or community was only a vessel. It had to be filled with a way of life liberated from the spiritual wounds of ghetto existence. The State of Israel was only an instrument, a neutral political entity which had to be imbued with the highest values distilled by the Jews from all the experience of exile.

"The command to serve the spirit," Buber insisted, in an address to the American Friends of *Ichud* in 1948, "is to be fulfilled by us today in this state, starting from it." [2] And he told the Jerusalem Ideological Conference in August 1947 that the generation living in Israel was "the first generation after two thousand years" that had "the prerequisite for fulfilling its task, that is, the independence of a strong nucleus." This gave the generation which had witnessed Israel's rebirth "the power to determine for itself in no small measure its institutions, its modes of life and its relations to other nations." [3]

But the goal should not be merely physical control of the historic territory, but what he termed "Zion"—a spiritual goal founded on, but higher than, the purely material or physical goal.

Israel should "take part in the redemption of the world" by being "a nation which establishes truth and justice in its institutions and activities." [4] He hoped that the State's establishment would be the "first step in the direction of Zion." [5]

"This quasi-Zionism, which strives to have a country only, has attained its purpose," he declared. "But the true Zionism, the love of Zion, the desire to establish something like 'the city of the great king' (Psalm 48:3 in the Holy Scriptures for Jewish worship; 48:2 in the King James Version), of 'the king' (Isaiah 6:5), is a living and enduring thing." [6]

Only in this way could the newborn State contribute to human civilization as a whole and avoid the dangers of a narrow, self-centered nationalism. It was characteristic of Zion that it could be built "only *bemishpat* (Isaiah 1:27), that is, only 'with justice.' " "A wrong way, i.e. a way in contradiction to the goal, must lead to a wrong goal." Israel was commanded by its history to seek the path of peace:

> The prophecy of peace addressed to Israel is valid not only for the days of the coming of the Messiah. It holds for the day when the people will again be summoned to take part in shaping the destiny of its earliest home; it holds for today.[7]

Only if the Jewish people in Israel preserved the spirit of justice as its guide "could it hope to bring forth something greater than merely one more state among the states of the world." [8]

As he told the Anglo-American Commission in Jerusalem on March 14, 1946:

> The responsibility of those working on the preparation of a solution to the Palestine problem goes beyond the frontiers of the Near East, as well as the boundaries of Judaism. If a successful solution is found, a first step—perhaps a pioneer's step— will have been taken towards a more just form of life between people and people.[9]

The test of "this dream which has as yet found no fulfillment, the dream of Zion," [10] would be Israel's ability to form ties of cooperation and partnership with the Arabs, who were also struggling for national liberation and a spiritual renaissance. It was typical of Buber's deep-rooted realism that he devoted so much of his time to the search for a practical Jewish-Arab understanding, while engaged in his constant quest for solutions to the deepest mysteries of man's existence.

Over a span of more than forty years he made many speeches and wrote many articles proposing ways of attaining better relations between Arabs and Jews. Most of these were about "topical" matters—in other words, the affairs or problems of the time at which they were written and to the solution of which they were addressed. Yet despite this immediacy, or perhaps because of it, they speak to us as well, many difficult months after the events and the problems they discussed have been solved or at least overtaken by history. They have not lost any of their force and wisdom. Perhaps that is the supreme test of their truth.

Buber's first major public stand on the possibilities of Jewish-Arab cooperation was made in 1921, during the Twelfth Zionist Congress, held that year in Carlsbad. As a member of the Political Committee of this Congress, he proposed forming a federation of Middle East states which would link the future Jewish community with its Arab neighbors. The reasons he advanced for this far-reaching proposal contained the kernel of all his thinking on the Jewish people's ties with the Middle East peoples during the turbulent years which followed.

He began by declaring:

Our national desire to renew the life of the people of Israel in their ancient homeland is not aimed against any other people. As they enter the sphere of world history once more, and become once more the standard-bearer of their own fate, the Jewish people, who have constituted a persecuted minority in all the countries of the world for two thousand years, reject with abhorrence the methods of nationalistic domination, under which they themselves have long suffered. We do not aspire to return to the land with which we have inseparable historical and spiritual ties in order to suppress another people or to dominate it. In this land, whose population is both sparse and scattered, there is room both for us and for its present inhabitants, especially if we adopt intensive and systematic methods of cultivation.

Our return to the Land of Israel, which will come about through increasing immigration and constant growth, will not be achieved at the expense of other people's rights. By establishing a just alliance with the Arab peoples, we wish to turn our common dwelling-place into a community that will flourish economically and culturally, and whose progress would bring each of these peoples unhampered independent development.

He expressed the wish that between the socialist Jewish community (which he at that time foresaw) and the working Arab people "there would spring up the deep and constant solidarity of genuine interests, which will eventually overcome the opposing interests of this difficult hour."

Then, he hoped,

out of the sense of these links there will arise in the hearts of the members of the two nations feelings of mutual respect and goodwill, which will operate in the life of both the community and its individual members. Only then will both peoples meet in a new and glorious historical encounter.[11]

This striking address shows that, with astonishing foresight, Buber sought the solution of the Palestine question within the wider dimensions of the Middle East as a whole fifty years ago. He was in a real sense, as Simon has said, "the pioneer of the regional concept." [12]

By setting up the aim of a broad confederacy of Middle East peoples or states, the Jews and the Arabs would, he felt, become allies in their search for independence and a national revival. Within this confederation all partners who wished to join could develop freely, maintaining their cultural and spiritual autonomy while cooperating economically for the benefit of the region as a whole.

In an address to the Fifteenth Zionist Congress, held in Basel in 1929, Buber made the same point even more emphatically:

> The maintenance of our existence is undoubtedly an essential prior condition of all our actions. But this is not enough. We also need imagination. Another thing we need is the ability to put ourselves in the place of the other man, the stranger, and to make his soul ours. I must confess that I am horrified at how little we know the Arabs. I do not delude myself into believing that at this time there is peace between our good and the good of the Arabs, or that it is easy to attain a peace of this kind. And yet, despite the great division between one and the other, and despite the fact that this division is not the result of merely an illusion or of politics, there is room for a joint national policy, because both they and we love this country and seek its future welfare; as we love the country and together seek its welfare, it is possible for us to work together for it. [13]

As the conflict in Palestine deepened, as the full intensity of the impending tragedy became clear to those with insight, Buber came out firmly in an address in Berlin in 1929 on the side of those who called for an attempt to come to terms with the Arabs:

> Those who favor only the power will argue against me that my demand for a responsible attitude toward our Arab neighbors is a 'purely moral' one. Yet it is actually a political demand, in the full meaning of this term. . . . It is unthinkable that those who hold dear the values cherished by the people of Israel will start their road by acting unjustly. He who does this

commits not only a moral, but a political sin. . . . Every immoral policy is a bad policy." [14]

Buber's approach to the key issue facing the Zionist movement in the period between the two world wars was naturally criticized as abstract moralizing which could never be accepted by practical politicians charged with the conduct of everyday affairs. However, it must be remembered that in the 1920s Weizmann's pragmatic attitude to the Arabs was still dominant.

The Weizmann-Feisal agreement (which provided for Jewish-Arab cooperation) was still fresh in people's minds; there were still some Arab circles willing to find a *modus vivendi* with the Zionist settlers; Jewish immigration to Palestine had not yet reached the peak waves of the thirties; and such thinkers as A. D. Gordon had generated a passionate neo-Tolstoyan idealism which found expression in the search for peaceful ties with the Arabs of Palestine, as well as in new agricultural and social forms. It was a time when many sincere and thoughtful Zionists were troubled about the impact their movement was having on the lives of the *fellaheen*.

Hence Buber's demand for an attempt to reach an understanding with the Arab national movement was timely and evoked a response from other people who were thinking along similar lines.

He was still in Germany, acting as spiritual mentor to the besieged Jewish community. He formed ties with Dr. Judah L. Magnes, head of the *Brith Shalom* (Covenant of Peace) group, and assisted him in his efforts to make contact with progressive Arab circles in Palestine and other countries. Meanwhile the group appealed to the Jewish population to exercise self-restraint in the face of Arab attacks and not to become involved in a chain reaction of violence.

But events were moving too fast for these warning voices to be heeded. In Germany what Buber later termed "the twelve-year reign of *homo contrahumanus*" [15] had begun. Jewish fugitives from Nazi terror began streaming into Palestine. This wave of desperate immigrants increased tension between the Jews and the Arabs. As Buber pointed out in his address to the American Friends of *Ichud*, "Israel and the Command of the Spirit," Zionist settlement in Palestine had been governed by "the principle of selective, organic development" based on the kibbutzim, *halutziut* (pioneering) and socialist, humanist values, until Hitler began exterminating millions of helpless Jews. Now "the harassed, tormented masses crowded into Palestine. Unlike the *halutzim*, for whom no sacrifice toward building the land of Jewish rebirth was too great, they saw in this land merely safety and security." Yet "who would have taken it upon himself to obstruct this onrush of the homeless in the name of the continuation of the selective method!" [16]

This flood of homeless refugees brought the already critical situation in Palestine to boiling point:

> Since a Jewish-Arab solidarity had not been instituted, either in the form of facts or even in an announced program of cooperation, the Arab peoples received the mass immigration as a threat and the Zionist movement as a 'hireling of imperialism' —both wrongly, of course. Our *historical* re-entry into our land took place through a false gateway.[17]

As the spokesman of the German Jewish community, Buber left for Palestine only in 1938, and was caught up in this tragic dilemma between the need to save the survivors of Nazism and the moral imperative to avoid injustice to the Arabs already living in the Holy Land.

As events in Palestine moved toward a crisis which everyone foresaw but no one could prevent, Magnes, Buber, and their friends did what little they could to avert the catastrophe. In August 1942 they founded the *Ichud* Association in order to bring moderate Jews and Arabs together. But the moderates on both sides, clearly in the minority toward the end of the British mandate, were unable to halt the deterioration of relations which resulted in the 1948 hostilities.

In 1946, at the height of the tension, Buber was intimately involved in a determined effort to find a solution which would avert war between Jews and Arabs. Aharon Cohen, the Israeli authority on the Arab world, has told this little-known story of a joint Arab-Jewish initiative, from the point of view of one who played a leading role in it at the time.

On November 11, 1946, an Arab body named *Falastin el-Jedida* ("The New Palestine") signed an agreement on cooperation and mutual assistance with the League for Jewish-Arab Rapprochement and Cooperation, of which Magnes and Buber were the spiritual mentors. The document set forth agreement on the following principles:

> Complete cooperation between the two peoples in all spheres;
> Political equality between the two peoples through the attainment of Palestine's independence;
> Jewish immigration according to the country's economic absorptive capacity;
> The affiliation of the independent Jewish-Arab Palestine to a pact with the neighboring countries in the future.

The League also expressed its readiness to support the activities of *Falastin el-Jedida*, which would include oral information and the publication of a journal called *Al Ikha* (Brotherhood). The Arab group in turn noted its support for the League's aims and activities. Identical versions of the agreement were drawn up and signed in Arabic and Hebrew.

The founder and leader of *Falastin el-Jedida* was Fawzi el-Husseini, a member of the well-known Husseini family and a cousin of the fanatically anti-Zionist Mufti of Jerusalem, Haj Amin el-Husseini. Fawzi, who was forty-eight at the time, had been active in the Arab national movement for many years and had taken part in anti-Jewish riots. For doing this he was jailed by the British Mandatory authorities.

In the course of time, however, and as tension grew until an explosion seemed inevitable, he decided that the only way to attain a solution was through an agreement with the Jews and an attempt to establish political equality between the two peoples.

At a public meeting in Haifa on July 22, 1946, he explained that his group thought an agreement could be reached, although there were many obstacles. The prime condition was "the principle of non-domination of either people by the other and the establishment of a binational state on the basis of complete political equality and cooperation . . . between the two peoples in the economic, social and cultural spheres."

This agreement should, he said, be granted approval by the United Nations, in order to ensure an independent, binational Palestine.

At another meeting in Jerusalem in August 1946 el-Husseini declared, "The official policy on both sides—Arab and Jewish —brings nothing but harm and suffering to both Arab and Jewish peoples. The Jews and the Arabs once lived in friendship and cooperation. There are Arabs and Jews from the previous generation who were suckled by the same mother. . . . I took part in the 1929 riots against the Jews. But over the years I came to realize that this road is pointless. The imperialist policy is playing with both of us, with the Arabs as well as the Jews, and there is no other way ahead of us except uniting and working hand in hand for our mutual benefit."

Fawzi and his friends began enlisting supporters. Among those who gathered around him were teachers, students, journalists, businessmen, and workers—both Moslems and Christians. They began plans for publishing their journal and acquiring a clubroom. El-Husseini was not deterred by warnings and threats. When extremist Arab circles sent someone to demand that he call off his campaign, he replied, "History will judge which of us followed the right path."

But the Arab leadership did not want to wait for the verdict of history. On November 23 Fawzi el-Husseini was murdered. He paid with his life for his daring and boldness. His murderers were never found, although everyone knew they were extremist Arabs who wanted to warn off any dissident elements who ventured to criticize the Mufti's anti-Zionist line.

As for the Jewish reaction to Fawzi's assassination, the Histadrut daily *Davar* reported on December 22, 1946, from the Zionist Congress at Basel:

> Laughter and amusement were aroused by the story told by the Hashomer Hatzair spokesman, Ya'akov Hazan, about an Arab who sympathized with Zionism and was murdered in Jerusalem because he believed in a Jewish-Arab agreement and favored immigration. Someone in the Revisionist ranks remarked: "Well, this one Arab has now been killed, and so there's no one left."

An article about this courageous attempt at Jewish-Arab cooperation was published in September 1964 in *New Outlook*, an English-language monthly published in Tel Aviv and devoted to improving relations between Jews and Arabs in the Middle East. I was one of the editors of *New Outlook* at the time, and translated the article from Aharon Cohen's original Hebrew. Buber was one of our sponsors and a constant source of inspiration in our work.

Before the article was published I brought it to Buber to check some of the details.

He read the proof copy I had brought and said, "Yes, I remember Fawzi well. He was a sincere man who was not afraid to say what he thought and to act on it. But the time was too extreme. Passions were too strong. The moderates in the middle had no influence compared to the extremists on both sides. And so they killed him.

"I remember his friends came and told us, 'Fawzi is dead. But we are ready to carry on. We are not afraid. Tell us what you want us to do.'"

He paused. After a moment I asked, "And what did you tell them?"

"We told them to go home. To go in peace. It was too late, you see. If they had gone on with his work they would have been killed as well. And we could not take this upon ourselves. We were sad and they were sad. We parted. And then a year later there was the war."

Buber strongly opposed the partition of Palestine because he saw that this would lead to an open, armed clash between the Jews and the Arabs. He was also concerned about the growing militaristic trend in the Jewish community and foresaw the harmful effect this would have on the new State's spiritual and moral life and particularly on the education of the younger generation. He personally favored a federation between the Jewish community and its neighbors. Other members of *Ichud* thought a binational state more suitable. However, as Buber wrote several years later, "this question is now an academic one, since history has decided against either solution." [18]

Buber was not a radical pacifist. He made this clear in his letter to Gandhi (see page 174). And several years after Israel's establishment he noted, in "Israel and the Command of the Spirit":

> I do not believe that one must always answer violence with nonviolence. I know what tragedy implies: when there is war, it must be fought.[19]

Buber fully accepted the political entity which emerged out of the 1948 fighting. "I have accepted as mine the State of Israel," he declared, "the form of the new Jewish community that has arisen from the war. I have nothing in common with those Jews who imagine that they may contest the factual shape which Jewish independence has taken." [20]

This was a clear reference to the American Council for Judaism, which tried many times to enlist Buber's support. But between his position and that of this anti-Zionist body there was an enormous abyss. The American Council did not accept Israel's independent existence and tried to undermine it from the outside. Buber accepted Israel's sovereign existence and criticized it lovingly from the inside. He sought a policy of peace and justice toward the Arabs because that was, he insisted, the only way a Jewish state could act according to its true nature. He wanted Israel to be more Jewish, not less.

Having attained its independence, he argued, Israel should act without delay to heal the breach with the Arabs. It should seek "to free once more the blocked path to an understanding with the Arab peoples." [21] He did not lose hope that a regional federation would one day come about. In 1958 he told the American Friends of *Ichud*:

> Today it seems absurd to many—especially in the present intra-Arab situation—to think now about Israel's participation in a Near East federation. Tomorrow, with an alteration in certain world-political situations independent of us, this possibility may arise in a highly positive sense. Insofar as it depends on us, we must prepare the ground for it.[22]

The best way of preparing the ground, he declared, was to take steps to ease the plight of the Arabs who had fled Palestine and become refugees. He considered it important that one of the young State's first concerns should be to act justly toward those who had suffered as a result of the war which had brought it into existence. This was important not only for the innocent people who had been the victims of this war, but for the moral life of the state itself. Professor Ernst Simon, in his essay "Buber or Ben-Gurion?" published in *New Outlook* in September 1966, pointed out that, like Machiavelli, Buber held that a state or nation will inevitably live by the *virtù*—the sign of fate—that rules the hour of its historical birth. Having won a victory on the battlefield, Israel should now show its generosity and restore the spiritual balance between violence and justice.

In a 1961 interview Buber had some pertinent things to say about an Israeli initiative on the Arab refugees:

> In political history the time and the tempo are almost decisive factors. . . . In 1949 Prime Minister Ben-Gurion invited several other people and myself to a talk, the subject of which was how to shape the image of the nation. . . . I said then, *inter alia*, [that] in my opinion, a government can exert a certain spiritual and moral influence on public opinion. For example, when, at a certain time, in a given situation, the Government takes a step which, at least outwardly, appears opposed to all national reasoning and logic, the man-in-the-street is liable

to ask, "Why was this done? What benefit will it bring to the state?" And then the Government comes and explains, "this certain step has latent in it a reason which transcends the purpose of the hour, and it is intended for the hours to come, for future generations, for the long range. This is how it is possible to try to shape a nation's image."

And at the same meeting I spoke very clearly and said, "Gentlemen, the Palestine Conciliation Commission is to meet in the next few days. Let us invite representatives of nations, even of churches, and say to them, 'We are ready to aid the solution of the Arab refugee problem. We bring this matter before you, so that we shall find a way out together, and Israel will play an active part in implementing the solution.' "

There was a discussion, and before we parted beside the door, Ben-Gurion said to me, "Mr. Buber, don't think that I am opposed to what you said. But you forget that in history there is something called early—and something called late." I thought for a moment, and then replied, "Yes! That is exactly what I meant. . . ." That was in 1949.[23]

Until the year of his death Buber continued to press for a massive Israeli initiative aimed at solving the problem of the Palestinian Arab refugees. In 1962 he was the only nonofficial Israeli to meet Dr. Joseph E. Johnson, the special United Nations envoy charged with examining this problem. Dr. Johnson, who is President of the Carnegie Endowment for International Peace, spent several hours with Buber at his home in Jerusalem and discussed the *Ichud* proposals for offering the refugees a realistic choice between staying in the Arab lands and receiving compensation or returning to Israel as full citizens.

Buber played an active role in the work of the *Ichud* group, defending the civil rights of Israel's Arab citizens and demanding that they and Jewish Israelis be given equal treatment.

He strongly opposed the military government imposed upon Arabs living in Israel and made many public demands for its abolition. A poster issued by *Ichud* in 1958 and signed by Buber, Simon, and other distinguished Hebrew University professors charged that the bulk of Israel's Arab population is subject to a military rule that denies them the basic rights of any free citizen. They have no freedom of movement or residence; they are not employed on the same basis as others in most organizations or government departments. Their entire life depends on the good graces of the military governors and their aides. Government ministries, in fulfilling their duties, help the Arabs in the fields of agriculture, health, education, etc.; but the system of military government casts its heavy shadow over all these benefits.[24]

Buber was extremely concerned about the danger of nuclear weapons entering the Middle East and did much to alert public opinion to the hazards this would create. He was in close touch with the Israeli Committee for a Nuclear-Free Zone in the Middle East, whose members included some of the most brilliant scientists in Israel.

In 1960 he attended and addressed the Mediterranean Colloquium held in Florence under the auspices of the mayor of that city, Giorgio La Pira. He made a tremendous impression on the delegates from Egypt, Lebanon, and other Arab countries. It had been agreed that specific topics such as the Arab-Israeli dispute would not be discussed and that the debate would be kept on a general level. Accordingly, he confined his remarks to a discussion of the difference between what he called "a small peace" and "a great peace."

"The small peace," he said, was really little more than a breathing space between two wars, a cessation of hostilities which did not change, for better or worse, the basic relations between the two sides. "The great peace," on the other hand, meant that both sides cooperated in improving their living and cultural standards and eliminating their differences. This implied a change of heart on both sides of the border when hostility existed, a willingness to forget longstanding animosities and to work together for the common good.

This was a theme he often returned to in the later years of his life, both in public statements and in private conversations. In a talk to a Jewish Theological Institute seminar in Jerusalem he summed up his views on the future relations between Israel and its neighbors, saying, "There cannot be any rebuilding of the Near East adequate to the great task of modern times without the real cooperation of all these peoples." [25]

But how could this cooperation come into being?

"Most of us," he said, "are so accustomed to political thinking that we view our era as one in which hot war has been succeeded by cold war and believe that on a certain day the cold war will cease too and there will be peace. I think this a great illusion. A peace that comes about through cessation of war, hot or cold, is no real peace. Real peace, a peace that would be a real solution, is organic peace. A great peace means cooperation and nothing else. What is less than this is nothing." [26]

He did not claim to possess any simple plan that would ensure this, and he did not think it could be attained by political means alone. But he did suggest one practical line of approach:

> The only thing, in my opinion, that could bring about a real peace, real cooperation, is the influence of the best Israel has produced, the new social forms of life, on the Arab people. The Arabs need this influence. They need a great agrarian reform, a just distribution of the soil, and the formation of small communities which would be the organic cells of this new economy and this new society.[27]

Always he sought to infuse every transient political moment with the demands of the spirit, which transcended and would survive this moment. He urged Jews and Arabs both inside and outside Israel to establish truly human relations on personal and individual levels, rather than as members of groups trapped in the stereotyped dogmas of political conflict. Always he emphasized what both peoples held in common and called upon them to use this common ground to discuss and settle the matters upon which they disagreed.

Speaking of the cold war between the West and the East, in a 1962 interview with *Life*, he remarked that "good merchants" settle their problems "by trying to distinguish between their opposing interests and their common interests.

"Now, let us take two societies opposed to one another. Let them sit together and come to a compromise. I do not think that a compromise must be as negative as that compromise we call 'coexistence.' It must be something positive, a kind of cooperation in solving the enormous problems that face mankind today. The way to reach that point would be for the two opposing sides to talk as good merchants. Let them make a list, so to speak, of those interests which are common and those which are antagonistic. If . . . they find that the common interests are really bigger, against all appearances, than the opposing interests, then they must try to reach an understanding to overcome the problems they have in common. . . . I do not see that any of the politicians ever tried it." [28]

What we need, he said to me one day, are merchants of peace —Jewish merchants and Arab merchants. He saw himself as a "merchant of peace." It was a tragedy that he was never given an opportunity to use his considerable diplomatic and persuasive skill to bridge the gap between Israel and the Arab world, and that no corresponding "merchant of peace" appeared on the Arab side. This was a tragedy for Buber. But it was even more of a tragedy for the Middle East—a region whose pain he felt so acutely and whose welfare he sought for most of his life.

Germany and Eichmann

"When my grandmother was sixteen," Buber told me, "she read German books in secret in her room, for Jewish girls in Galicia in those days didn't read Goethe and Schiller. Then, after she died, the books came to me, and I still have them.

"So you can see that I was brought up on German culture and literature. If I have a mother tongue, it is certainly German, although I speak several other languages. Yes, I am very German in many ways. But not Prussian! And that is of course the difference. We know what happens when the Germans behave like Prussians."

Many competent judges of German literature consider Buber a stylist ranking with the greatest writers in this language. The poet Fritz Diettrich said in a 1954 broadcast on Stuttgart Radio, "Buber has made our speech into so choice an instrument of his thought that he has taken his place by the side of Goethe and Schopenhauer as a master stylist." [1] Ludwig Lewisohn thought Buber belonged "to the very thin front ranks of living German masters of prose." [2]

And his translation of the Old Testament into German, undertaken together with Franz Rosenzweig in 1925, is generally agreed to be the finest since Luther's. Rosenzweig died in 1929 during the translation of the chapters in Isaiah on the suffering servant of God. Buber continued the translation alone, completing it in Jerusalem in 1961.

From 1923 to 1933 Buber was a professor at the University of Frankfurt, teaching Judaism and comparative religion. When the Nazis came to power in 1933, they excluded Jewish students from all institutions of higher learning. Buber's response, together with Rosenzweig, Ernst Simon, and other colleagues, was to set up adult education classes for those students. The famous Freies Judisches Lehrhaus (Jewish Academy), established in 1920, exerted a powerful influence on German Jewish life during that twilight decade, maintaining and serving as a focal point of communal morale.

Buber was dismissed from his professorship by the Nazis. But he was not deterred. From then until 1938 he displayed the full flower of his greatness as a communal leader. Ernst Simon said of Buber's efforts in the 1930s, "Anyone who did not see Buber then has not seen true civil courage." [3]

An address given by Buber to the students of the three German-Swiss universities, "The Question to the Single One," a dissertation on Kierkegaard which attacked the life-basis of totalitarianism, was actually published in Germany in 1936. In the preface to *Between Man and Man*, Buber noted that this was "astonishing," adding with a dry irony, "the fact that it could be published with impunity is certainly to be explained by its not having been understood by the appropriate authorities."

But he was not afraid to challenge Hitler's regime more directly. In the fall of 1934 Buber spoke at the Frankfurt Lehrhaus on "The Power of the Spirit." He openly criticized the pagan "glorification of the elemental forces as such." Christianity, he noted, instead of glorifying them, tried to conquer and control these elemental forces. But the third attitude was to hallow them, to sanctify them and thus ultimately to transform them. Judaism is, in Buber's opinion, "the most striking instance of this third relationship in the history of the Western world." [4]

"Heathenism," he declared, "glorifies elemental forces as such; they are considered sacred; they are declared holy, but not transformed. . . . This glorification, this divine rank of theirs, cannot be maintained because the spirit which has empowered them cannot draw upon inexhaustible depths. . . . In the end, heathenism necessarily breaks apart into spirit alien to the world and world alien to the spirit." 5

In contrast, Judaism offers a "reality system" in which

the elemental forces are connected with the living faith in a union holy from time immemorial. Thus, blood and soil are hallowed in the promise made to Abraham, because they are bound up with the command to be "a blessing" (Gen. 12:2). "Seed" and "earth" are promised, but only in order that—in the race of man scattered through the confusion of languages and divided into "isles of the nations" (Gen. 10:5; "isles of the Gentiles" in the King James Version)—a new people may "keep the way of the Lord to do righteousness and justice" (Gen. 18:19) in his land, and so begin rebuilding humanity.6

As Roy Oliver has remarked, "It would be difficult to find, in Hitler's Germany or elsewhere, a more radical challenge to paganism, racialism and false nationalism." 7 This attack was far more explicit than the essay on Kierkegaard. What is more, after delivering this address in Frankfurt, Buber dared to go to Berlin and repeat it in the Berlin Philharmonie, when he knew some two hundred S.S. men were in the audience.

The immediate reaction was a ban on Buber's speaking in public or to closed meetings of Jewish organizations. But Buber went on lecturing to closed sessions of non-Jewish anti-Nazi organizations, with the courageous assistance of a Frankfurt Quaker.

By 1938, however, he was totally silenced by the Nazis. The situation inside Germany had deteriorated to the point that the Frankfurt Lehrhaus could no longer be kept up. Buber himself was urged to go to Jerusalem. He struggled with his reluctance to leave Germany, and kept putting off his journey. He wanted to travel to Palestine as a tourist and not as an immigrant, so that he could return to Germany if the German Jews needed him. But finally, after increasingly urgent appeals from Jerusalem, he left.

His attitude toward Germany and the Germans has been mis-represented by some circles in Israel and world Jewry—often the same circles which disagreed so vehemently with his views on Israel's policies toward the Arabs. He is accused of adopting a lenient and forgiving position toward the guilt of Hitler's country-men. He was bitterly criticized when he agreed to receive the Goethe Prize from the University of Hamburg in 1951—this was before the Reparations Agreement, when feeling in Israel against the German people was at its height. And a particularly angry accusation was leveled against him when, in September 1953, he traveled to Frankfurt to accept the Peace Prize of the German Book Trade.

But very few of the people who so spitefully accuse him of "appeasing" the Germans have troubled to read his address on that occasion. In Paulskirche on September 27, 1953, he spoke with a blend of dignity and passion which was typical of his finest style. His sarcasm was the more scathing for being restrained; his eloquence the more moving because he was speaking in the city of the Lehrhaus for the first time in fifteen years—years which had seen the terrible war and the destruction of the German Jewry he had struggled to preserve.

"About a decade ago," he declared, "a considerable number of Germans—there must have been many thousands of them—under the indirect command of the German government and the direct command of its representatives, killed millions of my people in a systematically prepared and executed procedure whose organized cruelty cannot be compared with any previous histori-cal event." [8]

As one of those who remained alive, he felt he had "only in a formal sense a common humanity with those who took part in this action." These Germans had "so radically removed them-selves from the human sphere . . . that not even hatred, much less an overcoming of hatred, was able to arise in me. And what am I that I could here presume to 'forgive'!" [9]

Yet the German people had not acted monolithically. The "concrete multiplicity existing within a people" should not be obscured by "the levelling concept of a totality constituted and acting in just such a way and no other." [10]

Many of the Germans knew that "the monstrous event" of Auschwitz and Treblinka was taking place and did not oppose it. "But," Buber exclaimed, "my heart, which is acquainted with the weakness of men, refuses to condemn my neighbor for not prevailing upon himself to become a martyr." [11]

Next he thought of those who remained ignorant of the facts which were being withheld from the German public, and who did not try to discover the truth—the truth which they feared they could not face.

Finally, he said in a voice filled with emotion,

> there appear before me, from reliable reports, some who have become as familiar to me by sight, action, and voice as if they were friends, those who refused to carry out the orders and suffered death or put themselves to death, and those who learned what was taking place and opposed it and were put to death, or those who learned what was taking place and because they could do nothing to stop it killed themselves.
>
> I see these men very near before me, in that especial intimacy which binds us at times to the dead and to them alone. Reverence and love for these Germans now fills my heart. [12]

He was particularly concerned about the youth who had grown up in Germany since these events and played no part in the great crime against the Jewish people and all humanity. Within these young people he discerned "an inner struggle running for the most part underground and only occasionally coming to the surface." This was, he felt, only a part of "the great inner struggle of all peoples being fought out today, more or less consciously, more or less passionately, in the vital center of each people." [13]

And this crucial struggle was "the final battle of *homo humanus* against *homo contrahumanus*." [14] This typically contemporary conflict, which so concerned Buber toward the end of his life, was more than the cold war. It cut through the conventional groups of politically like-minded states and through all regimes and peoples, whatever their official alignment. (And indeed in conversation Buber would constantly draw our attention to signs of this struggle within both the world of free enterprise and the Communist camp.)

The outcome of this struggle would decide whether, despite everything, "a true humanity can issue from the race of men." [15] The true need and the very real danger was increasingly being perceived. And he had found more awareness of this central darkening rift in Germany, and especially among German youth:

> The memory of the twelve-year reign of *homo contrahumanus* has made the spirit stronger, and the task set by the spirit clearer, than they formerly were.[16]

The fact that such "a surviving arch-Jew" [17] as Buber could be awarded the Hanseatic Goethe Prize and the Peace Prize of the German Book Trade was significant. It represented a victory for the human spirit in its struggle against "the demonry of the subhuman and the antihuman." [18] By choosing a Jew to receive the highest German literary award, after all that had happened, under the weight of the memories that can never be effaced, the Germans had stressed "the high duty of solidarity that extends across the fronts: the solidarity of all separate groups in the flaming battle for the rise of a true humanity." [19] This duty was, Buber declared, the highest duty on earth at the present hour. Germans and Jews and the whole of mankind had to join in battle against the contrahuman, against the Satanic element in men, epitomized by the reign of the Nazis.

When he spoke these words, his voice cutting like a saber but radiant with his passionate vision of man's suppressed humanity, there were people in Paulskirche who wept. And yet he was accused of appeasing the Nazis—of forgiving the Germans too readily!

The simple truth is that Buber always rejected generalizations about races or national characteristics. He despised these inclusive statements and considered them superficial and, which was much more serious, dangerous.

"People say, 'The Germans are like sheep,' or, 'The Arabs understand only force,' " he said to me one day. "But did not people say all-embracing, negative things about us Jews? We, of all people, should beware of generalizations. Because a generalization is the beginning of prejudice. And the fact is that some Germans supported Hitler to the end, while others did not. There are Arabs and Arabs. And there are Jews and Jews. For my part, I cannot find it in me to condemn an entire people out of hand."

His refusal to close the door on reconciliation with Germany, and in particular with German youth, has aroused strong echoes in that country, where his works are widely read. It is significant that when German students were asked in 1960 to name the greatest spiritual figures of our time, Buber was placed third, along with Pope John XXIII.

But the views Buber expressed in his Frankfurt speech were not shared by most Israelis or even by many people in his own intimate circle in Jerusalem. Many of those closest to him were themselves former German Jews who had left the country after Hitler's rise to power.

If the Frankfurt affair showed how greatly Buber differed from the community on the question of post-Nazi Germany, the Eichmann trial set him on a lonely promontory isolated from even some of his closest and oldest friends.

Buber was not opposed to Eichmann's trial being held in Jerusalem. But, along with Dr. Nachum Goldmann, he thought the Israeli Government should have formed an international court to try this exterminator of Jews and other minorities. "I do not think that the victims should also be the judges," he said in January 1961. Further, broadening the composition of the court would, he felt, have stressed Eichmann's crimes against humanity as a whole, which were not less monstrous than his crimes against the Jews.

But about his opposition to the death penalty there could be no question. For crimes such as the Nazis had committed a death penalty was meaningless. The legal concept of punishment could not be logically applied, and man's imagination could not con-

ceive a fit penalty for such a man, as it could scarcely conceive
his crimes themselves. In the terrible shadow of Eichmann's actions his personal fate could not be measured against the lives of
the people he and the machine of which he was a part had taken.
Here the world of man-made law and retribution failed.

What mattered was the mystery of human darkness, of which
Eichmann was a repulsive symbol, and the unexplored point at
which man might be induced to turn back from the darkness, a
conscious act of wisdom which could spring, as Buber urged,
from the very depths of the antihuman, with the need to grapple
with *homo contrahumanus* and not to follow him into the full
darkness of the trap he has set.

It is important to emphasize that Buber's rocklike opposition to
the death penalty for Eichmann—an opposition which he
maintained both before and after the trial, and from which he
never wavered, throughout all the torrents of abuse and
vilification—did not spring from any feeling of compassion for
Eichmann himself. For Eichmann, Buber felt nothing but distaste
and horror. If there was one person Buber ever hated, it was
Eichmann, both for himself and as a symbol of everything against
which Buber had staked his entire life.

I remember vividly a conversation with him that drove this
home to me unforgettably. It was in February 1961, when Eichmann was in prison in Israel but before his trial had begun.

We were discussing a passage in *I and Thou*, one of my favorite passages in all his writings:

> Love is responsibility of an I for a Thou. In this lies the like-
> ness . . . of all who love, from the smallest to the greatest, and
> from the blessedly protected man, whose life is rounded in that
> of a loved being, to him who is all his life nailed to the cross of
> the world, and who ventures to bring himself to the dreadful
> point—to love *all men*.[20]

"But isn't it virtually impossible to love all men?" I asked. "Or
do you think we should dare the impossible?"

He was silent for a moment, and then said, "You know, even

Jesus" (he used the Hebrew expression *Yeshu Ha'notzri*—Jesus of Nazareth) "didn't love all men. Look at the Pharisees. . . . To understand is not always to love. Think of Hitler! Of Eichmann! Yes, I love many men to whom I am opposed. But not Eichmann! Perhaps I can understand him. But to *love* him—no, that I cannot do! This is really what you said just now: impossible."

More than once we discussed his attitude toward the execution of Eichmann, and he made it quite clear that he felt that he could make no exceptions to his basic opposition to the death penalty on principle.

"I do not accept the state's right to take the life of any man," he explained to me. "And so I must resolutely oppose a capital sentence on anyone, whoever he is. I remember expressing myself in public against it in 1928, in Germany. And I cannot now agree to it because it would be my own people that would carry out the sentence in its own country. But this is an issue of principle. It is more than a question of Eichmann and what I think of his horrible crimes. Anyone who thinks that I wish us to be lenient to Eichmann does not understand my basic position."

"What then should be done with him?" I asked. "You would not let him go free, I imagine."

"No, he should not go free," Buber answered. He sighed. "This is very difficult. He should be sentenced to life imprisonment. But we must remember always that he is a symbol of the Nazi holocaust, and not an ordinary criminal. So he should not be kept in a cell in a prison, like other people under similar sentences. It is not easy to explain."

(He seemed to be searching for the phrase he wanted, shaking his head as if still not satisfied he had found it.)

"He should be made to feel that the Jewish people were not exterminated by the Nazis, and that they live on here in Israel. Perhaps he should be put to work on the land—on a kibbutz. Farming the soil of Israel. Seeing young people around him. And realizing every day that we have survived his plans for us. Would not this be the ultimate and most fitting punishment?

"But this is not easy. There are problems of security, of vengeance. It is not a simple matter to sentence a man to life imprisonment and yet not to lock him up. But I believe a way could be found. We should apply justice tempered with imagination. And this would serve a far greater moral and historical purpose than killing him. That is too facile and commonplace a way out of this unique dilemma."

When Buber revealed that he intended asking for clemency, if Eichmann should be sentenced to death, there was a predictable outcry. He was accused of being unpatriotic, of turning the other cheek to the Germans, of behaving as if he were in a Diaspora ghetto and not in the sovereign State of Israel.

A characteristic attack was that by Shmuel Katz, a former officer in the Irgun Zvai Leumi, the right-wing underground group responsible for violent actions against the British Mandatory authorities. In a letter published in the daily newspaper *Haaretz* in February 1962, Katz wrote:

> When a man who is famous throughout the world as a philosopher exerts the moral influence attached to his name in order to save Eichmann's life, we are entitled and indeed duty-bound to examine his right to request us to accede to his plea. And we must ask where was the shock, the outcry, the use of his famous name, when in the past, in his immediate environment, in this country, people were being judged and hanged?

Katz accused Buber of doing less to save Irgun members sentenced to death by the British than he was doing now to save Eichmann from the gallows. It was true, he agreed, that Buber had signed a petition to the British High Commissioner asking for these death sentences to be commuted to life imprisonment. But he had only signed the petition, and the initiative had been taken by others. Now, in the case of Eichmann, Buber was taking the initiative.

"The contrast between what he is doing now and his reaction during the time of the British stares one in the face," Katz complained.

On December 15, 1961, Eichmann was sentenced to death. Buber asked for a meeting with Prime Minister Ben-Gurion and made an attempt to persuade him to agree to the sentence being commuted. He also wrote to President Ben-Zvi, whose prerogative it was to grant clemency or to confirm the death sentence.

But his efforts failed. On May 31, 1962, Eichmann was hanged at Ramleh jail, the body cremated, and his ashes scattered in the sea outside Israeli waters.

On June 4 Buber made a statement to the *New York Times* about the execution. In this interview, published the following day, he told Lawrence Fellows, the *Times* correspondent in Jerusalem, that the execution was "a mistake of historical dimension." He feared that the act of taking Eichmann's life might have served to expiate the guilt felt by many young persons in Germany over the actions of their elders in the years the Nazis were in power.

Because of this guilty conscience, Buber said, these young Germans were beginning to feel a resurgence of humanism. Without that conscience, an obstacle would have been removed to the advance of antihuman tendencies in them, and of antihuman forces that exist throughout the world, with neither conscience nor any real regard for humanity.

"It was not a question of mitigation," Buber told Fellows. "Neither was it just a question of the penalty of death. People are mistaken in thinking that I opposed this simply as a consequence of my opposition to the death penalty.

"For such crimes there is no penalty. I would not have dared to do what I have done if I had to think only about the crimes as such."

At this point Buber, who spoke English throughout the entire interview, read to Fellows the passage in his address in Frankfurt in which he charged German Nazis with "radically removing themselves from the human sphere."

He repeated his former assertions that he had no pity for Eichmann, or anything but approval for the trial as such. He also agreed that Jerusalem was the proper place for it, but once more said that it should have been conducted by an international tribunal, and that Israel's role should have been that of accuser, and not of judge.[21]

Several months after the execution I eame across an article by William Robert Miller, published in the *United Church Herald* on January 25, 1962. Miller, a member of the Fellowship of Reconciliation, suggested that

> it would do great honor to the State of Israel and to the Jewish community throughout the world if the High Court in Jerusalem were to . . . reverse the verdict, not because of extenuating circumstances, for there were none, but as a noble rebuke to the very idea that Eichmann represents, that men may choose to kill their fellow men. . . .
>
> Only the mighty power of love, working through kindness, could thaw the frozen spark of conscience in him and crush out of his soul the icy bestiality that surrounds it. . . .
>
> It is almost certain that this great opportunity will be missed, that the powers-to-be will let it slip by. Perhaps many of us will be glad to see it go by. For if Eichmann were spared for an experiment in redemption, and the experiment succeeded, it might well spring the lock on our own Pandora's box of guilt and force us to face up to our own sins.

This was at least a part of what Buber was trying to tell his fellow Israelis. But, as Miller prophesied, the opportunity was allowed to slip by.

The Teacher

"The real struggle," Buber said one day, "is not between East
and West, or capitalism and communism, but between education
and propaganda. Education means teaching people to see the reality around them, to understand it for themselves. Propaganda is
exactly the opposite. It tells the people, 'You will think like this,
as we want you to think!'

"Education lifts the people up. It opens their hearts and devel-
ops their minds, so that they can discover the truth and make it
their own. Propaganda, on the other hand, closes their hearts and
stunts their minds. It compels them to accept dogmas without
asking themselves, 'Is this true or not?'

"The trouble is that this is not only a conflict of ideology. It is
a conflict of tempo. The tempo of propaganda is feverish, ner-
vous. It is the pace of television and the radio. It is the pace of
the newspaper headline; the cry of the vendor in the street.
Whereas education goes at a slow pace. It is the pace of teachers
talking with their pupils. It is the pace of a man reading by himself in a room. It cannot be hurried or speeded up and remain
education."

"Then," I asked, "must propaganda win in the end? Must the
fast tempo drive out the slow always?"

"No," he answered. "Perhaps to some people speed is identified with progress, in the world of communications as in the world of motion. But this is not the way history is made. The authentic forces that change and shape the world are deep and under the surface. So they move slowly. Real history is the history of the slow pace. The question is whether there will be enough people who see the deceit in the feverish tempo, withstand its temptation, and commit themselves to the truth of the slower tempo."

Buber often returned to this theme of the struggle between education and propaganda. He saw clearly that it was a struggle for the control of communications, between those who wanted to use the new technology to encourage free expression and debate, and those who wanted to use it to impose a higher kind of electronic authority. And, as always, he was for the open against the closed, for the stammering question against the packaged answer.

He was basically a teacher—for me, the greatest teacher of our generation. He was an educator, in the true sense of this word and within the limits of his own definition of it. He did not try to impose a self-evident formula upon his pupils, but posed questions which forced them to find their own answers. He did not want his pupils to follow him docilely but to take their own individual paths, even if this meant rebelling against him, because for him education meant freedom, a liberation of personality. Perhaps too it is as a great teacher, embracing consideration of the whole of human existence in his approach to his pupils, that his influence on our time will be most enduring.

The right way to teach, he said, was "the personal example springing spontaneously and naturally from the whole man." This meant that the teacher should constantly examine his conscience. Indeed, every man should do this, but a teacher most of all, as he could not teach others if his own example was flawed.

The purpose of education was to develop the character of the pupil, to show him how to live humanly in society. One of Buber's basic principles was that "genuine education of character is genuine education for community." And he explained in his address "The Education of Character," given to the National Conference of Palestinian Teachers in Tel Aviv in 1939, how this could be achieved.

"For educating characters you do not need a moral genius," he declared, "but you do need a man who is wholly alive and able to communicate himself directly to his fellow beings. His aliveness streams out to them and affects them most strongly and purely when he has no thought of affecting them." [1]

The real teacher, he believed, teaches most successfully when he is not consciously trying to teach at all, but when he acts spontaneously out of his own life. Then he can gain the pupil's confidence; he can convince the adolescent that there is human truth, that existence has a meaning. And when the pupil's confidence has been won, "his resistance against being educated gives way to a singular happening: he accepts the educator as a person. He feels he may trust this man, that this man is . . . taking part in his life, accepting him before desiring to influence him. And so he learns to *ask*." [2]

He felt that it is not the teacher's task to tell the pupil what is right and wrong in absolute terms, to dictate what is good and what is evil in general. What the teacher should do is "to answer a concrete question, to answer what is right and wrong in a given situation." [3] Even better, the teacher should help the pupil to arrive at this answer for himself. But this does not imply unconditional agreement between teacher and pupil. Conflicts also have an educational value, so long as they occur in a healthy atmosphere of mutual confidence.

"A conflict with a pupil is the supreme test for the educator," [4] he asserted. But the teacher must use insight during this battle for the truth. If he wins the conflict, he has to help the vanquished to endure defeat; and if he cannot overcome the pupil's will, then he must find the word of love which will make the conflict part of the educational process.

In his usual direct and specific way he gave an example of this loving conflict deliberately aroused by the teacher:

At the time of the Arab terror in Palestine, when there were single Jewish acts of reprisal, there must have been many discussions between teacher and pupils on the question: Can there be any suspension of the Ten Commandments, i.e. can murder become a good deed if committed in the interest of one's own group? One such discussion was once repeated to me. The teacher asked: "When the commandment tells you 'Thou shalt not bear false witness against thy neighbor,' are we to interpret it with the condition, 'provided it does not profit you'?" Thereupon one of the pupils said, "But it is not a question of my profit, but of the profit of my people." The teacher: "And how would you like it, then, if we put our condition this way: 'Provided that it does not profit your family'?" The pupil: "But family—that is still something more or less like myself; but the people—that is something quite different; there all question of *I* disappears." The teacher: "Then if you are thinking, 'We want victory,' don't you feel at the same time, 'I want victory'?" The pupil: "But the people, that is infinitely more than just the people of today. It includes all past and future generations." At this point the teacher felt the moment had come to leave the narrow compass of the present and to invoke historical destiny. He said: "Yes; all past generations. But what was it that made these past generations of the Exile live? What made them outlive and overcome all their trials? Wasn't it that the cry 'Thou shalt not' never faded from their hearts and ears?" The pupil grew very pale. He was silent for a while, but it was the silence of one whose words threatened to stifle him. Then he burst out: "And what have we achieved this way? This!" And he banged his fist on the newspaper before him, which contained the report on the British White Paper. And again he burst out with "Live? Outlive? Do you call that life? We want to live!" [5]

In this example of constructive conflict between teacher and pupil we see again Buber's sense of the concrete. This earthiness, this genius for the moral lesson rooted in the everyday, was one of his most unexpected qualities and one which endeared him to those who considered themselves his pupils. And the conversation that he recorded above also illustrates another aspect of his character: his compassion for someone whose soul was being rent by a sincere moral dilemma. I have often seen him dart a look of tenderness and understanding at a young man or woman whom he had just challenged with one of his piercing life-searing questions, as if he were saying, "Yes, my young friend, I know this is causing you anguish and upsetting all your neat, agreed doctrines; but I am helping you to confront something you have shied away from, something you must face and overcome if you are to grow."

It was this concrete relationship with real problems of existence that brought so many people to seek him out in Jerusalem, particularly toward the end of his life. Of course, Buber was always identified with education in Israel. He was Professor of Social Philosophy at the Hebrew University from 1938 until he retired in 1951, at the age of seventy-three. In 1949 he founded the Israeli Institute for Adult Education, which trained teachers for work among immigrants in the camps. This was the period of mass immigration, and the new settlers were taught Hebrew and trained for life in the new land. Buber headed this institute until 1953 and continued showing an active interest in various spheres of education.

But his method was not pedagogical, in the narrow sense. He was little concerned with the how of teaching, with such matters as syllabuses, methods, and examinations. What concerned him was the why—how to give the pupil a sense of his identity, of his organic unity; how to show him the way to responsibility and love. This is what Buber looked for when judging the success of a teacher. And it was this emphasis which led teachers to come to him, slowly and singly at first, then sometimes in groups, not to consult him about technical problems but to ask him what they should teach, how they should reconcile conscience and faith.

In December 1962 one such group of twenty-five men and women teachers met Buber at his house for a discussion on the problems facing Israeli teachers. This discussion was published in the Histadrut daily *Davar* under the heading "How to Educate After What Has Happened in the World."

The conversation was opened by the secretary of the Israeli Teachers' Federation, Shalom Levin. He recalled that Buber had described the teacher as "the representative of the world and the messenger of history to the child." Faith in the world in which man lives was the aim of education, Buber had said. But, Levin went on, after what had happened in World War II, the terrible massacre of the Jews, we cannot have the same faith that we had before.

Another teacher outlined the special dilemma facing educators in Israel:

"We are living at a time when Israel is gathering in its exiles. The State is facing a political challenge, and this demands a considerable educational effort. But where is the common factor in our educational objectives which can bridge the gap between the generations—the generation of the Zionist immigration, the generation of the *sabras* [that is, the young people born in Israel] and the generation of Jews who survived the Nazi death camps? This last is a very special kind of immigration. Life has always been very difficult for human beings. But the crisis we have lived through is truly extraordinary—not least because soon after it we were called upon to set up a new independent state. I cannot perceive what should be our educational goal for the new generation. I do not see the sun in whose light I am supposed to exist."

To this Buber replied:

"This is a general question which has a bearing on what Mr. Levin said. I want to tell you about something that happened shortly after the State of Israel was established. The Prime Minister invited the intellectuals to offer advice on how the State should be shaped. At that time I asked the Prime Minister, 'For what purpose?' This has always been a fundamental question in Judaism.

"We have now had a state for several years; and no one has seriously tried to ask, what is it for?"

Teacher: "Our 'for what' is that we want to ensure our existence in this place."

Buber: "I do not believe this is a peculiar objective. After all, every living man wants to ensure his existence, to continue living."

Teacher: "The question also leads to the question of faith in man. The reality I find around me today is against the values I believe in. So the question is: How shall I educate my children? How can I preserve the values which have been sanctified from one generation to the next? Or shall I allow my pupils complete freedom to accept or reject these values?"

Buber remarked that he did not like the word "values," as it was too abstract. He suggested that the teachers should be more specific and explain what they meant by a conflict of values. The question was not whether there was faith or not, but in what was it possible to have faith?

One of the teachers explained the problem:

"Our youth are caught up in a crisis of values. We as teachers preach one thing, but the reality is very different, both here in Israel and in the world as a whole. We talk about work, *halutziut*, love of the homeland. But we feel that in our reality these things cannot be realized. Take for example the new settlers. Every family that comes to us brings with it the customs, the way of life, and the traditions of the country from which it comes. How then can we find the values we hold in common, so that we can bring the different Jewish communities together and not drive them further apart? What are our common national values? And how can we create the unified nation—which today does not exist?

"The teachers are good," he added. "The pupils are good. Yet there is a crisis. For example, we have always taught them to honor their fathers and their mothers. But in reality they do not."

Buber replied:

"You have touched on a very important point, which cannot be settled in one or two sentences. In my opinion, only life itself can answer your question. You ask how can we go about implementing the Ten Commandments in our time, in our country? Everything depends on the situation, on the correctness of each situation. The commandment to honor your father and your mother can take on different forms in varying situations.

"The same is true of 'Thou shalt not kill.' I once contemplated something and then realized that what I wanted to do was in effect the equivalent of killing. In the end it is the situation that interprets reality. It follows that there cannot be absolute answers to questions such as you have asked.

"The teacher must show the pupil the direction. He must point the way. But the pupil must make the journey himself. And you show someone the direction only when he wants to go the same way—the way of realization, of throwing his whole self into the journey.

"I consider the profession of teaching the most important in human society. But this is on the condition that the teacher should be a teacher on whom the fate of society rests. Clearly there are objective theories of education. But for myself I doubt whether these are valid in practice. The teacher can have an influence. And the most effective way to influence a pupil is through example. Not the overt example, but the hidden, which is provided unconsciously, without any didactic intention.

"Because the pupil learns not only during the study period but also while out on a walk, during a game, at a meeting with the teacher outside the schoolroom. We must try. We may even succeed. The main thing is that the pupil must learn all the time. As teachers, you must dare. Everything in life is based on daring. For a man to father children in these times is daring. For a man to believe in God today—that is daring. All the teacher must do is to point the direction. Then it is up to the pupil himself."

Here one of the teachers, who had been listening attentively, broke in and protested, "But surely it is not enough merely to point the direction? What about the agreed values which tell our pupils how to behave?"

Buber replied quietly:

"Let us try to understand what we mean when we use this word 'values.' Can absolute values be formulated at all? I wish I could do so. I think we must accept the world as it is. We are living in the middle of chaos. You cannot come along suddenly and say, Now let us invent some values! But if in your class at school there are some children from families of new immigrants, and you treat them in your everyday contact with them as it is prescribed in the admonition 'Love your neighbor as yourself,' then that will be *a* value, something definite and worthwhile.

"The teacher should not talk about it in this light. But if, for example, you would implement this and act in this way, then certainly something will come out of it, although we can only hope and cannot see where our actions will lead. The important thing surely is that the pupil says, 'Yes, my teacher said so.' This is the power of personal example. When there is a personal example by the teacher, then there can be cooperation with the pupil. And without cooperation it is difficult to achieve anything."

At this point another teacher raised the moral question of security in a country at war with its neighbors:

"The direction you spoke of does not depend on the free will of the individual. There is a determination of the situation, a historical development. I educate my children, and at the same time I know that this education is narrow and national. I teach psychology and also the Bible. And deep inside myself I think that good education is education which leads the pupil to identify with and cooperate with the world."

Buber: "Would you agree with me when I suggest that what is desired is an education toward humanism?"

Teacher: "Precisely. But our history compels us to teach our pupils that if someone comes to kill us, we must make haste to kill him first."

Buber: "I do not like talking about principles. I prefer to discuss different situations. But these are not fixed. Perhaps the situation of today will not be the same as the situation of tomorrow. For example, there have been some very extreme views on how we should defend ourselves. You might know that I am opposed to the military government for our Arab population, because I think it is the wrong way to ensure our security. I have always said that if you want to win the hearts of men, you must first acquire their confidence. This is a way of defending oneself—a way based on trust and real security.

"The main thing is knowing what to do in passing situations; how to see what this moment demands. In other words, we must replace the way of tactics, which is a short-term approach, with the way of strategy, which is thinking for the long term. Real defense consists of seeing far ahead, of taking the long view."

Here the discussion turned to ways in which the teacher could help the pupil express his personality.

Buber thought this was one of the most difficult tasks in education, because it required an intimate knowledge of each pupil and his particular makeup. The most important thing, he said, was to make it possible for the pupil to think for himself, to look at the situation facing him and respond to it according to his own understanding of it. This is what education should do. It should prepare the pupil for authentic independence. A hundred years ago, for example, Thoreau called for a struggle against slavery, in his essay "Civil Disobedience." This is what he felt the situation called for, and that was what he did in response to it. This is one way of answering the call of the critical situation.

Teacher: "By a civil rebellion?"

Buber: "I don't like the term 'rebellion.' I would rather describe it as 'civil disobedience.' In the situation we are in today, for example—the atomic bomb and all that this implies—a certain amount of civil disobedience is necessary. I said once that we should not leave everything to the politicians."

As the discussion neared its close, one of the teachers asked how the educator should put across his message in his daily routine.

Buber replied that the teacher should try to speak the truth at all times. He should see that the pupil heard the truth and not falsehoods.

Teacher: "But the teacher lives in a time of falsehood. His work does not bear fruit."

Buber: "You cannot be certain about this."

Teacher: "The generation dictates the direction. You have outlined the direction you think we should take—toward humanism. And this links up with the question that has perplexed us all these years: the question of war or peace."

Buber: "If it is a question of war or peace, you will not choose war."

Teacher: "No, certainly not."

Buber: "But this doesn't mean you will want peace under any conditions."

Teacher: "And how is it possible to educate for humanism when there is no hope? All the arguments put forward by the humanist and socialist philosophers count for nothing compared with the holocaust of our people in Europe."

Buber: "And wasn't there a Spanish Inquisition? And didn't the Turks massacre the Armenians?"

Teacher: "But not in such numbers."

Buber: "I do not think any basic change took place in the human race when the Nazis came into power. As you say, it is a question of proportion, not of basic content. The Nazi massacres were so horrifying because they were on such an unprecedented mass scale. But similar brutalities have occurred before in history. It is not essentially a new phenomenon. And it is certainly not a reason to lose faith and to despair of the human race."

Buber closed the meeting by summing up his concept of the teacher's role:

"Everything depends on the teacher as a man, as a person. He educates from himself, from his virtues and his faults, through personal example and according to circumstances and conditions. His task is to realize the truth in his personality and to convey this realization to the pupil."

When a young teacher enters a class of his own for the first time, Buber wrote in "The Education of Character," the class before him seems like a mirror of mankind, so heterogeneous, so full of contradictions, so inaccessible. The inexperienced teacher feels he has not sought these boys out. He has been put there and has to accept them as they are. No, he decides on second thought, he must accept them not as they seem to be at that first moment of confrontation, but as they really are, as they can become. But, he wonders, how can he find out what is in them? And what can he do to make it take shape, to bring out the latent potential in these unfamiliar semi-individuals?

And the boys do not make things easy for him. They are noisy, they stare at him impudently, they do nothing to help him come closer to them. He is tempted to maintain rigid discipline from the very beginning, to issue orders, to say no to everything rising against him.

But then something happens. The young teacher's eyes meet a face which strikes him:

> It is not a beautiful face nor particularly intelligent; but it is a real face, or, rather, the chaos preceding the cosmos of a real face. On it he reads a question which is something different from the general curiosity: "Who are you? Do you know something that concerns me? Do you bring me something? What do you bring?"

And the young teacher responds to this face out of the crowd of boys. He addresses it. But he does not set out self-consciously to teach, to instruct. He says nothing very weighty or important; he puts some such ordinary introductory question as, "What did you talk about last in geography? The Dead Sea? Well, what about the Dead Sea?"

Yet obviously there is something not completely usual in the question, for the answer the teacher gets is not the ordinary brief answer schoolboys give. The boy begins to tell a story:

> Some months earlier he had stayed for a few hours on the shores of the Dead Sea, and it is of this he tells. He adds, "And everything looked to me as if it had been created a day before the rest of creation." Quite unmistakably he had only in this moment made up his mind to talk about it. In the meantime his face has changed. . . . And the class has fallen silent. They all listen." [6]

This is how Buber taught those who were attracted by the passion and nobleness of his message. He looked for faces that were struggling for form and shape. Then he helped them achieve identity. And those whom he taught in this way, through the power of his person, not by preaching but through answering concrete questions, became his pupils during his life and after his life.

Tales of the Master

Buber and I were talking about the chances of peace in the Middle East. It was a warm summer afternoon; the shutters were half open, and we could hear the voices of children coming in from the garden.

We were discussing plans for a conference of Jews and Arabs in Tel Aviv when we heard cries from the garden and went out to see what was happening. Buber's grandson, Gideon, and his friends were playing "Nasser and Ben-Gurion"—the Israeli equivalent of cops and robbers.

Buber smiled, held up his hands, and said, "You see? This is where we must begin."

Someone who worked with him in the 1930s, after Hitler came to power, told me:

After Buber had made a speech in Frankfurt, the Gestapo came to his house to question him. They peered into the drawers of his desk and looked at his library. Then one of the officers asked him, "Do you have any radical literature here?"

"Yes," Buber answered. He took his own German translation of the Old Testament from the shelf and handed it to the officer. "Here!"

It was said in Israel:

When Buber first came to Jerusalem, his spoken Hebrew was

comparatively simple, and so most people understood what he meant. But over the years his Hebrew improved, and then no one any longer knew what he was saying.

I was with Buber one morning when the phone rang. In his usual direct way he picked up the old-fashioned receiver and barked into it, "Buber!"

Someone from the Hebrew University's English Literature Department was on the line. And the following conversation took place:

HEBREW UNIVERSITY MAN: Professor Buber, Robert Frost is here and we would like you to meet him.
BUBER: Frost? Frost? I don't think I know him.
HEBREW UNIVERSITY MAN: He is a famous writer.
BUBER: What does he write? Novels? Essays?
HEBREW UNIVERSITY MAN: He writes poetry.
BUBER: Oh, poetry? Then what does he want with me? I am a philosopher. You understand? And what can a poet and a philosopher have to say to one another?
HEBREW UNIVERSITY MAN (clearly growing desperate): But he is famous. He is a grand old man.
BUBER: I'm also an old man. There are many old men. That's no reason why they should meet.
HEBREW UNIVERSITY MAN: We thought—a photograph. A famous American and a famous Israeli.
BUBER: Oh, a photograph! Hmmm. Tell me, does this Frost really want to talk to me? Or is that your idea?
HEBREW UNIVERSITY MAN: Of course he does. At least I think so.
BUBER: Well, if this Frost asks to meet me, let him phone me himself! Do you hear? Then we'll see.

He put the phone down, turned to me, and laughed.

"Did you hear that? This poet Frost doesn't want to see me. It's all their idea. A photograph of two old men shaking hands—that's all they want!"

Buber never sought disciples who would follow him blindly
and turn his teachings into a new dogma.

A rather pompous visitor said to him, "Professor Buber, I want
you to know that I follow your philosophy faithfully. I consider
myself a devout Buberian."

Buber flashed him a quizzical glance, and replied, "If you call
yourself a Buberian, then you have not understood me!"

Buber had a warm relationship with Shmuel Yosef Agnon, the
great Hebrew writer, who also lived in Jerusalem. Agnon was extremely orthodox and wore a skullcap at home. Buber, of course,
did not observe strict Jewish ritual. But this did not prevent them
from enjoying one another's company and reminiscing about
their youth in Poland (Agnon was born in Galicia) and Germany.

One of the things that drew them together was their common
love for Hasidic folklore and legends. In the 1920s Buber and
Agnon actually decided to work together on a massive anthology
of Hasidic stories. Buber was living in Frankfurt at the time, and
Agnon began compiling the material in Homburg, only a few
miles away. But in June 1924 a fire destroyed all Agnon's manuscripts and papers, together with his priceless library of Hebrew
books. The flames which destroyed all Agnon's life work until
that date also consumed the first draft of the planned anthology,
which was never resumed.

Agnon was the only person who could make Buber go to synagogue. One Rosh Hashana—the Jewish New Year—I phoned
Buber and was surprised to be told, "He is out. He has gone to
synagogue."

That evening he called me and said, "Yes, I went to synagogue, for the first time in many years. Agnon came along and
insisted that I go with him. And I could not refuse Agnon! So I
went, more for Agnon's sake than for the synagogue, you understand. But I enjoyed it. I felt I was a boy again, in my father's
house."

When Buber addressed the Mediterranean Colloquium in Florence in 1960, he told the following parable:

"In the beginning Liberty, Equality, and Fraternity went hand in hand. Then their paths divided. Liberty turned toward the West, but changed its nature on the way. Equality turned toward the East; but it also changed during this journey. No one knows what happened to Fraternity. It seems to have been lost. . . .

"Now Liberty and Equality would like to rejoin each other and become what they were in the beginning. But they cannot do this unless we find Fraternity again."

All the participants in the Colloquium applauded these words. And an Iraqi delegate said to an Israeli, "If peace ever comes, it will be built by people like Buber."

Malcolm Diamond relates:

Buber's first public address in the United States in 1951 was critical of the failure of the State of Israel's policies to serve the ideal of Zion. At its end, there was a question period.

One of his listeners asked, "If, as you say, Israel has so far been nothing more than another political state in the Near East, this is, after all, not such a terrible thing. Why does it cause you to despair?"

Buber leaned toward the audience searching for his interlocutor. "Despair! Despair! In the darkest days of our history I did not despair—and I certainly do not despair now!"

And to me he said, "Rabbi Nachman of Bratzlav taught me the commandment: 'Never despair! Before we can achieve greatness,' he used to say, 'we must first descend to smallness, to a state of simplicity. Even in the deepest sinking there is the hidden purpose of an ultimate rising. So the most important thing during the time of smallness is not to despair. There is no such thing as despair,' Rabbi Nachman told his disciples. And he implored them, 'even when you fall into a state of ignorance and humiliation, do not despair!' "

The editor of the *Ichud* journal *Ner* was Rav Benyamin, a saintly man who devoted himself heart and soul to a reconciliation between Arabs and Jews. For several years I worked with

him on the English version of *Ner*, and I grew to love and respect him almost as much as I loved and respected Buber.

Rav Benyamin lived in near poverty. His flat contained only a
few sticks of furniture, and having shared many of his meals with
him and his wife, I knew what a frugal existence they led.

Hearing about this, the American Friends of *Ichud* sent some
money to him and specified that it was to be used to improve his
living conditions. But that month we were short of paper to print
the journal. Rav Benyamin went out without telling me and
spent all the money on paper.

When I told Buber this, he smiled warmly and said, "When a
man is determined to be a *zaddik*, a holy one, you cannot stop
him!"

Then, after a pause, he added, "And you should not try to stop
him."

When a group of *sabras* once pressed him to explain something
he had said, Buber replied good-humoredly with a tale of Rabbi
Barukh of Mezbizh, the grandson of the Baal Shem Tov:

One Sabbath a learned man who was a guest at Rabbi Barukh's
table said to him, "Now let us hear the teachings from you,
rabbi. You speak so well!" "Rather than speak so well," said the
grandson of the Baal Shem, "I should be stricken dumb."

Malcolm Diamond remarked to Buber one day that Freud is
reported to have answered a question concerning the meaning of
life by saying that it is work and love. Buber laughed and said
that this was good, but not complete. He would say: work, love,
faith, and humor.

I reminded Buber of this exchange with Diamond when I came
to see him soon after his eighty-seventh birthday. This was before he broke his leg and had to be confined to the bed from
which he never rose again. But already his health was failing and
his eyes in particular were troubling him.

"Yes, what I told Diamond is true," Buber said. "The real philosopher has to have a sense of humor, an awareness of the comic,
not only about the world we live in but also about himself. Most

people ask, 'What is going to happen tomorrow? Or the day afterward?' The philosopher asks, 'What will happen in another generation? Another two generations?' And in the same way let us imagine that our philosopher is ill, he has pains, he suffers like everybody else, perhaps there is a danger to his life. And yet, despite all this, if he is a true philosopher he will look at his own suffering a little from the side, a small distance away, with humor and without self-pity. Yes, without a sense of humor even a philosopher could not live in this world."

That was my last conversation with Martin Buber.

Buber, Hammarskjöld, and Schweitzer

In 1957 Buber published *Pointing the Way*. This was a selection of his essays written during the period from 1909 to 1954, dealing mainly with social and political questions, including the cold war which followed World War II.

At the beginning of 1958 this book came into the hands of Dag Hammarskjöld, who was then completing his first term as Secretary-General of the United Nations. Buber's observations on the reasons for the lack of international understanding in the 1950s were close to Hammarskjöld's own line of thought as the administrative head of the United Nations, and the book as a whole made a profound impression on him.

Hammarskjöld was particularly struck by the address Buber had given at Carnegie Hall in New York in 1952, at the conclusion of his lecture tour of the United States.

In this address, published now under the title "Hope for This Hour," Buber pointed out that since World War I "genuine dialogue between men of different kinds and convictions" had become increasingly difficult. Since then he had insisted that "the future of man as man depends upon a rebirth of dialogue." [1]

He quoted approvingly the words of Robert Hutchins on the civilization of the dialogue, the essence of which was communication, mutual respect, and understanding, even if there was no agreement.

But in order to attain this civilization of the dialogue, Buber said, there is an essential presupposition:

> It is necessary to overcome the massive distrust in others and also that in ourselves.

I do not mean thereby the primal mistrust, such as that directed against those with strange ways, those who are unsettled, and those without traditions—the mistrust that the farmer in his isolated farmstead feels for the tramp who suddenly appears before him. I mean the universal mistrust of our age . . . the demonry of basic mistrust. What does it avail to induce the other to speak if basically one puts no faith in what he says? The meeting with him already takes place under the perspective of his untrustworthiness. And this perspective is not incorrect, for his meeting with me takes place under a corresponding perspective. The basic mistrust, coming to light, produces ground for mistrust, and so forth and so forth.[2]

In Buber's opinion, this specifically modern mistrust differs from the ancient mistrust which is apparently inherent in the human being and has left its mark in all cultures:

> In our time something basically different has been added that is capable of undermining more powerfully the foundations of existence between men. One no longer merely fears that the other will voluntarily dissemble, but one simply takes it for granted that he cannot do otherwise.[3]

Because the assumed difference between the other man's opinion and what he says, between what he says and what he does, is seen as "essential necessity," I, the listener, do not really pay attention to what he is saying:

> I do not take it seriously as a contribution to the information about this subject, but rather I listen for what drives the other to say what he says, for an unconscious motive, say, or a "complex." [4]

What is for the other man an idea that is important becomes for me only an "ideology," an opinion cloaking the interest of his group. And here something sinister and characteristic of our time takes place:

> My main task in my intercourse with my fellow-man be-
> comes more and more, whether in terms of individual psychol-
> ogy or of sociology, to see through and unmask him.[5]

It is no longer only the honesty of other men which is in question but the inner integrity of their existence itself. This mistrust
destroys not only trustworthy talk between opponents but also
the feeling and immediacy of true meeting between people:

> Seeing-through and unmasking is now becoming the great
> sport between men, and those who practise it do not know
> whither it entices them. . . . For this game naturally becomes
> complete only as it becomes reciprocal, in the same measure as
> the unmasker himself becomes the object of unmasking. Hence
> one may foresee in the future a degree of reciprocity in existen-
> tial mistrust where speech will turn into dumbness and sense
> into madness.[6]

This sickness of existential mistrust means that one group of
men today can no longer carry on a genuine dialogue with another. And it causes contemporary mankind to lose confidence in
existence in general. The result is that man sets out on one of two
false ways: he seeks to be strengthened either by himself or by a
collective to which he belongs.

Buber was convinced that both these undertakings were
doomed to failure. The self-confirmation of someone whom no
fellow man confirmed could not long be valid. On the other
hand, "confirmation through the collective is pure fiction." [7]
While the collective accepts and employs each of its members as
a particular individual, it cannot recognize anyone in his own
being, independently of his usefulness for the collective.

The only salvation is to renew the principle of dialogue—
"the address of those called to speak to those really able and prepared to hear." [8] And this means, first of all, overcoming this
sickness of existential and universal mistrust.

Part of the problem is that people have become encrusted and encased by their opinions, which have been oversimplified and reduced to easy-to-grasp ideologies. If the mistrust which is poisoning the human organism is to be removed, this "ideological critique," [9] this superficial labeling and classifying of people into compartments of belief, has to be limited.

What Buber meant by this, he explained, was "a more comprehending, more penetrating realism." [10] Not merely the outer mask, but also the inner man should be perceived and understood.

"We wish to trust him, not blindly indeed but clear-sightedly. We wish to perceive his manifoldness and his wholeness, his proper character, without any preconceptions about this or that background." [11]

Only if this happens can a genuine dialogue begin between the two camps into which mankind is split in our century.

"It is self-evident," Buber added, "that these men will not speak merely in their own names. Behind them will be divined the unorganized mass of those who feel themselves represented through these spokesmen." [12]

This was an entirely different kind of representation from the political:

> These men will not be bound by the aims of the hour, they are gifted with the free far-sightedness of those called by the unborn; they will be independent persons with no authority save that of the spirit. [13]

Their task would be nothing less than "the rescue of man" through this authority of the spirit. Buber summed up their nature and their task in a magnificent passage:

> The representatives of whom I speak will each be acquainted with the true aims of his own people, and on these needs will be willing to stake themselves. But they will also turn understandingly to the true needs of other peoples, and will know in both cases how to extract the true needs from the exaggerations. Just for that reason they will unrelentingly distinguish between truth and propaganda within what is called the opposition of interests.

Only when out of the alleged amount of antagonisms just the real conflicts between genuine needs remain can the consideration of the necessary and possible settlements between them begin. The question one must proceed from will be this, apparently the simplest of all questions, yet inviting many difficulties: What does man need, every man, in order to live as a man? For if the globe is not to burst asunder, every man must be given what he needs for a really human life. Coming together out of hostile camps, those who stand in the authority of the spirit will dare to think with one another in terms of the whole planet.[14]

Buber was not naïvely optimistic about the chance that these representatives—if they could be found—would be able to renew the dialogue between opposing camps of mankind. Their success would depend on their unreserved honesty, their "goodwill with its scorn of empty phrases," their courageous personal engagement. But if there is hope for this hour, he said, it rests on the hopers themselves: those who feel most deeply the sickness of present-day man.

And the need for an immediacy of dialogue between men has another dimension; the conflict between trusting man and mistrusting him conceals the conflict between trust in eternity and mistrust in eternity. "If our mouths succeed in genuinely saying 'thou,'" Buber dared to hope, "then, after long silence and stammering, we shall have addressed our eternal 'Thou' anew. Reconciliation leads towards reconciliation." [15]

Buber certainly saw himself as one of these representatives of the spirit. Hammarskjöld probably also recognized his role in Buber's words. The Secretary-General of the United Nations had written in his diary in 1951, "Pray that your loneliness may spur you into finding something to live for, great enough to die for." [16]

Now, on the eve of his second term in office, he responded to Buber's plea for dialogue between men as he had earlier responded heart and soul to Albert Schweitzer's ethical code of conduct.

As Henry P. van Dusen points out in his fascinating study of Hammarskjöld, *The Statesman and the Faith*, he had been in Jerusalem three times in the preceding two years—in April and May 1956, in May 1957, and in December 1957. But he had made no effort to see Buber. Now, however, after reading *Pointing the Way*, he determined to meet him.

On April 10, 1958, Hammarskjöld was inducted for a second term as Secretary-General of the United Nations. Five days later he wrote to Buber in Jerusalem:

Dear Professor Buber,
    You do not know me personally, but I am afraid you have not been able to escape knowing about me.
    My reason for sending you these lines is that I just read the newly published American edition of your collection of essays, *Pointing the Way*.
    I wish to tell you how strongly I have responded to what you write about our age of distrust and to the background of your observations which I find in your general philosophy of unity created "out of the manifold." Certainly, for me, this is a case of "parallel ways."
    Once in a while I have my way to Jerusalem. It would, indeed, give me very great pleasure if on a forthcoming visit I may call on you.

Yours sincerely,
Dag Hammarskjöld

A day or two after he had written this, Hammarskjöld, discovering that Buber was in fact in Princeton, New Jersey, wrote and invited him to visit him at United Nations headquarters on May 1.

When they met they found, during an intense and warm conversation lasting over two hours, that they shared many of the same concerns about the worsening of the international situation. Buber has written, in his short memoir on his contact with Hammarskjöld, that "he who stood in the most exposed position of international responsibility" was concerned about the same things as "I who stand in the loneliness of a spiritual tower, which is in

reality a watchtower from which all the distances and depths of
the planetary crisis can be descried."

They were both pained in the same way by

the pseudo-speaking of representatives of states and groups of
states who, permeated by a fundamental reciprocal mistrust,
talked past one another out the windows.[17]

Hammarskjöld and Buber agreed that a genuine dialogue was
needed which would show that, in Buber's words,

the common interests of the peoples were stronger still than
those which kept them in opposition to one another. . . . For
there is no third possibility, only one of these two: common realization of the great common interests or the end of all that on
the one side and the other one is accustomed to call civilization.[18]

This shared anxiety about the fate of humanity was essentially
what bound the two men to one another then and afterward. At
that first meeting the talk was of philosophy and belief, of how to
bring people together into a true community of mankind based
on dialogue and mutual trust.

Hammarskjöld told Buber he was scheduled to talk at Cambridge University on June 5, when he would be awarded an honorary doctorate. And, he added, he wished to quote Buber's remarks on the need to combat the prevailing mistrust, from "Hope
for This Hour." Hammarskjöld's Cambridge address was entitled
"The Walls of Distrust," and in it he quoted from "Hope for This
Hour" at such length that he felt the need of this explanation:

I have done so because out of the depths of his feelings Martin Buber has found expressions which it would be vain for me
to try to improve.[19]

A few months later, in September 1958, Hammarskjöld was in
Jerusalem again. This time he visited Buber at his home, as he did
again in January 1959, when, over dinner, the two men had their
most intimate conversation. Buber sometimes spoke with me

about this evening—the last time he saw Hammarskjöld. And he has written that "in the center of our conversation stood the problem that has ever laid claim to me in the course of my life: the failure of the spiritual man in his historical undertakings." [20]

He illustrated this failure by Plato's abortive attempt to establish his just state in Sicily, which broke down when his friend and disciple, Prince Dion, was assassinated. This was a theme which always fascinated Buber. He returned to it again and again in conversation, and wrote about it in his essay "Plato and Isaiah," which formed part of the inaugural lecture he delivered at the Hebrew University in 1938.

I gained the impression that his relationship with Hammarskjöld gave him that contact with an active man of state which he had despaired of having with Ben-Gurion. Hammarskjöld was not an ordinary politician or diplomat. He suffered the inner torments of an ethical mystic who had to grapple with always complex and often sordid political problems. Something in his temperament bent sympathetically toward the philosopher who believed that love had to be expressed through action. Hammarskjöld had written that "in our age, the road to holiness necessarily passes through the world of action." [21] This was very much as the *hasidim* saw the world, and it formed the bridge between Hammarskjöld's world, rooted in the active life of global politics, and Buber's deceptively cloistered world in Jerusalem.

Buber had a high regard for Hammarskjöld's intellectual abilities. Hammarskjöld, he told me, was an outstanding interpreter of the medieval German mystics, and in particular of Meister Eckhart. "But he was not as austere as some people thought. In my talks with him I found him warm and capable of reaching a true understanding," he said.

"Do you know what Hammarskjöld told me?" he added. "That there were two books he kept near him and read passages from almost every day. One was the writings of Eckhart. And the other was—can you guess? Not the New Testament. But the Psalms. He had a deep knowledge of the Psalms, and when I referred to Psalm 73 he quoted part of it to me. This is, as you know, my favorite among all the Psalms. And it was one of those to which Hammarskjöld too felt closest."

During these two meetings in Jerusalem the conversation touched briefly on Israeli-Arab relations, and more specifically on the problem of the Arab refugees, on which Hammarskjöld was concentrating at the time.

The January 1959 visit was the last time the United Nations Secretary-General met Buber. It was also the last time Hammarskjöld came to Jerusalem. When he returned to New York he told a press conference:

> The moment I get time, I would like very much to translate some three or four essays from *Pointing the Way*. On very many points I see eye to eye with Buber; on other points, naturally, there must be nuances. But as to the basic reaction, I think that he has made a major contribution, and I would like to make that more broadly known.[22]

He was of course thinking of a translation into Swedish. He had first broached this possibility during the meeting at United Nations headquarters, mentioning "Hope for This Hour" as an essay he wished to translate, along with two or three others. Buber responded approvingly to this suggestion, although he knew Hammarskjöld was too busy to undertake any serious work at that time.

On June 15, 1959, Hammarskjöld submitted to the United Nations General Assembly a comprehensive report on the Palestinian refugee problem. This incorporated some of the ideas he had discussed briefly with Buber during their talks in Jerusalem.

In the same month he also wrote to the Nobel Prize Committee in Sweden proposing Buber for the Nobel Prize—but for peace, not for literature.

In this remarkable document of some fifteen hundred words he reviewed, with great admiration, yet with a high degree of objectivity, Buber's activities as a writer and as an exponent of "what might be called a humanistic internationalism built on basic elements of Jewish thought."

"However," he pointed out, "his literary production must probably be considered at an end, though he has become an increasingly active force in international debates . . . [and] has played an important role in Christian theological circles and in Jewry."

He called attention to Buber's "unique position in modern Jewish thought," but added that he was "scarcely accorded the status which an outside observer would think he merited."

He cited the reasons for opposition to Buber in the Israeli establishment, yet praised his Jewish idealism and steadfastness of character.

> Even though Buber's position in Jewry arouses opposition [he wrote], he stands out for those who have made a deep study of his works as a gifted interpreter of some of the loftiest and purest elements of Jewish tradition and Jewish spiritual life. If Ben-Gurion and his predecessors have taken up the legacy of militant nationalism which characterized historic Israel, Buber can be said to have given new life to essential features of the prophetic inheritance. One might venture to predict that this time as well the voice of the prophet will be shown to penetrate further into the future than the voice of the military leader.

He reviewed at some length Buber's writings, with special attention to *I and Thou*, which he called "a key work in Buber's philosophical writings," and "the work in which Buber best succeeded in presenting a coherent and pregnant formulation of his basic concept," mentioning also as important to an understanding of "the later development of his world of thought . . . such works as *Eclipse of God* and *Pointing the Way*."

Much of Hammarskjöld's statement, which is highly appreciative of Buber's greatness, sounds almost like an apology for the recommendation with which it closes, which is, in part, negative. For instance:

> Without examining the logical validity of Buber's formula and all its implications, one can accept it as the expression of an extremely fertile philosophy of life and can understand how in-

fluential it has become. It has touches of a mystical pantheism, while it still retains the depth and drama of the dualistic relationship with the divine. At the same time, in its relationship with man it is a translation of Kant's thesis of man as an object in itself, in terms which give this thesis a new human warmth and richness. . . .

Summing up the importance of Buber the philosopher in the context that interests us, one might say that—like Bergson, in another direction, but perhaps to the same high degree— he has been fruitful and inspiring through his philosophical writings in spheres intimately connected with poetry. Further, on the basis of his philosophy, as a shaper of opinion, he has become one of those who has most eloquently defended those forms of contact between people which poetry wants to serve: and in so doing he has remained firmly rooted in spiritual realities. It is quite possible that we are only seeing the beginning of a trend in both these directions, which he may have released.

Yet his conclusion is somewhat equivocal:

Under these circumstances it would seem that Buber could certainly be considered for a Nobel Prize. Nevertheless the objections are obvious: he is a man of eighty, with his life's work behind him, and his creation falls only indirectly within the spheres covered by the Nobel Prizes. In conclusion, one might say that perhaps he merits the greatest credit as the interpreter of an important culture, whose son he is, and this with such purity and force that already now, during his lifetime, he symbolizes it.

In spite of the admiration for Buber which these lines reflect, I would hesitate to see him rewarded with the Nobel Prize for Literature. A more natural form of recognition might be the Peace Prize.

New York, June 1959
Dag Hammarskjöld

As Dr. van Dusen remarks, this memorandum reveals as much about its author as about his subject. If Hammarskjöld had simply intended to recommend Buber for the Nobel Peace Prize, he would have written to the special committee appointed by the Norwegian Parliament, which makes this award, under the terms of Nobel's will. But he did not do this. He was himself a member of the Swedish Academy, which awards the prize for literature. And the main purpose of his memorandum was to give his opinion on Buber's candidacy for this prize.

Quite possibly he wished to recommend Buber, whom he so greatly admired, for this honor. But in writing the detailed memorandum his painful, lacerating honesty compelled him to confront the doubts he harbored, and to suggest as an alternative that the Peace Prize would be more appropriate.

Although his final recommendation obtained some distinguished support, and was duly forwarded to the Norwegian Parliament, the fact that Buber was an Israeli created a problem which eventually proved insurmountable. It was felt that the prize could not be given to an Israeli or an Arab, but should be shared between both parties to the Middle East dispute, if someone comparable to Buber could be found on the Arab side. Some names were considered. One such was Taha Hussein, the blind Egyptian writer. But, although he was a distinguished literary figure in his own country, he could hardly be said to have advocated peace with Israel to the same degree that Buber had called for an Israeli reconciliation with the Arabs.

After several tentative attempts to find an Arab equivalent to Buber whose nomination would at the same time not enrage the Arab governments, the idea was dropped. The Nobel Peace Prize for 1959 was awarded to Philip Noel-Baker, the British writer on disarmament and worker for world peace.

Buber was very disappointed. In 1949 the famous Swiss novelist and poet Hermann Hesse—himself a winner of the Nobel Prize for literature in 1946—had proposed Buber for the prize. "Buber," Hesse had written, "is in my judgment not only one of the few wise men who live on the earth at the present time. He is also a writer of a very high order, and, more than that, he has enriched world literature with a genuine treasure as has no other living author—the Tales of the Hasidim." [23]

That nomination had proved unsuccessful, and the 1949 award had gone to William Faulkner. Now Hammarskjöld's nomination failed for reasons which could only be termed political. It was ironical that Buber, who had displayed such courage in opposing Israeli chauvinism and encountered such unpopularity at home because of his stand, should lose the Nobel Peace Prize because of the committee's insistence on Jewish-Arab parity at Oslo. Giving him the prize would have encouraged circles within Israel who were seeking a path to the Arabs, and could even have reinforced some of the latent moderate trends in the Arab states. But this opportunity was lost. And with it went what was virtually Buber's last opportunity of winning a Nobel Prize.

He did not like to talk about it. And on the rare occasions when he did so it was with a tone of sadness and regret for the political obstacles which had prevented his nomination from being accepted. Then, after a downcast moment or two, he would shrug his shoulders and say, "Well, let us not think or talk about it. It is over and done with: in the past." That was Buber's way. The present was always waiting and more important than any setbacks behind him.

And there were other prizes to console Buber: the Erasmus Prize for contributions to European culture; and the Bialik Prize, the most important award for literature in Israel. When he was awarded the Bialik Prize in Tel Aviv he went out of his way to stress the fact that no other honor could have meant so much to him.

Ernst Blumenthal, a friend of Buber's from Jerusalem, learned about Hammarskjöld's memorandum in the summer of 1959, during a visit to Sweden. He revealed some of its contents to Buber. But he never told him about the final paragraphs and Hammarskjöld's reasons for not proposing him for the literature award and suggesting the peace prize instead. Buber's friends concealed this from him, and as far as we know he never discovered the truth.

It is not clear whether the Nobel episode created any breach between Buber and Hammarskjöld. What is certain is that there was no contact between them for the next two years. After this time Hammarskjöld resumed the correspondence. On August 17, 1961, he wrote to Buber in Jerusalem:

> The last few days I have been reading some studies of yours which I had not seen before. . . .
>
> After having finished reading these studies, I feel the need to send you again a greeting—after too long a time of silence, understandable only in the light of the pressure of circumstances. In what you say about the "signs," about the "questions" and the response and about the Single One and his responsibility, with reference also to the political sphere, you have formulated shared experiences in ways which made your studies very much what you would call a "sign" for me. It is strange—over a gulf of time and a bridge of differences as to background and outer experience—to find a bridge built which, in one move, eliminates the distance.
>
> I still keep in my mind the idea of translating you so as to bring you closer to my countrymen, but it becomes increasingly difficult to choose and of course I cannot envisage any more extensive work. Also, the more I sense the nuances of your German, the more shy I become at the thought of a translation which, at best, could render only a modest part of its overtones.

Buber was pleased that Hammarskjöld had written and that the silence between them had been broken. He replied at once with a handwritten letter, written in Jerusalem on August 23, 1961—the only letter Buber ever wrote to Hammarskjöld:

> Dear Mr. Hammarskjöld—
>
> I want to thank you for your letter.
>
> It is, for me, even more than what you said in our first talk, a token of true . . . understanding—rather a rare gift in this world of ours.
>
> Were I asked, which of my books a Swede should read first, I should answer: "The most difficult of them all, but the most apt to introduce the reader into the realm of dialogue, I mean: *I and Thou.*" As you may not know the Postscript to the new

edition, I am sending you a copy, together with a paper on language I gave last year.

> With kind regards,
> Yours,
> Martin Buber

Hammarskjöld accepted this suggestion and wrote to Buber on August 26:

> I am certain that I am reading you correctly if I see reflected in your reply a silent 'Aufruf' that I try a translation of this key work, as decisive in its message as supremely beautiful in its form. This decides the issue and, if I have your permission, I shall do it even if it may take some time.

He informed Buber that he was writing to the leading publishing firm in Sweden asking whether they would publish it. "If this all works out," he added, "may I tell you how much it would mean to me also by providing me with a justification for a broadened and intensified contact with you personally."

Hammarskjöld's Swedish publishers were enthusiastic about the idea, and he decided to begin work in earnest. He was due to leave New York on September 12 for the Congo, and he took along only two books: the copy of Thomas à Kempis's *Imitation of Christ* which was always on his bedside table in his New York apartment, and the copy of *Ich und Du* (the original German of *I and Thou*) which Buber had sent him in August. Before leaving New York he wrote Buber a short letter informing him that the Stockholm publishers had agreed to the project and adding that he intended to start work at once.

During the three days the United Nations Secretary-General spent in Leopoldville trying to stop the fighting between Tshombe's army in Katanga and the United Nations force, he seems to have worked on the translation. When he left the home of Sture Linner, head of the United Nations mission to the Congo, on the morning of September 17 he left there the copy of *I and Thou* and the first twelve pages of his translation into Swedish, with handwritten corrections on the first page. He told

Linner that he wanted to discuss it with him when he came back from Ndola, in Northern Rhodesia, where he had arranged to have face-to-face talks with Tshombe about the secession of Katanga.

That night, before Hammarskjöld's plane reached Ndola, it crashed in the bush. Everyone aboard was killed.

Buber heard the news of Hammarskjöld's death on the radio in Jerusalem. An hour later he received Hammarskjöld's letter about the Swedish translation of *I and Thou*, written and mailed in New York on September 12.

Hammarskjöld was one of the spiritual men whom Buber admired—a vigorous mystic who expressed his love in action, as the *hasidim* did. Another was Albert Schweitzer, of whom he always spoke with great affection.

Schweitzer, Buber said, was a great realist of the spirit who had courageously confronted the central dilemma of our time: that "spirit and life have fallen apart from one another more radically perhaps than in any earlier time." 24 The philosophy of reverence for life, which is perhaps Schweitzer's most lasting monument, answers this split in our consciousness by strengthening "the body-soul totality of the individual living man." 25 It is the *whole* human being who is to be healed, so that his spirit and his life can be joined once more.

Buber quoted with approval Schweitzer's insistence that man can no longer live his life for himself alone; that immaculate self-centered perfection is not enough; that each of us should give ourselves in some way as a man to other men. And he agreed with Schweitzer that the approach to life in our century should be both optimistic and ethical, so that contemporary barbarism can be opposed and civilization renewed.

This shared belief in man's unity with all life in nature and the universe drew Buber and Schweitzer together in a close friendship. Their ethical, life-affirming mysticism led Dag Hammarskjöld to consider them his spiritual mentors, who, originating in Europe, were observing the crisis of mankind from their respective vantage points, the Christian in Lambarene and the Jew in Jerusalem, and marking out the guidelines for survival.

After World War II Buber and Schweitzer cooperated several times on appeals against the spread of nuclear weapons. And in 1955, when Schweitzer turned eighty, the seventy-six-year-old Buber wrote him this letter:

Dear Albert Schweitzer—

Since my earliest years it has been a great encouragement, and in later years a comforting thought, that people like you exist. As you know, I have always been concerned with those who help mankind, and you have been one of the great helpers in so many ways. Every time one man helps another, the *hasidim* say, an angel is born. I hope, my dear Albert Schweitzer, that fate will long allow you to hear the wings of many angels beating about you.

Yours,
Martin Buber

Bertrand Russell

In 1951 I began writing to Bertrand Russell about Israeli-Arab relations. Russell did not know much about the Middle East, but he was deeply interested in seeing peace between Israel and the Arabs. And when he brought his acute mind to bear on the problems of the region he often showed astonishing insight.

In November 1955, for example, in a letter to me, he suggested the formation of "a small United Nations force to make sure the frontier is respected by both sides." This was fifteen months before the United Nations set up its Emergency Force to patrol the Israeli-Egyptian border, after the Sinai campaign.

Russell felt the conflict between Israel and the Arab world constituted "an intolerable danger to the peoples of these countries and the peoples of the world." He appreciated the sense of grievance on both sides. But he feared the danger that the dispute might become an item in the Cold War. Because of this, and out of his concern over the threat of nuclear weapons entering the Middle East, he urged the Arab and Israeli governments to put an end to the enmity between them through consultation. "Only short-sightedness," he wrote to me in 1962, "would lead the leaders of Israel and the leaders of the Arab world to overlook their common interests, their common culture and their common humanity."

I showed Buber one or two of these letters, as we wanted to publish them in *New Outlook*. I asked him whether he was familiar with Russell's philosophical writings.

"If you look at my essay on 'Society and the State,' " he replied, "you will see that I have quoted Russell's definition of power as 'the fundamental concept in social science, in the same sense in which energy is the fundamental concept in physics.' [1] This appeared in his book on *Power*, published in 1938. A remarkable book, which presented a new type of social analysis."

I looked up this essay of Buber's, and found he had described Russell's definition of power as "this bold concept on the part of a distinguished logician."

The next time I saw Buber I suggested that he should write to Russell with a view to common action for peace in the Middle East.

Buber gave one of his irresistible smiles, so genial and charming. But through it I detected a hint of opposition.

"And what good would that do, do you think? Two old men writing to one another. I am eighty-two, not so? And he must be eighty-five? Eighty-six?"

"Eighty-eight," I said. This was in 1960.

"You see, what did I tell you? Two old men . . . Let me tell you something—Russell has quite enough work to do in England. And I have more than enough to keep me busy in Israel. If we can each make a little progress, perhaps that might do something for peace. But we don't need to write to each other."

I said no more about it. But that year Buber became passionately engaged in the cause of Soviet Jewry. He attended an important conference in Paris together with Daniel Mayer and Dr. Nachum Goldmann, and signed several declarations demanding that the Soviet authorities grant the Jews of that country full civil and religious liberties.

In May 1961 the Soviet Union imposed the death penalty for economic offences, although these crimes had not been punishable by death since the 1917 Revolution. Disturbing reports began reaching Israel indicating that a high proportion of those involved in these cases and actually being sentenced to death were Jews, although it was difficult to find out whether they had actually been executed or not.

Russell was known to be in good standing in the Soviet Union and in touch with Premier Khrushchev. Buber decided to write to him and ask him to intervene on behalf of Soviet Jewry, and did so on March 4, 1962.

"I want to assure you," he wrote, "that my attitude to the whole issue of such death sentences would not have been any different if there had been no question of Jews being involved. But as one who has for many years followed with interest the problem of Jews in several lands, including the Soviet Union, I would like to stress that the fact that Jews are singled out in the eyes of the population as economic criminals is gravely dangerous for the general Jewish community in the Soviet Union. I feel we should do our utmost to minimize such dangers."

Buber proposed that Russell and he, together with Eleanor Roosevelt and François Mauriac, should sign the following cable to Khrushchev:

> News has come to us, through the Soviet and international press, that in the Soviet Union the death penalty has been instituted for economic and other offences, which it is not generally the custom to punish with death.
>
> The undersigned all belong to those who, as a matter of principle, are opposed to the death penalty. The Soviet Union has for many years been one of the countries where the death penalty did not exist, and this has aroused our sympathy. And just because of it, we are gravely concerned that as from about nine months ago increasing death sentences have been passed for economic offences and the like. We consider that this judicial custom does not agree with a great, progressive and cultured people, and we call on the Government of the Soviet Union to abolish this system of internal contest against economic offences. We zealously call upon you to prevent the execution of the death sentences which have already been passed by Soviet courts.
>
> We are further concerned by the fact that the majority of

those sentenced to death for economic offences, and whose names were published in the Soviet press, are Jews. In view of the fact that prejudices have not yet been rooted out from the wide masses towards some minorities living among them, these cases might eventually bare the entire Jewish community to grave dangers, these, of course, being contrary to the aims of the Soviet Union itself.

We are positive that you will see in this application no intention to offend the Soviet Union, nor harm the moral position she enjoys in the world. We are driven solely by the concern for the maintenance of universal human standards, as well as for the good name of the Soviet Union, so as to render easier international understanding towards world peace.

Buber added that if this appeal to Khrushchev were to have any practical chance of success, it had to be kept secret from the beginning.

Russell was then in London. But when he returned to his home in Wales and read the text of the cable he immediately agreed to sign it.

Russell did, however, request one change in the text of the cable, the deletion of the word "moral" in the phrase "no intention to offend the Soviet Union, nor harm the moral position she enjoys in the world." This was, he explained to Buber, because he felt "that governments such as the Soviet Union and the United States have no moral position in the world."

Buber agreed to this change and the revised cable was signed by Russell, Buber, and Mauriac and sent to Khrushchev. A copy was sent to the Soviet Ambassador in Tel Aviv. Mrs. Roosevelt decided to write a personal letter to Khrushchev.

Russell's intervention with Khrushchev on behalf of the Soviet Jews was one of the reasons the Jerusalem Municipality awarded him its first Literary Prize for Human Freedom in the spring of 1963, to be presented during the Book Fair which would be held in the city at the end of April of that year. I discussed the matter with Buber and the editorial board of *New Outlook*, and we decided to invite Russell to address a meeting of Arabs and Jews in

Tel Aviv under our auspices after receiving the prize in Jerusalem.

Russell replied, thanking me for the invitation but regretting that he was unable to come to Israel because of the work he was engaged in "and the energy required for travel at my age." It was arranged that his secretary, Ralph Schoenman, would accept the prize on his behalf and then be the guest of *New Outlook* during the remainder of his stay in Israel.

On April 22 Ralph Schoenman arrived, and we arranged for him to visit Buber at his home and to have several sessions with the *New Outlook* group in Tel Aviv. When I left him that night he was studying the text of a message from Russell which, he said, he would read at the ceremony the next day.

The following evening I turned up in City Hall for the presentation and took my seat in the press gallery. About twenty minutes behind schedule the officials and guests of honor filed in and took their places.

Schoenman was placed next to the mayor. He looked distinctly unhappy, I thought. And when he spotted me sitting among the other journalists he raised his eyebrows, shrugged, pointed one shoulder at the mayor and gave all the indications of trying to tell me something. But although I gestured back, I couldn't puzzle out his agitated sign language.

There was an air of anticipation in the hall, especially where I was sitting. The news had gone around that Russell had sent a message, an appeal for peace in the Middle East.

What followed was total anticlimax. When Schoenman finally rose to speak, he said a few words about Russell's pleasure in accepting the award and how honored he himself felt being in Jerusalem to receive it. Then, abruptly, he sat down. He could not have been on his feet for more than a minute.

The astonished audience filed out, while the press gallery buzzed with speculation. Just what had happened I learned later that night from Schoenman himself in his hotel room. A few minutes before the ceremony was due to start someone from the City Council had taken him aside and warned him not to make any political statements. Schoenman was taken aback, but was afraid that if he read Russell's statement there would be an unpleasant scene and so decided to omit the statement and to inform Russell of the pressure exerted upon him.

He was furious. And so was I. But if the evening that Schoenman was prevented from speaking remained a frustrating and irritating memory, the evening at Buber's home was ample compensation. It was in every way a memorable occasion. First Schoenman saw Buber alone for about an hour, and then they were joined by other members of Buber's circle for a discussion on Middle East peace and Israel's role in attaining this peace. We had invited Professor Ernst Simon and Dr. Simon Shereshevsky of *Ichud;* Professor Ephraim Urbach and Eliezer Livneh of the Israeli Committee for a Nuclear-Free Zone in the Middle East; Professor Amos Nathan of the Haifa Institute of Technology, also an expert on nuclear problems; Simcha Flapan of *New Outlook;* and two or three others.

Buber was in his element. I had never seen him so beaming, so fatherly and benign, toward the oldest of his colleagues as toward Ralph Schoenman and myself. He did not talk much. Most of the time he sat in his comfortable chintz-covered armchair in the center of the group, listening intently, as he always did. But when a knotty point arose, or the discussion strayed from the main issue, it was Buber who, with a phrase that did not order or insist but suggested, proposed, hinted almost, led the group skillfully back to the main flow of the talk.

It was a superb performance, and it confirmed what I have often thought—that Buber was the perfect chairman of a committee composed of factions hostile to one another, or a delicate international conference. He had all the tact, composure, and rapier-like subtlety of a first-class statesman. If anyone could have brought Arabs and Israelis around a table to a common understanding, Buber could have—if he had been given the opportunity.

The discussion that night centered on the growing fear that nuclear weapons would be introduced into the region. Schoenman gave Russell's views on the reality of this danger. We spoke about various ways of arousing opinion in Israel, the Arab states, and the world, and decided whom we would ask to sign an appeal to the Arab and Israeli governments to keep atomic weapons out of the Middle East.

Russell had already written to the heads of state of Iraq, Saudi Arabia, Algeria, Israel, Egypt, Syria, Jordan, Lebanon, Ghana, Tanganyika, and Yugoslavia expressing his concern about the possibility that the arms race between Israel and the Arab world might spread to embrace rockets and nuclear weapons.

"I am convinced," he had written, "that unless the Arab world or Israel find a way in which to make a dramatic gesture for the purpose of ending the arms race in the Middle East, only terrible conflict can ensue, leading to the intrusion of Cold War powers who will exploit the problem for their own ends. The result may be nuclear devastation." [2]

He called upon each leader in the Middle East to declare his willingness to admit international supervision and control of all nuclear plants and delivery systems for rockets. This declaration could be made, he suggested, under the aegis of the United Nations, the great powers, or of any group of nations neutral toward both the Arab world and Israel. African states could well lead in this task, he felt—which was why he wrote to Nkrumah and Nyerere.

But there was no serious response to Russell's private appeal to these eleven heads of state. Those who replied showed little willingness to accept international control, and each tended to blame the other side exclusively for the gathering arms race.

Ben-Gurion had not yet replied to Russell's letter when Schoenman arrived in Jerusalem. He received Russell's secretary, and the two had a heated argument which led to no meeting of minds on the need to keep atomic weapons out of the region.

Shortly afterward, on June 30, 1963, Ben-Gurion resigned as Prime Minister. One of his last official acts was to draft a reply to Russell's original letter of April 8. Israel, he declared, had to increase and strengthen its deterrent force, because of the Arabs' threats. Instead of agreeing that nuclear weapons should be banned from the entire Middle East, Ben-Gurion proposed the general and total abolition of all weapons in the region—a program so grandiose and messianic that he could be quite certain it would never be accepted by anyone. This apparently idealistic proposal is a perfect example of what Buber meant by propaganda, as opposed to education.

Because his letter to the Middle East heads of state evoked so little response, Russell then wrote to various eminent scientists and humanitarians asking them to sign an appeal to the Arab and Israeli governments. This was one of the subjects discussed at Schoenman's meeting at Buber's house.

As a result of these discussions an appeal to the Arab states and Israel to accept international supervision of nuclear and rocket weapons systems and plants, and an internationally supervised embargo on further arms shipments to the region, was drawn up and published in *New Outlook* in February 1964. It was signed by ten internationally known and respected scientists and scholars: Professor Max Born, Danilo Dolci, Pastor Martin Niemoller, Professor Linus Pauling, Professor C. F. Powell, Professor Eugene Rabinowitch, Professor Joseph Rotblat, Professor Abdus Salam, Jean-Paul Sartre, and Dr. Albert Schweitzer.

After the high point of Ralph Schoenman's visit and the intense behind-the-scenes work on the anti-nuclear appeal there was no direct contact between Buber's circle in Israel and Russell's in England. There was no break or disagreement, just a diversion of energies. Buber grew older and more tired, and so, we must assume, did Russell, although his vitality and intellectual grasp continued to be truly phenomenal. In 1965 Buber died, and five years later Russell—two of the greatest men of our century, whose brief interaction upon each other I was privileged to witness and, in a humble way, to foster.

Gandhi and Tagore

Buber was always interested in the Orient. At university he studied ancient Chinese philosophy, especially the teachings of Lao-tzu and Chuang-tzu. In Germany and later in Jerusalem he went out of his way to meet scholars from China and India and to question them about the political and spiritual paths their countries were taking. Toward the end of his life his granddaughter, the wife of Professor Agassi, a specialist in Chinese studies, was in Hong Kong and sent him extracts from Chinese papers about the Communist struggle. He read these avidly and sometimes discussed them with me.

This interest found expression in some of his lesser-known writings. In 1909, at the age of thirty-one, he had translated some selected *Talks and Parables of Chuang-tzu* into German. This little book was introduced by an essay called "The Teaching of the Tao," the "path" toward a life of unity and harmony.

Nearly half a century later, in 1957, when Buber came to choose essays for the collection entitled *Pointing the Way*, he included "The Teaching of the Tao," although, he said, he could no longer feel that it expressed his beliefs. In the foreword he asked the reader to bear in mind that this essay belonged to "a stage that I had to pass through before I could enter into an independent relationship with being."

When he was younger, he explained, he sought "the unification of the self with the all-self, attainable by man in levels or intervals of his earthly life." The Chinese of antiquity had seemed to him to offer a guide to this mystic and ecstatic experience, in which a person lost his individuality through absorption into the universe.

But later he had a shattering experience with a young student during World War I, the story of whose suicide is told in this book in the chapter "Meeting and Living." This stimulated an approach to his philosophy of dialogue which developed until it attained mature expression in 1919. He came to see that this attempt to be "elevated above life" was actually a flight from reality, and to perceive that a man who followed Oriental-style mysticism was turning away from his true existence, "the existence into which he has been set, through conception and birth, for life and death in this unique personal form": his whole existence as he lives it day by day, in both the hours of joy and exaltation and those of anguish and hardship. The mysticism of the Tao, Buber wrote in 1957, "is certainly an exalted form of being untrue: but it is still being untrue." [1]

However, even after coming to this belief, Buber continued to be fascinated by the Far East and by Oriental thought. But his interest was now attracted less by the "religious" aspects of this thought than by its political and secular implications. One of the first results of this inquiry was a remarkable article called "The Spirit of the East and Judaism," published in 1916—first in his own monthly *Der Jude* and then, later the same year, in his book *On the Spirit of Judaism*.

Today, after all that has happened in Asia since then, including the war in Vietnam, this article remains astonishingly prophetic even for Buber:

> The age we live in will one day be known as the age of the Asian crisis. The leading peoples of the East are enslaved— some outwardly, some inwardly—by Europe. These peoples have not preserved their most sacred assets, their great spiritual traditions; at times they themselves have forsaken them. The

subjugation of India, the self-imposed Europeanization of Japan, the debilitation of Persia, and, finally, the disruption of China—where we were wont to think the spirit of the East would dwell unblemished and secure—all these represent stages in this process. The soul of Asia is being destroyed, and Asia itself is cooperating therein. The world is about to lose a valuable possession that is irreplaceable.

The Jew, Buber asserted, has remained an Oriental:

He was driven out of his own country and dispersed throughout the countries of the West. He was compelled to sojourn under skies he did not know, on soil he did not plough. He endured the martyrdom of debasement; he learned to speak the tongues of the people in whose midst he dwelled. Nevertheless he has remained an Oriental.[2]

This Orientalism of the Jew, he wrote, is hidden and concealed. But if he has the wisdom to perceive it and to allow it free play, then the people of Israel who are returning to the Land of Israel can undertake a great mission: to merge the spirits of East and West in a new synthesis, serving as intermediaries between Europe and Asia. The people of the Orient were wakening and becoming liberated, precisely at the time that the Jewish people were returning to their homeland in the East. He attached profound symbolic significance to this historic coincidence:

Jerusalem is still—even more than it has ever been before —what it was thought to be in days gone by: the meeting-place for all the peoples. It is the juncture between the East and the West. It was to Jerusalem that ancient Asia turned its troops, when in the days of Nebuchadnezzar and Cyrus [the Babylonian Exile], it embarked on a campaign of conquest in the West: and it was there that the Europe of Alexander the Great and the Romans marched when they were set on capturing the East. As a result of the drive of the Orient towards the West the first Jewish state collapsed and met its destruction; while as the result of the West's drive towards the Orient the second Jewish state was destroyed.

From that time on the importance of the Land of Israel for

the world has grown ever greater and more profound. . . .
The time has come to seek out peace for Jerusalem, for it spells
peace for all the peoples.[3]

If we remember that these words were written in Germany at
the beginning of World War I, when there were only a few
thousand Jews living in Palestine, and when Asian countries were
largely dominated by European powers, we cannot but agree
with Professor Hugo Bergman, one of Buber's closest friends and
colleagues, who declared:

> We must stand in awe of the powerful vision contained in
> the words of the young Buber.[4]

Buber was one of the first Jews to understand that the new settlers in Palestine and their children could fulfill their destiny only
if they rediscovered their Asian and Oriental heritage. This was
one of the basic ideas put forward by his *Ichud* group as a fundamental step toward an Arab-Jewish dialogue.

In 1947 some progress toward this "Asian consciousness"
seemed to be made when Nehru convened the Asian Relations
Conference at New Delhi and invited the representatives of
twenty-five nations from all parts of Asia to take part.

The Jewish community of Palestine was also represented,
through a delegation headed by Professor Bergman. At the opening session he read the following declaration on behalf of this delegation:

> These are the greetings of representatives of an old religion
> and an old Asian people, driven from its Asian motherland
> eighteen hundred years ago at the point of the sword, but a
> people which has never ceased to be linked in thought and
> daily prayer with this Holy Land, which is at the same time
> the Holy Land of Christianity and Islam. We are happy and
> proud to take part as an old Asian people at this conference,
> and shall strive to be a loyal member of this great family of na-
> tions.[5]

But the Council of Representatives of all Asian peoples, elected
at New Delhi at the end of this conference, never met. Fierce

warfare broke out in India between the Hindus and the Moslems. And the following year the greatest Indian of his times, Mahatma Gandhi, was assassinated.

Gandhi had caught Buber's imagination when the Mahatma began his struggle in India in the 1920s. Buber was particularly impressed by Gandhi's insistence on honesty in politics, exemplified in February 1922, when the All-India Committee forced him to take the words "truthful" and "nonviolent" out of its program statement, and he remarked, "If I stood before the prospect of finding myself in a minority of *one* voice, I humbly believe that I would have the courage to remain in such a hopeless minority. This is for me the only truthful position."

In a 1930 essay about the Mahatma's political activities, "Gandhi's Politics and Us," Buber mentioned his admiration of Gandhi's 1922 statement, adding:

> I know of nothing in modern Western public life to put by its side, unless it were, for all the difference in its source, the words of the American Thoreau in his classic treatise on the duty of civil disobedience.[6]

Surely one of the reasons why Buber so greatly admired Gandhi's stand was—consciously or not—that he himself was often called upon by his conscience to come out against official Zionist and Israeli policy. How many times Buber remained in "a hopeless minority," as he was for example in the Eichmann case!

But the great difference between him and Gandhi was that the latter's field of activity was political, engaged as he was in a direct struggle with the British authorities, whereas Buber was first and foremost a spiritual leader who tried to influence political developments indirectly through his moral position.

He discussed this difference between them in the essay previously mentioned, quoting a key statement in which Gandhi outlines his position, in the article "Neither a Saint nor a Politician":

> I seem to take part in politics, but this is only because politics today strangles us like the coils of a serpent out of which

one cannot slip no matter what one tries. I desire, therefore, to wrestle with the serpent.[7]

Buber noted this statement approvingly and called it "memorable." It is obvious that he shared this point of view and was wary of becoming entangled in the coils of political intrigue. Certainly his experiences of internal Zionist politics during the 1921 Zionist Congress and other high-level conferences permanently disillusioned him about the role an intellectual could play in shaping this movement's policies. He always held himself slightly aloof from complete involvement in the current political whirlpool, and, as I have noted, he was criticized for this by some of his followers, who cited the example of Bertrand Russell's active participation in the Campaign for Nuclear Disarmament's demonstrations in Britain during the early 1960s.

So, reading between the lines of this essay, we can perceive that Buber was curious to find out how Gandhi managed to reconcile his spiritual integrity with the day-to-day political struggle, and whether he succeeded in evading the stranglehold of the dangerous serpent.

In effect, Buber suggested, the real question that should be asked is: Can religion be introduced into politics in such a way that a political success can be obtained?

Answering his own question, he showed that there is a basic distinction between religion and politics: "Religion means goal and way, politics implies end and means." The political end can be recognized visibly by what the world considers "success"; whereas even in the highest experiences of mankind the religious goal remains "that which simply provides direction."

Religion is not necessarily consummated in history. Where religion appears to succeed, in worldly terms, it is really no longer religion that prevails, but "the politics of religion." Instead of introducing religion into politics and purifying the latter, politics becomes part of religion and corrupts it. This, Buber says, is the opposite of what Gandhi intended.

While Gandhi's own attitude is religious in the most genuine

sense, Buber found that at that time—when he had just announced his campaign of civil disobedience—he was forced by
circumstances to ally his religion with the politics of others, in
order to obtain approval for his policies:

> He cannot wrestle uninterruptedly with the serpent; he must
> at times get along with it because he is directed to work in the
> kingdom of the serpent that he set out to destroy.[8]

And this is the source of the tragic character of Gandhi's greatness: "the contradiction between the unconditionality of a spirit
and the conditionality of a situation, to which situation, precisely,
the masses of his followers, even of the youth, belong." [9]

Was not Buber, in writing about Gandhi, really telling us
about himself?

He too had realized that at one pole religion is threatened by
"the ice of isolation" if it separates itself from human activity in
building up the community; yet, if it enters "the rapid fire of political activity," it is threatened by evaporation. For only in "the
great *polis* of God" [10] would religion and politics be blended into
a life of world community, in an eternal harmony in which neither religion nor politics would exist separately from the other.

This was the crucial dilemma, as Buber accurately saw it. Gandhi attempted to resolve it by lifting politics to a more spiritual
plane. But in doing so he faced the tragedy into which every
prophetic man is driven—and which Buber, another prophetic
man, tried unsuccessfully to avoid by staying detached from politics.

The conclusion Buber came to on the basis of Gandhi's experience was that the West could learn something from Gandhi's
philosophy, but that "we cannot simply follow in his steps."

One should neither plunge into politics nor consciously avoid
it, he suggested. Politics, after all, is part of life itself, and is deformed just as civilization as a whole is deformed. Yet, like work,
"public life is redeemable." The "political serpent" that Gandhi
spoke of is not essentially evil; it is merely misled; "it, too, ulti-

mately wants to be redeemed." It belongs to the world of man, and so we must grapple with it "in naked responsibility." [11]

The West, despite Gandhi's belief that it is purely materialistic, cannot and must not abandon its concept of modern civilization. And the East too will not be able to shun it by adopting such artificial symbols as the spinning wheel. The real task is to master these materials, to humanize our material existence. If we hallow this world, the world we all inhabit, whether we come from East or West, then and only then can the two hemispheres come together. Any return to a simplistic pre-industrial concept of life is barred, Buber says emphatically:

> The flaming sword of the cherubim circling the entrance of the Garden of Eden prohibits the way back. But it illumines the way forward. [12]

It is clear that this essay, written in 1930, reflected and continued a discussion Buber had held with another great Indian, the writer Rabindranath Tagore, several years earlier. He referred to this conversation briefly in his address "China and Us," delivered at the fall 1928 conference of the China Institute in Frankfurt-am-Main.

When I read this lecture in *Pointing the Way*, I asked Buber how he had come to meet Tagore. He replied, "Have you ever heard of Hermann Keyserling? He was a German philosopher, eccentric and rather naïve, although well-meaning. He had the idea of setting up some kind of University of Human Wisdom, with distinguished men from all parts of the world. In any event, one of the people he wanted to take part in this was Tagore, who had won the Nobel Prize for literature. He invited Tagore to visit Europe, and I went to one of his lectures.

"Afterward I was told that the Grand Duke of Hesse had invited me to have dinner at his residence together with Tagore. I refused. And when people said to me, 'How can you refuse an invitation to meet Tagore?' I answered, 'A dinner at the Grand Duke's is not the occasion on which I would like to meet Tagore.'

"Well, years went by. And then I received a letter from Professor Winternitz, a well-known authority on Sanskrit in Prague. He wrote that Tagore was staying with him and would like to meet me. So I went to Prague, and we had a really long discussion on Judaism, Zionism, and the future of Palestine.

"Suddenly, in the middle of our talk, Tagore said to me, 'You, the Jews of Palestine, belong to the West. But why do you need the West? Come, throw all these machines and cannons into the sea! You do not need all this industrialization. Cast off all this and then let us, East and West, sit down and contemplate truth together!'

"Oh, he was very sincere. A wonderful man . . . But I answered him and said, 'I think it would be a mistake to believe that the peoples of Asia can choose a path different from that taken by the West. The growth of technology and the industrialization of society are irreversible processes. And we cannot simply say, "Come, let us cast all this off!" '

"And I told Tagore a little story. You know I like stories! 'There was once a man,' I said, 'who wanted to place a heavy symbol at the peak of a great mountain which had not yet been climbed. He took the symbol, put it on his back, and began climbing upward, with a tremendous effort. While he was climbing, straining and sweating, another man saw him. And this other man cried out to him, "You fool! Throw away that symbol, and you'll be able to climb much quicker!" '

"The same applies to the technology which we wish to raise to the summit. We cannot suddenly throw it down and think that we will now climb more easily. Because we intend either to reach the top of the mountain with it or to fall down with it! Mankind cannot now give up technical and scientific development. The real problem is how to humanize technology. This is a problem which the East will not be able to escape. And this is a difficult task: perhaps the gravest that has ever faced the human race."

"And what did Tagore say to this?" I asked Buber.

"Oh, he looked at me, rather surprised, I think. He had a marvelous face, you know. He looked at me, and said, 'Yes, is that what you really think?' And he remained sunk in thought, without speaking. . . . Whether I convinced him or not I don't know."

On November 26, 1938, Gandhi published an article in his journal *Harijan* criticizing the Jewish reaction to Hitler's persecution and the Zionist attitude toward the Arabs. Gandhi urged the Jews of Germany to launch a campaign of passive resistance against the Nazis, rather than to flee to Palestine and try to establish a Jewish homeland there against the will of the Arabs.

"If I were a Jew and were born in Germany and earned a livelihood there," he wrote, "I would claim Germany as my home even as the tallest Gentile German may, and challenge him to shoot me or cast me in the dungeon."

Gandhi felt that the Jews of Germany could offer *satyagraha* —personal witness, to the point of martyrdom—far more effectively than the Indians of South Africa had:

> The Jews are a compact, homogeneous community in Germany. They are far more gifted than the Indians of South Africa. And they have organized world opinion behind them. I am convinced that if someone of courage and vision can arise among them to lead them in nonviolent action . . . what has today become a degrading manhunt can be turned into a calm and determined stand offered by unarmed men and women possessing the strength of suffering given to them by Jehovah.

In his opinion, the Jews should adopt the same passive approach to the Arabs:

> They can offer *satyagraha* in front of the Arabs and offer themselves to be shot or thrown into the Dead Sea without raising a little finger against them.

But the Jews should not try to settle in Palestine unless they first won the good will of the Arabs, as "Palestine belongs to the Arabs in the same sense that England belongs to the English, or France to the French. It would be wrong and inhuman to impose the Jews on the Arabs."

Gandhi's article prompted Buber to reply, in what is perhaps the most definitive exposition of his stand on the Jewish people's right to their national center in Palestine.

He began by pointing out that the situation of the German Jews under the Hitler regime was scarcely comparable to that of the Indians in South Africa, who were being deprived of their civil rights but were not being tortured and murdered in concentration camps. He did not believe that passive resistance against the Nazis could be effective.

"An effective stand may be taken in the form of nonviolence against unfeeling human beings in the hope of gradually bringing them thereby to their senses," he wrote, "but a diabolical steamroller cannot thus be withstood." [13]

It was obvious, he went on, that when Gandhi was in South Africa protesting against the lot of his fellow Indians, he took it for granted that he had Mother India to turn to. The one hundred and fifty thousand Indians living in South Africa were nourished by the fact that there were more than two hundred million Indians living in the mother country, whether they were conscious of this or not. But if the hundreds of millions of Indians were to be scattered over the face of the earth, should "a Jewish Gandhi—assuming there could be such—" teach the Indians, as Gandhi was trying to teach the Jews, "that the India of the Vedic conception is not a geographical tract, but that it is in your hearts?" [14]

This train of thought led Buber to a sublime vision of the relation between the Jewish people and their land:

A land about which a sacred book speaks to the sons of the land is never merely in their hearts; a land can never become a mere symbol. It is in the hearts because it is a prophetic image of a promise to mankind: but it would be a vain metaphor if Mount Zion did not exist. This land is called 'Holy'; but this is not the holiness of an idea, it is the holiness of a piece of earth. That which is merely an idea and nothing more cannot become holy; but a piece of earth can become holy just as a mother's womb can become holy.[15]

Without the Land of Israel—without "a piece of earth wherein one is in the midst of an ingathering and not in dispersion"—the Jewish dispersion would be intolerable because it would amount to dismemberment. For this reason Jewish destiny was indissolubly bound up with the possibility of ingathering in Palestine: "Every nation has the right to demand the possession of a living heart." [16]

The Jews did not base their claim to Palestine on the Bible. On the contrary, they sought freedom in the land so that they could act in the spirit of the Bible:

> More than three thousand years ago our entry into this land was in the consciousness of a mission from above to set up a just way of life through the generations of our people. . . . No other nation has ever been faced at the beginning of its career with such a mission. Here is something which allows of no forgetting, and from which there is no release. At that time we did not carry out what was imposed upon us: we went into exile with our task unperformed: but the command remained with us and it has become more urgent than ever. We need our own soil in order to fulfil it: we need the freedom of ordering our own life: no attempt can be made on foreign soil and under foreign statute.[17]

Hence the Jews could not renounce their claim to Palestine, for "something even higher than the life of our people is bound up with the Land, namely the work which is their divine mission." [18]

He added that he belonged to "a group of people who, from the time Britain conquered Palestine, have not ceased to strive for the concluding of genuine peace between Jew and Arab." This group sought the support of well-meaning persons of all nations. "But now," he told Gandhi, "you come and settle the whole existential dilemma with the simple formula: 'Palestine belongs to the Arabs.' "[19]

Yet what do we mean by saying that a land belongs to a people? "By what means did the Arabs attain to the right of ownership in Palestine? Surely by conquest, and, in fact, a conquest by settlement." Thus settlement by force of conquest justified the Arabs' right of ownership to Palestine, in Gandhi's view, whereas a settlement such as the Jewish one did not justify any participation in the right of possession. "This wandering nation, to whom the land once belonged, likewise on the basis of a settlement by force of conquest, and who were once driven out of it by mere force of domination," was now striving "to occupy a free part of the land, or a part that might become free without encroaching on the living room of others, in order at last to acquire for themselves a national home—a home where its people could live as a nation." But instead of helping to establish a genuine peace, "giving us what we need without taking from the Arabs what they need, on the basis of a fair adjustment as to what they would really make use of and what might be admitted to satisfy our requirements," Gandhi had declared that the land did not belong to the Jews.[20]

But the soil too should be asked about the right to the land:

Ask the soil what the Arabs have done for her in thirteen hundred years and what we have done for her in fifty! . . . It seems to me that God does not give any one portion of the earth away so that the owner thereof may say as God does in the Holy Script: 'Mine is the Land.' Even to the conqueror who has settled on it, the conquered land is, in my opinion, only lent—and God waits to see what he will make of it." [21]

Buber expressed his belief in

the great marriage between man (Adam) and earth (Adama). This land recognizes us, for it is fruitful through us, and through its fruit-bearing for us it recognizes us. Our settlers do not come here as do the colonists from the Occident, with natives to do their work for them; they themselves set their shoulders to the plow, and they spend their strength and their blood to make the land fruitful.[22]

But the Jewish settlers did not want the land to be fertile only for themselves:

The Jews have begun to teach their brothers, the Arab peasants, to cultivate the land more intensively; we desire to teach them further; together with them we want to cultivate the land—to "serve" it, as the Hebrew has it. The more fertile this soil becomes, the more space there will be for us and for them. We have no desire to dispossess them; we want to live with them. We do not want to rule, we want to serve with them.[23]

In March 1922 Gandhi himself had written, "Have I not repeatedly said that I would rather India became free even by violence rather than she should remain in bondage?"

This indicated that for Gandhi the desire for India's freedom was even stronger than his faith in nonviolence. "For this," Buber declared, "I love you." [24]

We do not want force. We have not proclaimed, as did Jesus, the son of our people, and as you do, the teaching of nonviolence, because we believe that a man must sometimes use force to save himself or even more his children. But from time immemorial we have proclaimed the teaching of justice and peace: we have taught and we have learnt that peace is the aim of all the world and that justice is the way to attain it. Thus we cannot *desire* to use force. No one who counts himself in the ranks of Israel can desire to use force.[25]

Yet, Buber asserted, although he would not have been among the crucifiers of Jesus, he would also not have been among his supporters:

For I cannot help withstanding evil when I see that it is about to destroy the good. I am forced to withstand the evil in the world just as the evil within myself. I can only strive not to have to do so by force. I do not want force. But if there is no other way of preventing the evil destroying the good, I trust I shall use force and give myself up into God's hands.[26]

The letter to Gandhi closed with a confession of his credo:

There is nothing better for a man than to deal justly—
unless it be to love; we should be able even to fight for
justice—but to fight lovingly.[27]

Dr. Magnes also wrote a letter to Gandhi, independently of
Buber. These two letters were published as the first pamphlet issued by a group founded by Magnes, which he called "The
Bond." However, Gandhi replied with only a postcard in which
he said he was too busy to make a detailed answer to their letters.

So far as I know there was no further direct or indirect contact
between Gandhi and Buber until the former's assassination in January 1948.

Despite their difference of opinion on the Palestine question,
Buber continued to have the highest regard for Gandhi and was
shocked by his assassination. Einstein once remarked that Gandhi
"confronted the brutality of Europe with the dignity of the simple human being." Buber would have agreed with this. But he
also felt, I think, that Gandhi was a uniquely Indian phenomenon
that could not readily occur again in a different social and ethnic
context, such as the Jewish struggles against Hitler and against
the British Mandate in Palestine. And, much as he admired Gandhi, he would not have wished to adopt his specific blend of politics and morality.

Dialogue with Christians

One of the charges constantly leveled against Buber by his Jewish critics is that he was more popular among Christians than among Jews. It was indeed a curious paradox which made him a focal point of admiring circles in Western Europe and the United States, with many devout Christians making pilgrimages to Jerusalem to see him, and with the youth of West Germany voting him third in their list of the world's greatest men, while in Israel he was surrounded by a wall of indifference and was seldom invited to address conferences on Biblical research and Jewish studies, which would have seemed his natural element.

When he was referred to in the "patriotic" Israeli press, it was often in sarcastic and belittling terms. The editor of the afternoon paper *Maariv*, Yosef Lapid, observed that during the 1948 war with the Arabs "Buber's house was located between the two fronts, and in the exchange of fire Arab bullets hit his precious library—the treasurehouse of his ideas about 'brotherhood.' " [1] The facts here are correct, but the way they are presented is typical of the sneering tone with which most right-wing or orthodox religious journals wrote about Buber's ideas.

I have never been able to understand why Buber's popularity among Christian circles should be held against him by Jews who reject his approach. If Buber's philosophy is corrupt and unworthy, as they claim, why should they mind if it is taken up by the Christians? And if they do not find Buber wise and pertinent, why should he be censured because Christian thinkers claim that he was one of the wisest men of our century? A people which rejects a prophet living in its midst can hardly complain if he is taken up by others of another faith.

The reasons why Buber appealed so greatly to various Christian denominations and only to a fraction of organized Jewry are, I think, fairly obvious. During the first half of the twentieth century the main movement in world Jewish life was not a religious but a secular one: the Zionist struggle for a Jewish presence and ultimate statehood in part of Palestine. Everything else was subordinated to this. There was little serious religious searching or ferment in this period. The rise of secular Jewish nationalism in fact reinforced conservative, sentimental religious tendencies. In Christianity, on the other hand, the period of both world wars and the confrontation with Communism and Fascism has sparked an unprecedented open-ended experimentation and questioning from which no sect has remained immune. And so it happened that the words of a German Jew, transmitting the teachings of Eastern European *hasidim*, struck a chord in the hearts of Catholics and Protestants who were sensing, unspoken, the same restlessness and change in orientation from the more authoritative aspects of codified religion to the more personal.

One of the men who came under Buber's spell was Roy Walker, an Englishman born in Sussex in 1913. It is instructive to read his own account, in a letter to me, of his first contact with Buber:

> During World War II a friend had strongly recommended to me that I read *I and Thou*. I did not do so. I was not then interested in Jewish writing, being still strongly under the influence of Gandhi. However, when I saw that Buber was to address a meeting in the Conway Hall in London, I realized this was a rare opportunity and decided to go along.
>
> What he said impressed me at the time, but it did not remain long in my conscious mind. But what did remain was the ex-

traordinary experience of sitting in a large audience, feeling that every word was addressed to me personally, and knowing at the same time that everyone else in the hall either did or could, at will, experience the same thing. (Only many years later, when I read of the same quality in the Baal Shem, did something of the real significance of this experience begin to dawn upon me.) But at the time I was so impressed that I did something unique for me. I decided to go to another meeting two or three nights later (at Woburn House) where Buber was to speak in Hebrew to a Jewish audience. I know no Hebrew, alas, and so I knew that this time I would not understand one word he said.

Yet the experience was exactly the same: a personal communication, independent of the 'sense' of the words spoken, more like listening to a kind of musical soloist of genius than a man making a speech.

Nevertheless, I still read nothing of Buber's. I did once write a Christmas editorial round one of his New York speeches, and I had a kind postcard from Buber about it.

But it was only fifteen years later, in the stress of a crisis in my personal life in which I did not know which way to turn, that I came across *Between Man and Man* in paperback in a Scarborough bookshop. Before I had read more than the first two pages—which I did not very well understand—I experienced total certainty that this was what I was searching for. So began my study of Buber's writings.[2]

Roy Walker took his mother's surname of Oliver, to mark his new orientation and commitment. He began seeking out Buber's books, and found, just as I had, that "my experience of reading him has been more like that of listening to a living voice than with almost any other author accessible to me." [3]

These readings of Roy Oliver's eventually led to his very interesting study *The Wanderer and the Way*, dealing with the Hebrew tradition in Buber's works. The impact Buber had on Roy Oliver—the way he changed his life, as he had changed mine —has been echoed by other believing Christians.

I and Thou in particular has exerted enormous influence. The

British theologian J. H. Oldham, a leader in the ecumenical movement, wrote that this key work of Buber's should be read again and again and allowed to mold our thinking slowly. "I am convinced," he added, "that it is by opening its mind, and conforming its practice, to the truth which Buber has perceived and so powerfully set forth that the Church can recover a fresh understanding of its own faith, and regain a real connection with the actual life of our time." [4]

And Paul Tillich wrote in an article entitled "Martin Buber and Christian Thought" that

> Buber's existential "I-Thou" philosophy should be a powerful help in reversing the victory of the "It" over the "Thou" *and* the "I" in present civilization. . . . The "I-Thou" philosophy . . . challenging both orthodox and liberal theology, points a way beyond their alternatives. [5]

Buber himself was slow to realize the impact his thinking was having on Christian circles. Perhaps his first awareness of this was during World War II, after he had moved to Jerusalem. The British military chaplains serving in the Middle East held a conference in Jerusalem. And the discussions at this conference revealed that a strong group of forward-looking Christians considered Buber's views profoundly relevant to their own lives, and felt *I and Thou* to be the most accurate statement of their own religious approach.

"Several of these chaplains came to see me," Buber told me. "And they said, 'We have read your books. And we are trying to apply them to our work as Christians.' I was surprised by this. In Germany I had met many Christian scholars and thinkers. But since I had come to Jerusalem I thought, Now this is over and I will spend the rest of my life quietly here. But suddenly it seemed that the seeds I had sown in *I and Thou* were bearing fruit. Some Christians and some Jews were listening to me."

One of the Christian theologians most strongly influenced by Buber is Dr. John Robinson, Bishop of Woolwich from 1959 to 1969 and later Dean of Trinity College, Cambridge. In the prologue to his book *Exploration into God* Dr. Robinson recalls how the chaplain at his school had taken Nicolas Berdyaev's *The Destiny of Man* to a religious discussion group. Robinson read it, and it fired his imagination.

This contact with a new kind of religious thinking led Robinson to study the philosophy of religion at Cambridge after he had finished classics. Here his instructor, H. C. L. Heywood, recommended that he read Buber's *I and Thou*, saying, as Robinson himself reported, "that it might transform me." And, he added, "It did." [6]

Robinson chose Buber's book and its relation to "the vastness of the Christian doctrine of God" as the subject of his Ph.D. thesis. This thesis, which regrettably remains unpublished, was completed in 1945 and is entitled *Thou Who Art*, a reference, the author tells us, to his belief that the truth as a Christian knows it is always a relationship he must be in, as a subject in response to a "Thou."

The future Bishop of Woolwich and leader of the British "Death-of-God" school began his doctoral dissertation by pointing out that the traditional theology of the Church, as epitomized by the *Summa Theologica* of Saint Thomas Aquinas, has always relied on Greek thought for the intellectual formulation of its insights. But these traditional philosophical categories do not do justice to the "living" God of the Biblical revelation:

> They are static and impersonal, and quite inadequate to that creative center of loving will and energy of which the Scriptures speak.

Is there, then, an alternative philosophy which can enable us to formulate a doctrine of God in different categories—"drawn from specifically personal existence and more fitted, therefore, to describe the grace and challenge of that peculiar encounter of two wills in love which the Bible sees as the norm of the Divine-human relationship"?

Robinson answered his own question by asserting that the writings of Martin Buber and others, in their analysis of the I-Thou relationship, have supplied precisely these categories.

"If there is one point at which I am convinced of the validity of Buber's emphasis," he added, "it is in his insistence that truth is to be found, not in the thoughts of a solitary individual, but always and essentially in the meeting between the 'I' and the 'Thou.' "

Robinson outlined Buber's idea of the I-Thou and I-It relationships. To explain how these operate in everyday life, he took the example of a chimney sweep coming to his house to clean the chimney:

> I meet him as the possessor of a chimney that is full of soot: he meets me as one who is skilled in removing that soot. Apart from that we might never have met, and the chances are that my contact with him will be limited strictly to the transaction of sweeping.

This relationship would be *functional*, or I-It, as contrasted with the I-Thou relationship to which men aspire when seeking deeper ties with man or God.

The classical theory of personality paid no attention to man's responsibility to exist in the peculiarly personal, as opposed to the merely functional or instrumental relationship with other persons, such as the chimney sweep's with the owner of the blocked chimney. Yet, Robinson stressed, "there is a kind of relationship which is 'proper' to existence as a person."

The classical definition of personality has broken down in our time because this element of relationship was missing. Hence the work of a modern school of writers, of whom the best-known is Martin Buber, takes on considerable significance. This school— "one of the most original and positive movements in recent and contemporary philosophy"—has reopened the entire question of personality and personal relationships. What it has achieved, Robinson wrote, is, in fact,

> nothing less than the reversal of the traditional starting point of all Western philosophy, especially as it has been formulated since the days of Descartes.

The traditional point of departure has been the idea of "individual substance"—the self-conscious Ego, as expressed in Descartes's famous saying, *Cogito ergo sum*—"I think, therefore I am."

Buber, Robinson pointed out, reversed this position when, at the very beginning of *I and Thou*, he stated, "There is no 'I' taken in itself"—no *"Ich an Sich."* The primary things, Buber insisted, are not individual substances but relationships. In our dealings with others the I-Thou relationship is the "distinctively personal" and the I-It the "functional and instrumental."

For Buber, then, the primary fact is not the Ego but the "Ego-in-relationship." Only what is relational is real. Robinson finds this approach far more gripping than the writings of Boethius and similar thinkers on personality. He complains that they are "depressingly abstract and uninspiring." They tell us little of what it is like to meet a person and form a real relationship.

It is a mark of Buber's work, on the other hand, that it makes an intense appeal to those who read it, even if they have little philosophical training and find his way of expressing himself perplexing. They come away from reading him feeling "that here at any rate is to be found something real and living, something which they have actually experienced and known for themselves."

Robinson noted the speed and eagerness with which the idea of the "Thou" relationship was being accepted and applied to matters far removed from the world of academic philosophy. He felt this showed

> that men are finding in it something which they can really make their own, which they can constantly verify in their own living, and which can lead to a really creative understanding of their personal and social situations.

While other thinkers had come close to the I-Thou conception, Buber's great contribution, in the author's view, had been to recognize its central importance and to expound it as "the clue, not only to the nature of personality, but also to the interpretation of truth and reality."

Other thinkers had seen glimpses, but only Buber had been radical enough to realize fully this powerful new theory of personal relationships.

Robinson's thesis applied Buber's approach to Christian theology, with particular reference to the doctrine of the Trinity and the Person of Jesus.

The thesis is a fascinating document which would well repay publication, because in addition to the intrinsic value of Robinson's appraisal of Buber's views on personality, it is possible to trace the seeds of the ideas which matured in *Honest to God* eighteen years later.

An American Christian cleric who was also deeply influenced by Martin Buber was the late Reverend James A. Pike, former Bishop of the Episcopal Diocese of California and later Theologian in Residence at the Center for the Study of Democratic Institutions in Santa Barbara. A dynamic and controversial writer and lecturer, Bishop Pike often clashed with church authorities and was in the forefront of those demanding a more liberal and radical interpretation of the Gospels for our century.

In 1963 he visited Israel as the guest of *New Outlook*, whose seminar on Israeli-Arab relations he opened. I arranged a meeting between Buber and the guest speakers from abroad, at Buber's home. Buber was in one of his most genial moods. When Bishop Pike entered the room, Buber and he began exchanging what can only be described as ecumenical banter. I remember that Buber said something about the discussion that evening being kept private and not being disclosed to the newspapers. Pike laughed and said, "Of course. The journalists always get in the way. Even the New Testament tells us, 'They could not see Jesus for the press!' "

After Buber's death, I asked Bishop Pike to recall his contact with Buber over the years. What follows is the account he wrote especially for this book:

It is doubtful that many Jews who lived past the time of the
first century A.D. have been commemorated in the stained glass
windows of Christian Churches. I know of only two. One is
Samuel Joseph Isaac Schereschewsky, whom we placed in the
panel of a window of Grace Cathedral in San Francisco in
1959, and who is the subject of a statue in the reredos of the
National Cathedral in Washington. But he had become a
Christian—and a bishop. . . . The other was . . . Dr. Martin
Buber. While I was Bishop of the Episcopal Diocese of California we completed the Cathedral, and in planning windows for
the additional bays of the Nave we decided to include Dr.
Buber. . . .

Such a recognition would be appropriate in any case (Dr.
Buber had been a strong influence on contemporary Christian
theology, not the least among Anglicans), but it was particularly meaningful to me because of our personal friendship and
the influence he has been upon me.

It began . . . about 1951 . . . in connection with development of an entirely new program of religious education. . . .
The writings of Dr. Buber had been strongly influential in the
development of the philosophy behind this vast project.

At that time Professor Buber was visiting New York as the
guest of Columbia University which I served as chairman of
the Department of Religion and as Chaplain. I was able to arrange a day of dialogue with Dr. Buber and the professional
staff of the Episcopal Church's Department of Christian Education (responsible for developing the new education materials). . . .

About three years later our conversation continued—but
this time sitting in the garden of Professor Buber's modest
home in Jerusalem. . . . At the time I was visiting both Israel
and Jordan, talking to government officials, Church leaders and
other private citizens, with the purpose of grasping the meaning of the conflict in the Middle East, coming at the subject
with no presuppositions. Near the end of the various conferences on both sides of the Mandelbaum Gate, I had a long talk
with Dr. Buber which was most helpful indeed, because of its
objectivity and the warmth of his human concern for all parties involved. . . .

Then in 1960 a conference on the Status of Jews in the Soviet Union found us in Paris together. He opened with a memorable address on "What Is a Jew?"—a difficult question, which even his presentation did not satisfactorily answer for me. But particularly memorable for me was a luncheon three of us had: Father Jean Daniélou (noted scholar in early Christianity), Dr. Buber, and myself.

The whole conversation is still vivid to me. For example, Dr. Buber said at one point, "You Christians say that the world has been saved by Jesus," then added—not with forensic zest, but with a wistful sadness, "But, unfortunately, the world is not yet saved." And again: "I understand" (and indeed he did, as much as anyone can) "what you Christians mean when you say that there are three persons in one God; but why do you have to say it that *way*?" Both these comments germinated my statements of two points in an article I wrote shortly thereafter for the *Christian Century*[7] which evoked the first of several sets of heresy charges.

In January 1963 once again I was back in Dr. Buber's house in Jerusalem in connection with my participation in public meetings sponsored by *New Outlook*. . . . A group of us had a long evening visit with Dr. Buber. . . . I will always treasure our theological discourse that evening, but even more, the further opportunity it gave me for the revelation of the man himself—a man of modest courage, contagious compassion, sensitive identification with a tradition, and at the same time complete intellectual honesty. I recall that I shared with him something going round my Church at that time:

Q. Who are the principal theologians of the Episcopal Church?

A. Martin Buber and Paul Tillich.

—neither of them Anglicans! The amusing side of this not entirely inaccurate answer was . . . muffled for him by the fact that he was obviously humbled by being even mentioned in such a connection. Nor was it a humility acted out for my benefit. It was entirely disingenuous—though in fact inappropriate.

In making my plans for a sabbatical leave to be spent principally at Cambridge University, but to include a period of study in Israel, my anticipation of the latter was largely focused on the opportunity it would afford me to sit again at the feet of Martin Buber. . . . But . . . even the awe and wonder ever left in me from the climbing of Masada did not make up for the fact that there was to be no talking with Dr. Buber. He had passed away some months before my plans called for me to be there. . . .

> Bishop James A. Pike
> Santa Barbara, California
> November 1967

Although Buber's thought has been so influential for the Christian Church, this does not mean that all his ideas could be accepted wholeheartedly by even the most advanced theologians. As Professor William Hamilton, one of the most prominent American "Death-of-God" theologians, put it:

Like all Christian intellectuals of my generation (by that I mean those for whom the word war means World War II) Buber has been both a help and a problem. I suppose, in many ways, his *Eclipse of God* is the most impressive statement of the alternatives for the radical theology. Perhaps a Jew can never genuinely close the door on transcendence, as the Christian radicals are trying to do. . . . I guess I would have to say that Buber has moved me but not helped me.[8]

In writing this Hamilton was undoubtedly thinking of the passage in *Eclipse of God* in which Buber relates his conversation with an unnamed "noble old thinker." Buber had been reading the proofs of a preface of a new book, and since it was a statement of faith he wished to read it carefully once again before it was printed. The old man, at whose house he happened to be staying, asked him what he had in his hand. When Buber told him, he asked him to read it aloud to him. The old thinker listened in a friendly manner but clearly in growing amazement.

When Buber had finished reading, his listener said, first hesitatingly, then ever more passionately:

"How can you bring yourself to say 'God' time after time? How can you expect that your readers will take the word in the sense in which you wish it to be taken? What you mean by the name of God is something above all human grasp and comprehension, but in speaking about it you have lowered it to human conceptualization. What word of human speech is so misused, so defiled, so desecrated as this! All the innocent blood that has been shed for it has robbed it of its radiance. . . . When I hear the highest called 'God,' it sometimes seems almost blasphemous."

In writing of it, Buber says that he cannot remember exactly but can only indicate in a general way the answer he gave:

Yes, it is the most heavy-laden of all human words. None has become so soiled, so mutilated. Just for this reason I may not abandon it. Generations of men have laid the burden of their anxious lives upon this word and weighed it to the ground; it lies in the dust and bears their whole burden. . . . We cannot cleanse the word "God" and we cannot make it whole; but, defiled and mutilated as it is, we can raise it from the ground and set it over an hour of great care.[9]

We still need words, Buber is telling us. We still need them as symbols for what we cannot comprehend. And although he had written of the incident in 1932, the fact that he chose it to illustrate *Eclipse of God*, a volume based on lectures delivered at various American universities in November and December 1951, shows that he still felt this way toward the end of his life. While he seldom used the term "God" in conversation, preferring to talk of "the Eternal Thou," he was not yet prepared formally to relinquish its use as a symbol of man's longing for the ultimate. This is what Professor Hamilton means when he says that Buber is both "a help and a problem" for today's radical Christian theologians.

On the question of Jesus too Buber did not go as far as some Christians would have liked him to. It is true that he felt close to the human being Jesus. In *Two Types of Faith*, published in 1950, he wrote:

From my youth onwards I have found in Jesus my great brother. . . . My own fraternally open relationship with him has grown ever stronger and clearer, and today I see him more strongly and clearly then ever before. I am more than ever certain that a great place belongs to him in Israel's history of faith and that this place cannot be described by any of the usual categories.[10]

Elsewhere, in *Between Man and Man,* he describes a discussion with some Christian friends on Easter 1914. And he recalls that he told them, "We Jews know Jesus from within, in the impulses of his Jewish being, in a way that remains inaccessible to the peoples submissive to him." [11]

Buber certainly felt spiritually close to Jesus, but not to Paul. It was a feeling that grew in him after he came to live in Jerusalem, in the landscape where Jesus spent his last days. Herbert Weiner recalls a conversation with Buber on the impact the modern land of Israel had on Christian religion. Weiner suggested that Christians living in the State of Israel could not but confront the historical and therefore the Jewish component of their religious origins.

Buber agreed and added, "I would say that living here makes you for Jesus and against Paul." [12]

I know from talks with Catholics and Protestants living in present-day Israel that this is precisely what they themselves discover—another instance of Buber's remarkable ability to penetrate the deepest feelings of people from other faiths and nations.

But although he venerated Jesus as virtually a spiritual ancestor of all Jews, and specifically of himself, he saw him quite distinctly as a man. Buber could not possibly accept the orthodox Christian view of Jesus as the son of God. Nor could he see him as the Messiah who had come two thousand years ago to redeem the world. In an address in Jerusalem commemorating his Christian friend Leonhard Ragaz, he made this unmistakably clear:

I firmly believe that the Jewish community, in the course of its renaissance, will recognize Jesus; and not merely as a great figure in its religious history, but also in the organic context of a Messianic development extending over millennia, whose final goal is the Redemption of Israel and of the world. But I believe equally firmly that we will never recognize Jesus as the Messiah Come, for this would contradict the deepest meaning of our Messianic passion. In our view, redemption occurs forever, and none has yet occurred. Standing, bound and shackled, in the pillory of mankind, we demonstrate with the bloody body of our people the unredeemedness of the world. For us there is no cause of Jesus; only the cause of God exists for us.[13]

Again Buber is being, from the Christian standpoint, "both a help and a problem." But the truth is that, as Chaim Potok pointed out in his article "Martin Buber and the Jews," "though he addressed himself to the world, Buber regarded his thought as firmly rooted in Judaism and he persistently refused to sever his writings from their Jewish moorings." [14] Despite his virtual ostracism by the ultraorthodox Jewish community, including the *hasidim* whose heritage he had brought to the Western world's attention; despite the growing adulation by progressive Christian thinkers, Buber remained first and always a Jew drawing his strength from Judaism, speaking to the whole community of mankind, but, it was clear to anyone who knew him, hoping that it would be the Jews who would respond. It is unfair to blame him if, by and large, the Jews ignored him and it was the searching, radical element in the Christian church which first listened to him.

Talking with *Sabras*

Buber was always interested in young people. He enjoyed his work at the Hebrew University because it brought him into contact with Jewish youth from all over the world, and in particular the *sabras*—the Israeli-born young people whom Buber considered a new phenomenon in Jewish history and a clue to the nature of Israeli society in the future.

Israeli youth, however, did not take easily to Buber for a long time. He was associated in their minds with German culture, and in any event with an era in Jewish history which no longer interested them. His writings were difficult to understand and were available only in English or German. And, perhaps the greatest psychological block of all, he was the spokesman of a group which most *sabras* believed wanted to appease the Arabs and hence was antipatriotic and "soft."

But in 1961 a change began to take place. The World Zionist Organization published a volume of Buber's essays on political and social topics, in Hebrew. This had a considerable impact, and his views on Israel's national goals and on educational problems were widely discussed. In the same year he also played a major role in what became known as "the revolt of the intellectuals" against Ben-Gurion's role in the Lavon Affair.

Buber began to be, if not completely understood and accepted, at least appreciated. *Sabra* writers and intellectuals started seeking him out and coming to visit him. Members of kibbutzim asked him to advise them on education and the aims of communal living. Like Bertrand Russell in England in the 1960s, here was suddenly a great man who had been ignored for decades by his contemporaries and was now being taken up in his old age not by the middle-aged establishment but by the young people who were critical of the establishment.

When Aharon Megged wrote his novel *Fortunes of a Fool* he took as his motto a quotation from Buber:

> Whatever the significance of the term "truth" is in other spheres, in the inter-human sphere its significance is that people reveal themselves to one another as they truly are in their being. . . . Wherever this is absent, the human also is not true.[1]

I was translating the book into English for Victor Gollancz and Random House and told Buber about the use of this passage as a motto. He was pleased and saw it as a sign that some modern Hebrew writers were studying his work closely and responding to his emphasis on building relationships between people and groups, instead of perpetuating divisions based on dogmas.

He thought a great deal about the spiritual life of young Jews born in Israel. And he had a theory which, he thought, explained the *sabras'* growing interest in his point of view.

"When I came to Palestine in 1938," he said to me, "the young people were mainly interested in the political parties and the struggle for a Jewish state. This was of course perfectly understandable, in view of the objective geopolitical conditions at that time. But at the same time this politicization of the young was exaggerated and excessive. Their life was encrusted by politics, and the spiritual and moral side suffered.

"After the State was established in 1948 the political parties were also the main thing for a while. But then I noticed that a new generation was developing for which the parties were not the most important thing. Although many of these young people belonged formally to the parties, they were basically more interested in themselves, in their work, in founding a family. They were concerned really with what they considered 'living,' and drew away from ideology and the political struggle.

"In some of these young people this took the negative form of careerism. But many did not act from motives of careerism. Their emphasis on family life was healthy. It was a reaction to the previous situation, in which everything had to be sacrificed to the nation and there was little private life or individuality.

"Now, I think (and every year that goes by makes me more confident of this), we are seeing a third phase: a search for faith in place of the cynicism and heresy which characterized the former generation.

"Notice," Buber said, "that the young people born after World War II or during the time of our own war with the Arabs in 1948 are different. It is not yet easy to pin down what is happening. This is a more elusive generation. But something is developing. I sense a dissatisfaction. We do not know what will come out of this. But it is easy to understand it. Because, as Hamlet said, something is rotten in the state. And these young people feel it. They cannot put their fingers on it precisely. But it bothers them. Their unhappiness is growing.

" 'Is this what the human world is like?' they ask themselves and one another. There is a boundary to this human world, and around it a broad world that has lost its humanity. There is a lack of fulfillment from politics, the life of the individual, and the life of the family. Something is missing. 'Is this all?' they look at you and ask.

"But when you question them, they cannot put into words what is missing. There are longings—a nostalgia for something they have never had. Longings without a name. And in this dissatisfaction there is a seed, a holy seed. But it needs time to grow. It is not yet a movement, only vague aspirations, a wish, a reaching out. But this is a good thing. And this modest beginning, which has almost gone unnoticed, is very precious to me.

"These young people are concerned about the realities facing the inhabitants of Israel—all the inhabitants of this land. They are not as interested in party politics as they used to be. They seek a new reality. They seek the truth that lurks in Judaism." (Here he raised his voice, to almost a cry of triumph.) "Yes, there is such a truth! It yearns to be made flesh. These young people's souls are thirsty for true Judaism, for what they have lost. They are the ones who interest me. And they know this. They know how I welcome them." (His voice became warm and fatherly.) "I get many letters from young people, with questions. They ask me to explain things. And I reply to every letter. Yes, every single one. At my age it is good to have some young allies."

"Is it religion they seek?" I asked Buber.

"I am not talking about the authority of religion," he replied. "It is the nature of longings like these that they are against authority, against dogma. They are dreaming of something they cannot describe. And when young people have dreams like these the nameless will take on a shape sooner or later. I do not think that I will see it. But perhaps I can help it along while the plant is still fragile.

"In my opinion our generation is one of transition. Ten years ago young people did not come to me like this. We did not have talks like this. We will probably have to wait another two or three generations before the final form becomes clear. But it is in the air. We must wait for it to flourish.

"Youth likes to be in a state of genesis, of beginning. A young man wants to be able to say, 'I am the first! Not just continuing something my father has done, even if this was glorious in itself.' Zionism—well, it has been accomplished. Now the young people want to do something new, to create something that springs from themselves."

He was silent for a moment. Then he said very quietly, "I do not know if I will see the decisive change. But in my heart I feel I have a pact with my grandchildren—and perhaps with my great-grandchildren."

During the last few years of his life Buber had many talks with young people who came to him for counsel. I helped to arrange some of these meetings. Others were arranged by the kibbutz movements. Buber had a perennial interest in the kibbutzim and always enjoyed meeting boys and girls from these settlements.

I have records of some of these talks, drawn up afterward by the participants. They give a touching picture of his affection for these young people and his efforts to help them clarify their own sense of powerlessness and loss.

In June 1963 several young members of Kibbutz Afikim, in the Jordan Valley, called on Buber. The discussion was opened by Ya'akov, the educator of the fifteen- to eighteen-year-olds.

"I was not born on the kibbutz," he said, "and so I can see things more objectively. I see many things that the members who have been living on the kibbutz for a long time, and the children born in it, don't notice. I can appreciate the values here. But I also look at flaws in the relationships between people.

"For example, if a member of the kibbutz is ill, his comrades do not rush to his side, because there is a Health Committee and they know it will look after him. The individual feels himself freed from taking a personal human interest."

Buber: "Has it always been like this? It is worth talking to veteran members of the kibbutz and finding out—and asking them what has changed. A conversation between individuals, and each one with his own heart. This can only come about if there is complete frankness. This is not common, as you know.

"During this talk you should uncover the bitter truth which as a rule people do not want to hear; yet when it is heard some of them are influenced by it. If this truth influences even a small number of the members, then there will be a passionate discussion on how to change the situation."

Ya'akov: "At a party one veteran member said, 'Once we had nothing, and we had everything. Now we have everything, and we have nothing.'"

Buber: "We find this in individualistic society as well. A man is often better when times are hard."

At this point Pinchas, another instructor, tried to change the direction of the discussion. "We really wanted to talk to you about the children growing up in the kibbutz, how to educate them to mutual assistance, to righteousness, to truth and justice."

Buber replied, "As long as you do not recognize the roots of this problem in yourselves, how can you change it in your pupils? Every genuine action begins with the recognition of the historical truth—in other words, what has actually happened. If this is to succeed, it cannot be done without admitting past mistakes."

Hedva: "What you propose is very difficult. There will be opposition. The members of the kibbutz do not remember the bad things about the past, and don't want to remember."

Buber: "Yes, there will be opposition. And it is easy to fail. But it is also possible to succeed."

Hedva: "The older kibbutzniks will not understand that we are doing it for their sake, for the sake of the whole kibbutz. They blame the younger generation for the change that has taken place."

Buber: "But the younger generation of today was educated by them. And it is important to study the problem for the generations that will come afterward."

Ya'akov: "There are already finished 'products' of this education, young kibbutzniks aged twenty to thirty; there is already an image of the son of the kibbutz. The young kibbutznik is known for his honesty and straightforwardness. He is usually ready to sacrifice himself for a cause. What he lacks is the ability to understand another person. A kibbutznik will help someone else. But he won't understand him.

"We rub against one another too much every day. Perhaps this is the reason. We don't know how to listen to one another."

Buber: "And is there friendship between you?"

Ya'akov: "There are close ties of friendship."

Patchi: "But it is more a silent understanding, a feeling one person has for the other, and not an understanding based on a real dialogue."

Z'mira: "I was born on the kibbutz. In my group there were twenty-five boys and girls, and I didn't have a single friend among them."

Buber: "And did you feel the need for friendship?"

Z'mira: "I didn't feel it then. But I do now. Ya'akov's question springs from a desire to try to educate the youngsters of today in a different way."

Buber: "The decisive thing is whether the young people are ready to talk. If someone treats them with trust, shows them that he believes in them, they will talk to him. The first necessity is that the teacher must arouse in his pupils that most valuable thing of all—genuine trust.

"This means that at a time of despair the young boy or girl will come to the one he trusts and say, 'I do not know why I am still living and what I am living for.' There does not have to be constant personal contact between them; but there must always be the possibility of contact.

"In every man there is something special that cannot be expressed, or that can only be expressed in certain moments, at the depth of a profound despair that cannot be given a single name. And here is the place for what I call trust."

At the same meeting Pinchas spoke about his problems as the instructor of a group of immigrant children. He explained that the children stayed on the kibbutz until late adolescence. Then, at the age of seventeen or eighteen, they usually left. Another disadvantage arose from the fact that many came to the kibbutz at thirteen or fourteen from various places and widely different backgrounds. Some were from broken homes, for instance, Pinchas explained.

The children of the kibbutz, he said, understood that these newcomers from problem homes had to be absorbed into the life of the kibbutz, but, practically speaking, the established kibbutzniks were not ready for this. It was very difficult to get them to accept the immigrant children.

Buber: "This is a display of collective egoism. I think you can only fight this through a revolution of the young people themselves. There are only two ways: the way of explanation and the way of revolution.

"The way of explanation means telling them that what they are doing is detrimental to their way of life. You must explain this both at formal gatherings of the young people and in private conversation. You can prepare the ground and atmosphere for the group meetings through these private talks. But it needs a certain knowledge of psychology. I would suggest that you try this approach first of all.

"Then comes the way of revolution—in other words, the solidarity of the kibbutz with the immigrant group, against the uncooperative boys and girls of the kibbutz itself. But I don't propose that you should follow this path at once. I am, generally speaking, for experiments—for trying. During my long life I have often said, 'The chances are not very good, but it is worth trying.' "

Later in the same conversation the young kibbutzniks spoke more intimately about their personal lives and asked Buber what principles they should follow.

He replied, "I have no rigid principles. There is what has to be done here and now. I have only a direction and my senses, and I act according to the situation."

Hedva: "But our life in the kibbutz is based on principles."

Buber: "When I educate young people, I try to explain to them that there are things for which it is worth living. A real educator has an influence even without speaking. And another thing you must do if you want to teach others: you must see your environment, the conditions, the circumstances. You must see how to live now. Even the Ten Commandments have to be translated to make them fit a given situation. If I am commanded to honor my father and my mother, then from time to time, in the given circumstances, I have to interpret for myself what this honoring means. And this interpretation will be different at different times. Otherwise it is impossible."

Pinchas: "You said you were against rigid principles. But that in itself is a principle. What is a principle, in your opinion?"

Buber: "A principle means that you always have to act in a prescribed way."

Pinchas: "Is 'Help your comrade' a principle?"

Buber: "If you turn this into a principle, you will be wrong. There are times when you cannot help and cases in which it is wrong for me to arouse within myself the feeling that I want to help someone, because he does not want it. You must weigh things anew every time."

Ya'akov: "And what shall I judge by?"

Buber: "By the situation and the way you see it. I am sorry. I cannot make it any easier for you."

Pinchas: "I want to tell you about something that happened to me. In our youth group there is a boy from Rumania whose parents are deaf and dumb. The boy came to our kibbutz when he was thirteen. Now he is seventeen and a half. He stammered when he came to us.

"In our kibbutz the boys are 'adopted' by foster families during the time they are with us. This boy stole a large number of stamps from the family which had looked after him for two years. When we discovered that the stamps were missing I faced a serious problem.

"In a frank conversation with him he admitted taking the stamps. Then came the dilemma: what to do with the boy? To hand him over to the police would be a final step. But, all the same, what should we do with him? He had not been accustomed to freedom in Rumania. It appeared that through our good and free education we had harmed him.

"In the end the owner of the stamps complained to the police. The boy remained on the kibbutz. I didn't have the courage to take him back to his parents. And, besides, I wanted to take the difficult road—to struggle with the problem."

Buber: "A man must do what he can until he comes to a point that he knows is the border. If I had been there, I would have preferred to take the hard road—not to bring him to the police.

"We cannot do without the police, in the same way that we

cannot do without a state and so on. But we should try to do as much as we can without them. These institutions are based on coercion, on force, and not on truth. Again it comes down to what we were saying before—that there are no rigid principles."

In another conversation with young kibbutz teachers he spoke about the need for human relationships in the kibbutz. The teachers asked him how it was possible to develop close relationships between individual members in such a densely packed society without the members being lost in the sea of people.

To this Buber replied, "There is a clear and important distinction between *closeness* and *relation*. Although the members of a kibbutz work for the same cause, this does not mean that there is an automatic link between any member and his neighbor.

"This is partly a question of size. In my opinion, a kibbutz can attain its purpose only if its numerical size does not prevent every member knowing all the other members. What can the communal nature of the kibbutz be when I meet someone whom I am told is a member of my kibbutz and I have never seen him before?

"A kibbutz of six hundred or seven hundred people is no longer a commune, an organic unit, but a social monster. Any place which threatens to become as large as this should be organized on the basis of smaller groups, interlocking with one another. Then the individual can feel part of his group, within which he can discuss his problems without feeling lost in the efficient, smoothly run collective.

"It is important also that there should be a possibility of meditation, of contemplation. There should be enough space around a man so that his individuality can remain intact. If the density does not allow a man to look at his comrade, to have some perspective, he will not be able to acquire any relation to him. And then the fact that they follow the same cause will not be enough to avert a poverty in human bonds."

To another group of *sabras* who asked him what his system of thought was, and whether he could teach it to them, he answered, "I have no system, no method. I do not believe in formulas. I believe in people. And so I cannot give you any easy recipes that will solve all the problems. If anyone comes to you and says he has the solution, he knows how to solve all the problems, my advice to you would be, do not trust him!

"I know only things which are concrete and can be realized. And when they are realized by living people, they become truth."

Buber and the Young Protesters

In the Haight-Ashbury district of San Francisco there used to be a café called "I and Thou," decorated with psychedelic paintings in brilliant soft colors.

And when Nelson Algren was explaining the kind of world he would like to see, he told H. E. F. Donohue, "What we should do is all get together and have a second-person world. You know, everybody calls everybody 'you'. . . . Have an 'I' and 'Thou' world." [1]

I don't know whether the owner of the San Francisco "tribal refuge" was familiar with Buber's writings. And Nelson Algren told me that he has never read *I and Thou*. Yet somehow this basic concept of Buber's has permeated their consciousness and is used to express their instinctual longing for closer relations within society.

Listening to students in the United States, Britain, and France talk about their resentments and dreams, I have been impressed by the way they echo motifs and even phrases from Buber's thought.

Paul Lawson, deputy editor of the London magazine *Oz*, wrote:

> We don't have a position from which we hand things out on a plate. We don't have a plate to put anything on. It's more like having a graph with a number of positions on it: we can

change our position, alter our frame of reference, as we constantly do. . . . We're not didactic; we don't pontificate. We offer things to people, and they can take them as they like.

A student at Yale says:

I don't want revolution on the streets. I want to work on an intellectual revolution, changing ideas, making a cultural revolution. Mass movements are stupid; what we have to do is to live as close as possible to our private conception of life.

And Des Wilson, Director of "Shelter," the British Campaign for the Homeless, explains why young people are rebelling:

It is because they no longer feel that their voice can be heard. It is because they care more than any generation has cared before—about peasants dying in their millions in both North and South Vietnam, about the starving in Africa and Asia, about the poor and homeless at home—and find that while their energy and enthusiasm are welcomed, their ideas and their leadership are not. . . . It is because there is no longer a basis for trust between young and old, little basis for understanding, and no proper dialogue.[2]

It is not, I think, that many of these rebellious young people have come into contact with Buber's ideas, as expressed in his writings and speeches. To most of them Buber is known only in a most superficial way, by the titles of one or two of his books. It is rather, I am convinced, that Buber in the 1920s was one of the first profound thinkers to sense the slow deep-running currents of change among post–World War I youth, and to realize that these were different not only in intensity but also in kind from the customary restlessness of young people in all eras and cultures. I was deeply involved in the protest movement within Israel, and so I know how sympathetic Buber was to young people who wanted to express their opposition to bigotry and injustice. We could always rely on him for assistance and practical advice. But he would not give this blindly, and if he thought the form of protest we had chosen was sterile, he would not hesitate to tell us what he thought.

About a year after I first met him I came to his house in a state of indignation, bursting into his quiet room and complaining that he and the other rather elderly people in his circle were not doing anything, that they did not make any demands on us younger people, and that the peace movement was altogether too polite and passive. What we needed, I told him, was action.

Buber looked across his desk at me.

"And if you were given a free hand by us, 'the old people,' as you call us, what would you do?" he asked.

"I can't say exactly," I replied. "Demonstrations. Protests. Some kind of action. Not just talking and issuing statements."

He pondered this for a moment, and then said, "I don't disagree with you. And I certainly think we could all do more—young and old. But the question for me is, what is the purpose of our action? Will we do something for the sake of the action itself, because we want to feel we are doing something—or will it have some life that continues after our protest?"

Buber got up, walked over to the bookshelves and came back with an Old Testament.

"To show you what I mean. . . . Do you know the words of Jeremiah to Baruch the son of Neriah? They are in chapter 45 of Jeremiah: 'Seekest thou great things for thyself? Seek them not.' And what I mean is, do we want to have a demonstration because it will be noisy and exciting, because it will attract attention and be in the newspapers, or because we really think this is the way to influence the people who have power?

"I am not against demonstrations. I am just asking, could not our energy be directed more effectively? Instead of a hundred people marching along the street to the Knesset [Parliament], perhaps it would be better if each of them would make contact with a single Arab family. Then there would be ties of friendship between a hundred Jewish and a hundred Arab families, and these ties would have more effect than a demonstration which would be over in two hours."

I did not agree with him then. But in the course of time I came to understand more profoundly what he meant.

In 1958 Buber spent three months at Princeton University, where, Malcolm Diamond tells us, "he was curious about every detail of American culture, from the complexities of its religious manifestations to the working of its supermarkets." [3] He must have come away with some positive impressions of American youth. For I had a revealing conversation with him in the fall of 1962, just after the Cuban missile crisis.

Buber had been tremendously impressed by the way Kennedy and Khrushchev had forged a personal relationship in the heat of this crisis. "If these leaders had decided on war now," he remarked to me, "then the young people on both sides would have fought one another. But in the coming years perhaps the young Americans and the young Russians may build up the same kind of urgent relationship as Kennedy did with Khrushchev—because of the danger of not doing this, and because they realize their real interests are greater than their differences.

"If this happens, the leaders of each side will know that they cannot order their young people to kill the young people from the other side. And then the politicians will have to come to terms. Because the situation then would be civil disobedience by the young soldiers on both sides. When we reach this point in human development, many things will happen. . . . And perhaps it would be the beginning of a worldwide movement of young people determined to live together instead of killing one another over minor points of difference."

Buber's fondness for Thoreau's essay "Civil Disobedience" made him quote it to us often. I remember his telling me about an incident during his visit to Princeton. "One of America's greatest intellectuals," he said, "invited me for a talk. He assumed that there would be another world war—took it for granted, in a defeatist way. He talked about the chances of victory. At the beginning of the war things would go badly for the Americans, he thought, but then later they would gain the upper hand and win.

"I said to him, 'Do you think that if another world war came, it would be like the wars we know from history, up to and including World War II—with stages, first a bad stage and then a good stage? No, it would be one great destruction for everyone!' "

And then, looking at me, Buber added, "Rather than take part in such a 'victory,' young people of all nations would be justified in following the way of civil disobedience, as Thoreau suggests."

Buber was one of the fathers of what is called today "situation ethics," exemplified in the youthful revolt of the last half of the twentieth century against absolute dogmas. This is a philosophical and moral position which says that only the individual faced with a moment of crucial decision can decide what he should do, this decision coming from the depths of his being and not from some external inherited code of behavior.

In line with this approach, Dr. Joseph E. Fletcher, of the Episcopal Theological School in Cambridge, Massachusetts, the leading American exponent of situation ethics, argues that "the morality of smoking marijuana depends on circumstances. Social drinking is not immoral, social smoking is not immoral, social pot is not immoral—unless they are used to excess." [4]

This is the kind of reasoning that ruled Buber's social philosophy, though he would not have approved of the use of drugs as a personal outlet. While he would have been tolerant of many harmless freakish acts, amused rather than irritated by the exuberance which produced them, he had two reservations about youth's struggle against the accepted standards of their elders that would apply to the confused outlets sought by many young people in the last half of the twentieth century.

He did not condone violence in support of peaceful aims— and particularly not violence directed against oneself.

And, before the use of drugs in the attempt to seek enlightenment had become widespread among young people, he had opposed the practice in his comments on Aldous Huxley's famous experiments with mescalin, described in *The Doors of Perception*.

In the *Review of Metaphysics*, March 1958, Buber took issue with Huxley in an essay called "What is Common to All," later reprinted in *The Knowledge of Man*, in which he attacked this attempt to flee from "the common world." Huxley, he pointed out, had to avoid the eyes of people present in the room with him, "people who are otherwise especially dear to him," [5] because they belong to the world of selfhood that Huxley claims mescalin enables him to leave.

But, Buber says, the person who takes mescalin or any other mind-expanding drug does not really emerge into some kind of cosmic experience of the universe. He does not escape the entanglement in the net of his material being, as Huxley thinks he does during a trip. What happens is that the drug taker merely escapes into "a strictly private special sphere given to him as his own for several hours." [6]

This flight is, however, self-defeating:

> The "chemical holidays" of which Huxley speaks are holidays not only from the petty I, enmeshed in the machinery of its aims, but also from the person participating in the community of logos and cosmos—holidays from the very uncomfortable reminder to verify oneself as such a person.[7]

This is the crux, the core of Buber's opposition to Oriental mysticism and religious asceticism. "To verify oneself as a person" means to meet oneself, to go deeper into oneself, not to flee from oneself or from what Huxley suggests are "the possibly repugnant surroundings." [8]

Buber is firm on this point. "Man may master as he will his situation, to which his surroundings also belong; he may withstand it, he may alter it, he may, when it is necessary, exchange it for another; but the fugitive flight out of the claim of the situation into situationlessness is no legitimate affair of man." [9]

The paradises that man creates for himself by taking drugs or through mysticism are not genuine states of ecstasy and understanding. Their true name is "situationlessness," like the dream state and like schizophrenia. In their essence, says Buber, these states of being are "uncommunal," and the people who directly surround us are not transformed with them. In effect, the "illuminating trance" is a self-deceptive illusion which is selfish, sterile, and unlikely to produce anything of lasting artistic or human value.

In such statements as this Buber left behind him words of wisdom for young people hooked on LSD and other drugs, words that said in effect, "Do not try to escape in this way from our common world. The problems of the world will not dissolve or melt in the shining radiance of the visions you will see! Try rather to live in the real world: the world of Auschwitz, Vietnam, Biafra. To live in it—to confront it—to meet it. Anything else is a diversion, nonauthentic, a deflection of energy."

He had an instinctive sympathy with and understanding for the kind of young people who supported Eugene McCarthy in the 1968 United States presidential elections, and for such statements as that of the journalist who wrote, "The university is turning from a place in which the old instruct the young to a place in which the young will instruct the old." The slogan someone scrawled on the walls of the Sorbonne during the 1968 student occupation—"It is forbidden to forbid"—might almost have been spoken by him. His own apparent conviction that many of the middle-aged and old people who run things cling to values which are not only obsolete but clearly lunatic and which must inevitably lead to wars, racism, atomic destruction, and other acts of violent inhumanity anticipated that of contemporary youth.

Indeed, many years before any of today's fashionable young rebels voiced their dissatisfaction, he sounded some of the first quiet warnings about what would happen to the world if it became ruled by mistrust instead of dialogue, if men allowed themselves to become objects and lost their I-Thou sense.

To be "beat," said John Clellon Holmes in his book about the Beat generation, meant "to be at the bottom of your personality looking up."

That is almost as perfect a description of Buber as I have ever read. And it may sound fanciful, but I really believe this old man with his white beard, his knitted cardigan and old-fashioned pepper-and-salt suit, was at heart as "beat" as they come—this century's equivalent of Blake and Dostoevski.

Eighty-five

On February 8, 1963, Buber became eighty-five. Tributes flowed in from abroad and from Israel. His house was filled with flowers. Ben-Gurion sent a cable: "I honor you and oppose you." On the fourteenth—his birthday according to the Jewish calendar— the Hebrew University and the Israel Academy gave a luncheon for him, attended by members of his family.

All during that week people streamed through the house on Lovers of Zion Street. There were deputations, formal messages from great institutions, brief visits from people Buber hardly knew but whose life he had touched in some way. Young people and kibbutzniks came in bearing bunches of fruit or books as gifts.

Professor Norman Bentwich, who visited Buber then, recalls:

> Buber enjoyed the tribute, but did not let it turn a hair of his head. He told me he was still writing and editing. But, he said, the time was not right for world peace or for a new universal religion. There was no practical basis. He thought it might come in the second or third generation after ours.[1]

The highlight of the celebrations came on the night of his birthday, with a midnight serenade by five hundred students of the Hebrew University. This was a custom followed in some European universities when the students particularly wanted to honor a professor. Someone had the idea of doing this in Israel for the first time, as a tribute to Buber.

But it was not certain whether he could stay up so late. The chairman of the Jerusalem Students Association, Ben-Zion Eliash, phoned and told Buber the students were planning a special celebration for him. "But," he asked anxiously, "won't 11:30 at night be too late for you?" "Not at all," Buber replied. "I will be happy to welcome you to my home at midnight."

That night the students assembled with burning torches outside Beit Hillel, a students' center near Buber's home. Professors Simon, Rothenstreich, and Zelinger took their places at the head of the procession, and it marched off, trumpets blaring, some students singing, others clapping their hands in rhythm as they walked.

At about half-past eleven they came to Buber's house, which was brightly lighted and decorated with flowers. Buber was waiting on the porch, together with his family, some of his great-grandchildren, and some of his oldest friends. He was wearing a heavy, furry coat and beaming with pleasure like a schoolboy on a late night out.

When the students saw him they waved the torches and burst into "Martin's a jolly good fellow" and "Happy birthday, dear Martin." Someone blew a trumpet even more loudly than before, and Buber's neighbors in Talbieh came out to see what was happening and stayed for the fun.

A delegation of seven students—six men and one girl— moved onto the porch to greet the old man on behalf of the five hundred in the street. The girl, Esther Fleishman, went up to Buber and placed a garland of flowers, like a Hawaiian *lei*, around his neck. Then she bent over and kissed him on each cheek. The students cheered and yelled, while Buber smiled at the delegation and said, "What, is there only one woman student?"

By this time it was midnight and time to make the presentation. Ben-Zion Eliash spoke on behalf of the students. "When we were born," he said, "your name was already a legend. We are only sorry that we were too late to be your pupils at the Hebrew University, and that we have not had the honor, the pleasure, and the privilege of being taught by you."

Then he informed Buber that he had been made an honorary member of the Jerusalem Students Association. As the crowd shouted and clapped, he handed Buber his membership card as "an honorary student."

Buber was moved. With the garland around his neck, his white beard shining in the glare of the lights, he looked radiantly happy. Now he sat down, or, rather, was persuaded to sit down, and surveyed the crowd affectionately.

"I will tell you a secret," he said. "I have six or seven honorary doctorates from various universities. But this is the first time I have been made an honorary student! And of the Hebrew University too!

"There was a Dutch professor" (I knew he was thinking of Johan Huizinga) "who wrote a book about the natural playing man—someone who enjoys play as an expression of freedom. Well," Buber said, "perhaps we can also recognize what I would call the natural studying man—someone for whom learning and study are equally an expression of human freedom. This student man is someone who aspires to know the truth, in order to erect upon it a structure worthy for people to inhabit. If this is your aspiration, I am delighted that you have made me a partner in it, by accepting me as a student in Jerusalem."

The end of Buber's short speech was greeted by cries of "Long life!" and "Till a hundred and twenty!"—the traditional Jewish salutation.

"Don't you think that's a little too much?" Buber asked. "Well, perhaps we can reach a compromise."

One student called out, "Professor Buber, when you were a young man did you ever take part in a midnight serenade like this?"

Buber's eyes twinkled as he answered, "Yes, I did. In Germany, where this was often done for popular professors. But I only went along a few times. And for a very good reason—I didn't like most of my professors!"

It was half-past twelve already, and the leaders of the students decided it was getting too late for the old man. They shook hands with him warmly and filed off the porch back to the main body of the crowd.

Buber was laughing and chatting with his friends, relaxed and very much enjoying himself. He showed no sign of being tired or wanting to go to bed. But his granddaughter Barbara Goldschmidt, who, with her husband Ze'ev, lived with Buber, took his arm gently, and with a last wave he was gone. The students dispersed quietly, with only an occasional bugle call to disturb the Jerusalem night.

The next day I phoned Buber to find out if he was all right and if the midnight festivities had not been too much for him. No, he assured me; it had been delightful and had taken him right back to his own days as a student in Germany and Austria. The students were fine youngsters, he said, a credit to the Hebrew University.

"And do you know what pleases me most?" he said. "That this shows they are starting to understand what we have been saying all these years. This is the heartwarming thing. Who knows, perhaps the pact I am always talking about—the pact between my generation and our grandchildren born in Israel, and their children—perhaps this pact has already been signed."

"The Doors of the Shadow of Death"*

All through 1963 and the first half of 1964 Buber showed remarkable vigor. He was genial, optimistic, sunnier than I had ever seen him, cheered by the increasing interest of young people who often came to see him.

"The many letters and visits from young people warm me," he said. "They are fine youngsters. I feel they are listening to me. I feel they are trying to understand what I have been saying. And I feel more hopeful because this is the new generation that is growing up here."

Seeing Buber with them, leaning back in his armchair and beaming at them like a kindly Viennese uncle, was heartwarming. His family and friends tried to guard him against overfatigue, so these young people were usually asked not to stay too long. But almost always, when the agreed time limit would arrive, Buber would dismiss it with a wave of his hand and say, "Oh, it's still early. And we haven't finished our discussion." And he would turn back to his young boys and girls, eliminating by his warmth and unobtrusive wisdom the sixty or seventy years that lay between them.

A great event at this time was his journey to Amsterdam in

* Job 38:17.

July 1963 to receive the Erasmus Prize, one of Europe's highest awards, presented to people who have contributed to the spiritual unity of Europe. Previous winners included the philosopher Karl Jaspers and the painter Marc Chagall. In its announcement the Board of the Praemium Erasmianum Foundation called Buber, "with his impressive and versatile series of writings, one of the great leaders of this century."

The Erasmus Prize was awarded by His Royal Highness Prince Bernhard of the Netherlands, who delivered an address on Buber's life and thought. Prince Bernhard emphasized Buber's universality and the actuality of his message, and pointed out that he had "substantiated with deeds" what he had avowed and taught.

"You have worked," he said, "for the breaking down of barriers between individuals, between peoples and between religions by starting the conversation. . . . You have taught us that what matters is not what happens to people but how people act. You have taught us that the true purpose of life is revealed only in acts carried out by people in the name of God. . . . There is no contrast between the holy and the profane. Everything in the world, and in particular in our daily lives, can be hallowed. . . . It is the task of every one of us to become what we really are and to live by the divine power which is within us."

The prince announced that Buber had decided to devote the major part of the twenty-eight-thousand-dollar Erasmus Prize to a far-reaching study of the crisis and destiny of European Jewry before, during, and after World War II.

And he concluded by saying, "Out of the era in which the integration of the Jews produced names such as Heine, Freud, Einstein, Chagall, Kafka, and—Buber, a tragedy emerged which extinguished the lamps of humanity in Europe. But out of the darkness glowed a new flame, which we all witnessed with interest, surprise, and joy. Amid this source of light we find again—or, rather, still—Buber."

In his reply Buber outlined his concept of "faithful humanism," which differed from the humanism of Erasmus's day. Today, he said, humanity and faith no longer appear as two separate spheres. They permeate one another and join forces, so that we can truly say, "Our faith is based on humanity, our humanity is based on our faith."

What is special about mankind, the *humanum*, is "the faculty innate in man to enter into encounters with other beings." It is our duty to recognize, honor, and develop this *humanum*, which, like religious experience, is rooted in the soil of the encounter. Indeed, Buber declared, "the fundamental religious experience itself may be considered to constitute the highest attainable reality of the encounter."

Only if we foster this positive "faithful humanism" can we overcome the crisis of mankind caused by "technology which has passed beyond our control and the unrestricted domination of means that have overreached their aims." From the land of Erasmus, Buber said, he greeted the counterforce of the new faithful humanists, "those who are pushing forward and those who are only ripening, throughout the world."

Although occasions such as these lifted Buber's spirits and his hopes that his message was being understood, there was a slow change in the second half of 1964. I noticed it for the first time one late summer afternoon when I was alone with him in his study. In the middle of a sentence he stopped—as if reflecting on what he had said—and did not finish the thought. We sat quietly, comfortably, without any feeling of unease. Then he said gently, "Yes, lately I have been forgetting. Let us sit silently for another little while. And then you must go, and I shall go and lie down."

Before I went home that day I asked Barbara Goldschmidt whether such lapses of memory were common lately.

"So you've also noticed it," she exclaimed. "I have seen it once or twice, and it has troubled me."

We agreed that, without alarming Buber, we would try to cut down his outside visitors and get him to rest more. But in trying to do this the greatest obstacle was his own vitality and his wish to meet everyone who wanted to see him.

At the end of April 1965 Buber slipped in his bedroom and broke his leg. He was taken to the Hadassah Hospital and operated on. After being in the hospital for a month, he returned home and was confined to bed. The old man had suffered considerable pain and was weak. From time to time he lost consciousness. It was clear that he was sinking and that the end could not be far away.

And now, as he lay dying on Lovers of Zion Street, a macabre farce was played out by the members of the Jerusalem City Council. Buber had lived in Jerusalem for twenty-seven years. Of all the city's inhabitants he was probably the most famous in the world as a whole. Yet he had never received any civic honor. Several leading men and women had been given the freedom of the city. But Buber was not among them. Now the City Council met hastily to consider a proposal to award him the freedom of Jerusalem.

The debate on that occasion makes shameful reading, even today. The motion was supported by the members of Mapai, the central labor party. But it was strongly opposed by the right-wing Herut faction and the ultrareligious councillors. Herut stated that Buber was not worthy of this honor because he had opposed Eichmann's execution. The religious groups, for their part, complained that he was not an orthodox Jew and did not attend synagogue regularly.

Despite this opposition, there was a slight majority in favor of making Buber a freeman of Jerusalem. The mayor rushed to his bedside to inform him of the decision. Whether Buber would have been gratified by this news or not under normal circumstances I do not know. But now it was too late; he was beyond caring.

On Sunday, June 13, 1965, I went to the Ma'asiyahu detention camp to visit a young friend of mine, named Uri, who had been sentenced for illegally entering an Arab village which was out of bounds to Jews. Uri knew Buber slightly. I had arranged for him to meet Buber and was trying to persuade him to study his writings, in the hope that this would channel Uri's passionate rebellion against injustice away from mere random acts of bravado into an effective protest.

Before going to the detention camp I went to a bookstore to buy something for him. The moment I entered the store my eyes were caught by a photograph of Buber: the thick white beard I knew so well, the eyes which could be so melancholy and then glow with quick warmth. I felt a stab of pain in my heart.

The photograph was on the cover of *Daniel*, an early work published in 1913 and now translated into English by Maurice Friedman. I bought a copy for Uri and a copy for myself.

The bus ride to Ma'asiyahu was slow and hot. Sand spun against the half-open windows. The bus driver swayed in rhythm to the Oriental music coming through his radio. I tried to read some of *Daniel*, but the heat, the music, and the thought of Buber lying semiconscious in Talbieh made reading his words impossible.

At half-past one the driver turned on to the news and made the radio louder. (Everything stops in Israel for a few minutes when the news comes on, in the early afternoon and twice in the evening. It is automatic, a reflex reaction to life in a tense country, where someone you know might have been killed on the border or a code word after the weather forecast might mean that someone in the room with you gets up silently and leaves without anyone asking where he is going, because they all know.) And the first item was that Martin Buber had died that morning at 10:45.

It was strange after that going into the detention camp, built, it seemed, of dust and barbed wire, holding the paper portrait of a man who had just died as if it were a banner. And seeing Uri, looking thin and tired in khaki, and telling him the news. We spoke quietly about the last times we had seen Buber.

"When will the funeral be?" Uri asked.

"Tomorrow, probably," I answered.

"I would like to go," he said.

I went to talk to the prison governor. I explained to him what

Buber had meant to Uri and myself, and asked him if he would let Uri attend the funeral. He thought for a moment in the hot office.

"I didn't agree with Buber myself," he said. "But all the same —yes, he can go."

The moment Buber's death was known President Zalman Shazar came to the house on Lovers of Zion Street to pay his respects. Buber's son, daughter, grandchildren, and eight great-grandchildren were already there. They had been summoned early that morning, and were at his bedside when he died. His wife, Paula, had died in 1958 at the age of eighty-one.

After Shazar came the heads of the Hebrew University—the president, Eliahu Elath, and the new rector, Professor Nathan Rothenstreich—Buber's former colleagues; and students.

The Israeli Cabinet was in session, for its usual Sunday morning meeting, when the news came through. Prime Minister Levi Eshkol asked the Ministers to stand in memory of Buber. Then he himself delivered a short eulogy and sent condolences to Buber's family on behalf of the Israeli Government.

In his will Buber left no instructions about his funeral or where he wished to be buried. The arrangements were agreed upon by the family and the Hebrew University, of which Buber was a Professor Emeritus. It was decided that the funeral would take place the next day, Monday, June 14. The body would lie in state on the Hebrew University campus, before the burial on Har Ha'menuchot—the Hill of Rest—in Jerusalem, in a section reserved for former professors of the university.

Rhoda and I went up to Jerusalem next morning. We drove straight to the new Hebrew University campus. It was half-past nine when we got there, and the atmosphere was tense and silent, without the usual hurry and bustle.

At ten o'clock the stretcher bearing Buber's body was brought from the Hadassah Hospital. The body, which in Israel is buried without a coffin, was covered by a *talit*—a black and white prayer shawl. It was carried by President Elath of the Hebrew University; Rector Rothenstreich; the outgoing rector, Professor Yoel Rakach; and Professors Ernst Simon, A. Fahan, Benyamin Mazar, Alexander Dushkin, and Zvi Werblovsky. The stretcher was placed on a black cloth in the square before the Wise Auditorium, and covered with the flag of the university. The pallbearers, the writer Shmuel Yosef Agnon, and a representative of the students formed a guard of honor, which was changed every fifteen minutes until twelve noon.

And now something remarkable took place. It had been announced that all studies at the Hebrew University between twelve and two would be canceled, so that students could attend the funeral. But already now, at ten o'clock, life at the university had stopped. Hundreds of students lined the broad piazza, with its ancient Corinthian columns, stone paving, and fountains.

Young men and women waited patiently for up to two hours to file slowly past Buber's body or to take a place in one of the guards of honor. And, side by side with them, also waiting quietly in this ritual of grief and loss, were faces one knew by sight or reputation—former colleagues of Buber from Frankfurt, kibbutzniks who had come under his influence as young men in Prague or Berlin, veterans of the peace movement, Catholic monks from the monasteries of Jerusalem, Arab Moslems and Christians, German students at the university, the representatives of foreign embassies, *sabra* writers, young men or women whom I and others had brought to Buber, and for whom he had found an hour, as he had for me that first time I had gone to him.

It was an assembly that stirred our hearts: the best of Israel, the finest people and aspirations in the country, all that was true and idealistic and in search of what Buber called "Zion." It was, I thought as I looked around the unique gathering, a living symbol of what Israel could be if men like Buber could prevail. And perhaps only his own passing could have brought these people together in a silence which linked them and their memories of the man who bridged the disparity, the habitual rifts between them, and made them part of the same potential Israel, the Israel of the meeting and the "between."

The first speaker to eulogize Buber was Prime Minister Eshkol.

Mordechai Martin Buber, he declared, was "the most distinguished representative of the Jewish people's reborn spirit." With his passing an era in our spiritual and national revival had come to an end:

"Today the people of Israel mourns a light and a teacher, a man of intellect and action, who has revealed the soul of Judaism with a new philosophical daring. Humanity as a whole mourns together with us one of the spiritual giants of this century."

Eshkol noted that Buber had come to the Zionist movement in its very beginnings, and that he had been rooted in the Jewish national liberation movement. He had always stressed the value of education for the Jewish renaissance, and his fame as a great teacher had spread far and wide. Buber, said Eshkol, gave the young Jewish intelligentsia of Europe a sense of their destiny both as Jews and as human beings. "I do not know," he concluded, "whether anyone among us who is concerned with the spirit belongs to the whole world as Martin Buber does. And Buber was anchored to the depth of his being, to a depth that few can reach, in the people of Israel, the revival of Israel and the love of Israel."

Professor Samuel Hugo Bergman was overcome by emotion as he stood beside Buber's body. I could see him struggling with tears before he was able to speak—not, as he said, on behalf of any institution but "as one whose friendship with Buber lasted sixty-three years."

Bergman began by quoting the words spoken by Elisha when he saw his master Elijah being taken up to heaven in a whirlwind: "My father, my father, the chariot of Israel, and the horsemen thereof!"

Then he recalled what Buber had written in *Der Jude*, the organ of German Jewry during the 1920s: "We carry within ourselves a lofty image of Judaism, and we want to implement it."

"This was in Europe, where the Jews had a different image," Bergman remarked. "And Buber lifted up this image."

In Israel things were different. But Judaism still had to be implemented, to be realized. And, Bergman said, the students in Israel could learn from Buber how this could be done:

"Implementing Judaism does not mean performing existing, static commandments. It means struggling for Judaism, fighting for it, each one of us in his own life. Buber knew how to fight for Judaism and even how to be unpopular. But he was able to defend his kind of Judaism courageously, both inside Jewry and outside it."

During the 1930s and the nightmare of Hitler Buber had comforted his German Jewish brethren by teaching them the values of Judaism.

"Perhaps you students don't care much for Jewish studies," Bergman said, looking around him. "But it gave our brothers in Germany the strength and spiritual might to withstand the Nazis."

Bergman recalled his own disagreement with Buber in 1953, when the latter had accepted the invitation to visit Frankfurt-am-Main and receive the Peace Prize of the German Book Trade.

"We, his friends, hesitated," Bergman said in a musing voice, as if he were still wondering, even then, who had been right. "We were not sure the time had come to be in Germany again. Buber went. But he did not touch the money. He donated it to bodies working for peace with the Arabs. But after going to Germany he told me, 'For me this was an examination, a test of maturity.' "

On this issue, and on Eichmann, Buber had stood virtually alone against the Israeli public. Yet, Bergman declared, Buber's opposition to Eichmann's execution was "the stand of a great teacher."

And Bergman finished his speech with a cry from the heart, an outpouring of personal grief and loss which moved all of us as he turned toward the body of his dead friend:

"I take my leave from you. You were a blessing to us. May your memory be a blessing to us, and a guide to coming generations. You have done your share. We shall try to follow in your footsteps and to realize the meaning of Judaism, each of us according to his ability. We thank you, dear Martin Buber."

After a short speech by Professor Rothenstreich, Buber's only son, Rafael, said *Kaddish*—the traditional prayer for the dead. Then the body was carried to the hearse by a distinguished group of pallbearers: President Shazar; Prime Minister Eshkol; Agnon; Eliahu Elath; the Speaker of the Knesset, Kadish Luz; Ya'akov Tsur; Yigal Allon; and Professors Gershom Scholem, Ephraim Urbach, and Ernst Simon.

From the Hebrew University campus the hearse drove past the Convention Center and through Sderot Ben-Zvi to the Har Ha'menuchot cemetery. Rabbi Aharon Phillip, of the Emet Ve'emuna congregation, whose membership was largely German Jewish, performed the funeral service.

At the graveside Professor Scholem spoke about the three qualities which had met together in Buber's personality: he was a man of conversation and dialogue, a man of advice and action, and a man of hope and optimism.

"Buber had a profound intellect and an unrivaled depth of penetration," Professor Scholem said. "He was a great talker. But he was also a great listener. And he listened not only to the other person, but also to voices which reached him from afar. These he tried to translate into everyday language. And," he added, "he was a teacher who wanted his pupils not to do as he had done, but to follow their own paths. His pupils were rebels, which was exactly what he wanted."

Professor Simon described Buber as an envoy and an emissary whose people had not sent him. "He took this mission on himself, and fulfilled it successfully. But his people never summoned him to act as its envoy. He was alone when he fought, and the support he was given was small—even smaller in times of peace than in times of crisis and disaster.

"This unbeckoned envoy," Simon went on, "sought his roots constantly. For most of his life he sought those who were ready to let him fulfill his mission and speak on their behalf. During his last years he did indeed begin to find people like this among the young generation—Jews and Arabs alike."

The Independent Liberal Party and Mapam laid wreaths on the

grave. Then three Arab students, representing all Arabs studying at the Hebrew University, came forward and placed a wreath of roses, carnations, and gladioli on the freshly turned earth.

The Knesset held a memorial session for Buber, at which the Speaker, Kadish Luz, surveyed his career in Jewish public life and noted that he had blended theology, utopian socialism, poetry, and moral purity into a unique personal harmony.

Meanwhile tributes were starting to come from abroad. On the day after his death *The New York Times* published an editorial which deserves to be quoted in full:

MARTIN BUBER

Martin Buber was the foremost Jewish religious thinker of our time and one of the world's most influential philosophers. He was a theological bridge-builder long before ecumenism achieved its present popularity. He served as a kind of patron saint for such towering Christian intellectuals as Paul Tillich, Reinhold Niebuhr, Jacques Maritain and Gabriel Marcel. For many in the Jewish community, the bearded old man in Jerusalem was the quintessential scholar, the teacher and exponent of a tradition that reaches back to the Biblical ages.

If today the ancient cold war between the faiths is being replaced by dialogue and friendly personal confrontation, much of the credit must be given to Martin Buber. It was he, with his doctrine of "I-Thou" personalism, who showed the way. For Buber, the God of Abraham was no icy abstraction or loveless Prime Mover but a Person, infinitely lovable and loving.

Love, he said again and again, is the key to the mystery of existence and points the way to divinity. "Every particular Thou is a glimpse through to the eternal Thou." Men find God by discovering each other; there is no other way. Yet, he was careful to distinguish between God and man—the difference between them, he said, is the difference between finitude and infinity.

Sometimes, Buber taught, men find God even when they believe they are escaping from Him or denying Him. "When he who abhors the name and believes himself to be godless, gives his whole being to addressing the Thou of his life, as a Thou that cannot be limited by another, he addresses God."

Because Martin Buber lived, there is more love in the world than there would have been without him. And for him that was the reason above all others for the gift of life.

In the United States Senate, Senator Abraham Ribicoff asked that this editorial be inserted in the *Congressional Record*. And he added:

> Professor Buber was the most distinguished contemporary Jewish philosopher. Religious scholar, teacher, and writer, he furnished inspiration to people of all faiths. He served as bridge-builder between Judaism and Christianity in an era that abounds with divisive forces.
>
> With deep regret we mark the death of Martin Buber. With sincere thanks we appraise his remarkable life.

Senator Jacob Javits asked the Senate's consent to have the entire obituary from *The New York Times* printed in the *Record*, and added his own tribute:

> His pursuit was the pursuit of peace and man's understanding of man. His stress was moral commitment.
>
> Dr. Buber succeeded in weaving together the philosophy of an ancient faith with modern knowledge into a fabric and pattern of thought which will lead man to contemplation of his mortal role.
>
> The small flame that was the life of Martin Buber has flickered and died. But the light he cast will long continue to illumine men's lives.

The news of Buber's death was announced at the commencement exercises of the Jewish Theological Seminary of America, being held in the assembly hall of Hunter College, in New York City. A murmur of grief and shock ran through the two thousand people in the audience when Alan M. Stroock, president of the seminary corporation, broke the news and asked them to rise for a moment of silence.

Dr. Louis Finkelstein, chancellor of the Jewish Theological

Seminary, told the gathering that Buber was "one of the foremost religious philosophers of our time, the first of the great philosophers of the Hasidic movement who was able to interpret this movement to western Jews and the world at large."

Paying tribute to Buber's scholarship, Dr. Finkelstein said it had "tended towards universalism," a universalism which had been exemplified in the ideals of the prophets. "He was," Dr. Finkelstein added, "one of the few philosophers who was extremely erudite, and who managed to weave into a single structure traditional Judaism and modern psychiatry."

In Tel Aviv the United States Embassy transmitted to Mrs. Golda Meir, then the Israeli Minister for Foreign Affairs, the following message from Secretary of State Dean Rusk:

> The death of Martin Buber is a great loss to the American people and to all humanity. Martin Buber was a searcher of the mystery of existence and a lover of mankind. His spirit will always remain wherever men actively seek a better understanding with their neighbors. I wish to express to you and to the people of Israel my sincere sympathy.

In London *The Times* noted that "to Buber Hasidism had the supreme merit of being alive in contrast to the formalism he had felt in the synagogues of Vienna. Hasidism was vital and enthusiastic."

The *Guardian* quoted Buber's saying, "Being true to the being in which and before which I am placed is the one thing needful."

The paper recalled that Buber had abandoned Oriental-type mysticism because sporadic moments of absorption into the infinite were retreats from life in the here-and-now, a turning away of man's existence qua man. "This activist, personal, world-affirming mysticism," the *Guardian* said, "is Buber's singular contribution to contemporary philosophy and theology."

West German Chancellor Ludwig Erhard expressed "deep and sincere sympathy in the name of the German Federal Republic and in my own name." Although Professor Buber was gone, he said, there would always remain "the inextinguishable spiritual presence of this great man." "The spirit of Christian-Jewish understanding which informed his work," Erhard declared," has become part of German spiritual history."

Bruno Marek, the Mayor of Vienna, Buber's birthplace, said that "the city of Vienna remembers in grief and reverence her deceased great son, who as a scholar and philosopher of religion contributed so much to an understanding of the various creeds."

In Israel Buber's long-standing adversary, David Ben-Gurion, said, "I admired his spiritual aloofness, especially during the days when I differed with his political views—as with regard to relations with the Arabs."

Agnon recalled what he had said several years earlier:

> Many times I have wanted to write about Buber, not in order to glorify him, but for the sake of those who should know him and yet do not know him. And why should they know Buber? Because he is a teacher and a guide for the many and the individuals, in writing and in speech, in a conversation of friendship, in a crowd and in solitude.

In their obituaries most Israeli papers noted that Buber uncompromisingly rejected all practices that did not spring from the depths of the personality, and that this was of course a fundamental departure from the traditional point of view which held that the *mitzvot*, or religious commandments, had to be observed first, with the rest of Judaism following from this observance.

Meanwhile Buber lay buried beneath the rocks of Jerusalem. On his tombstone is a quotation from Psalm 73, one of his favorite psalms: *Va'ani tamid imakh*—"I am continually with Thee."

A few weeks before he died, the members of his family found, looking through his papers, the handwritten manuscript of a poem in German: *The Fiddler*. It had evidently been intended as his farewell to life:

> Here on the world's edge at this hour I have
> Wondrously settled my life.
> Behind me in a boundless circle

The All is silent, only that fiddler fiddles.
Dark one, already I stand in covenant with you,
Ready to learn from your tones
Wherein I became guilty without knowing it.
Let me feel, let there be revealed
To this whole soul each wound
That I have incorrigibly inflicted and remained in illusion.
Do not stop, holy player, before then![1]

He had been prepared for death, his rich, profound life "wondrously settled." But we, his friends and disciples, were not ready for the loss of the greatest teacher we had known. No one, we knew, could take his place. All of us together had to try to make up for the poverty we had suffered. To let the world continue to reverberate with his spirit. So that when the time came that people were ready at last to understand, Buber would still be there to speak to them.

The memories of those of us who knew him well are rich with his wisdom. I remember how one day he was talking about the need to devote one's entire personality to the struggle for truth, and how, searching for the word he wanted in Hebrew, he came out with one derived from the word *kol*, which means "all." "Allness," he said to himself and then delightedly to me, chuckling with pleasure at his new discovery. "Man in his allness. Tell me, is there such a word in English? If not, there should be!"

The word "allness" (which, of course, is a perfectly good English word) describes Buber's nature better than any other I know. What he said about Aharon Cohen was true of himself: his thought, speech, and actions were fused into one unified life directed toward conciliation and dialogue. Erasmus, the great Dutch thinker who gave his name to the prize Buber won in 1963, said that "true religion is peace—and we cannot have peace unless we leave the conscience unshackled on obscure points on which certainty is impossible." Buber acted in this light: always seeking common ground, always bringing men together on this narrow ridge of mutuality so that they could clarify what kept them apart. He sought to humanize the masses, so that individuals would emerge out of the shapeless throng. "Make the crowd no longer a crowd!" he wrote in 1919. Love, he believed, would redeem the crowd and create the seeds of true community, of a humanism which could perhaps become a universal, nonsectarian faith.

In his last years he often spoke about this kind of humanism, which he called variously "faithful," "devout" or "believing" humanism. But I think I came close to seeing into his purpose when, in a moment of inspiration, I said to him, "What you are speaking about is Hasidism permeated by humanist ideals, humanism permeated by Hasidic fervor. In short, a Hasidic humanism."

He pondered this a moment, and then looked up with a smile. "Yes, I think that is very near. . . . A humanist who acts with *hesed*, with loving-kindness. That is the kind of man we are looking for, is it not? And perhaps he will come about—not now but in another two or three generations."

This then was Martin Buber: poet philosopher, visionary prophet, Hasidic humanist. Yet there was something else about him which I have tried to catch in this book. He was a man of the border. By this I mean that he perceived like a geographical fact the borders which divided men of differing beliefs. For two hostile groups to become reconciled it is necessary for men from both sides to meet at the border which separates them. As the Japanese poet Teika says:

> Both friends and strangers meet
> At the Barrier Post of Meeting! [2]

So, Buber knew, the border was both threat and promise. Man's short-sightedness or peaceful vision would decide which one it became. He himself unhesitatingly took his place on the frontier looking toward the other side. The British theologian Ronald Gregor Smith, who translated *I and Thou*, understood this when he wrote in his introduction to *Between Man and Man*:

> Buber's wisdom may be described as the power to step over artificial boundaries, for the sake of true humanity.[3]

And as the truest symbol of the twentieth century is the border, the barbed wire fence of the heart, Buber will remain one of those rare men who both recognized it and showed us the way to bridge it.

Notes

See Bibliography, p. 235, for complete information.

The Asylum

1. *The Way of Man*, pp. 38–39.

Meeting and Living

1. *Between Man and Man*, pp. 13–14.
2. *Ibid.*, p. 14.
3. *Tales of the Hasidim: The Later Masters*, p. 301.
4. Letter from Anthony Wedgwood Benn to the author, March 6, 1967.
5. *Pointing the Way*, pp. 3–5.

Answering for Ourselves

1. *Between Man and Man*, p. 40.
2. *Ibid.*, p. 82.
3. *Ibid.*, p. 16.
4. *Ibid.*
5. *Ibid.*, p. 17.
6. *Ibid.*
7. *Ibid.*, p. 16.
8. *Ibid.*, p. 17.
9. *I and Thou*, p. 11.
10. *The Way of Man*, p. 17.
11. *Ibid.*, p. 29.
12. *Ibid.*
13. *Ibid.*
14. *Ibid.*, p. 30.

The Need to Say No

1. *Davar*, December 19, 1961.
2. *I and Thou*, p. 75.
3. *Between Man and Man*, p. 54.
4. *The Way of Man*, p. 16.

Childhood: The Horse

1. Told orally by Martin Buber to the author. Several of these stories were published in a little Hebrew book called *P'gishot* (Meetings), which appeared shortly before his death.
2. *Between Man and Man*, pp. 22–23.

The Way to Hasidism

1. *Memoirs of My People*, p. 517.
2. *Ibid.*
3. *Ibid.*
4. *Ibid.*
5. *Ibid.*, p. 515.
6. *Ibid.*
7. *Ibid.*
8. *Ibid.*
9. *Ibid.*
10. *Ibid.*, p. 516.
11. *Ibid.*

12. *Ibid.*, p. 518.
13. *Ibid.*
14. *Ibid.*
15. *Ibid.*
16. *Ibid.*
17. *Ibid.*
18. *At the Turning*, p. 44.
19. *Ibid.*
20. *Memoirs of My People*, p. 519.
21. *Ibid.*
22. *Ibid.*
23. *Israel and the World*, p. 159.
24. *I and Thou*, p. 16.

The Narrow Ridge

1. *Der heilige Weg*: quoted by Will Herberg in *The Writings of Martin Buber*, p. 19.
2. *Between Man and Man*, p. 184.
3. *Ibid.*, p. 200.
4. *Ibid.*
5. *Ibid.*, pp. 200–201.
6. *Ibid.*, p. 201.
7. *Ibid.*, p. 203.
8. Professor Ernst Simon, "From Dialogue to Peace," *Jerusalem Post*, June 18, 1965.
9. Autobiographical note accompanying announcement of *The Way of Response: Martin Buber*.
10. *Maariv*, October 21, 1960.
11. J. H. Oldham, *Real Life Is Meeting* (New York: Sheldon Press, 1942), p. 28.
12. *The Prophetic Faith*, p. 175.
13. *Ibid.*, p. 64.
14. *Ibid.*, p. 175.

Hebrew Humanism

1. *Israel and the World*, p. 241.
2. *Ibid.*
3. *Ibid.*, p. 245.
4. *Ibid.*, p. 246.
5. *Ibid.*
6. *Ibid.*, p. 247.
7. *Ibid.*
8. *Ibid.*, p. 248.
9. *Ibid.*
10. *Ibid.*, p. 252.
11. *Haaretz*, September 17, 1965.

12. *Davar*, December 19, 1961.
13. "Notes on Martin Buber," *Haaretz*, June 18, 1965.
14. *New York Times*, June 20, 1965.
15. *Israel and the World*, p. 251.
16. *Ibid.*
17. *Ibid.*

Facing the Middle East

1. Introduction to *Am v'Olam* (People and World), p. 27.
2. *Israel and the World*, p. 257.
3. *Ibid.*, p. 261.
4. *Ibid.*, p. 260.
5. *Ibid.*, p. 262.
6. *Ibid.*
7. *Ibid.*, pp. 237–39.
8. *Ibid.*, p. 256.
9. Proceedings of the Anglo-American Commission on Palestine, 1946, Central Zionist Archives, Jerusalem.
10. *Israel and the World*, p. 262.
11. Address to the Twelfth Zionist Congress, Carlsbad, 1921, *Am v'Olam*, p. 287.
12. Professor Ernst Simon, "Buber or Ben-Gurion?" *New Outlook*, February 1966.
13. *Am v'Olam*, p. 306.
14. "The National Home and Our Policy in Palestine," *Am v'Olam*, pp. 311–12.
15. *Pointing the Way*, p. 234.
16. *Israel and the World*, p. 255.
17. *Ibid.*
18. "Character Change and Social Experiment in Israel," in *Israel: Its Role in Civilization*, edited by Moshe Davis (New York: Harper & Brothers, 1956), p. 211.
19. *Israel and the World*, p. 256.
20. *Ibid.*, p. 257.
21. *Ibid.*
22. *Ibid.*
23. Interview with Rafael Bashan, *Maariv*, January 27, 1961.
24. Cited in *The Arabs in Israel* by Walter Schwarz (London: Faber & Faber, 1959), p. 11.

25. "Character Change and Social Experiment in Israel," in *Israel: Its Role in Civilization*, p. 211.
26. *Ibid.*, pp. 211–12.
27. *Ibid.*, p. 212.
28. *Life International*, September 10, 1962.

Germany and Eichmann

1. Quoted by Maurice S. Friedman, *Martin Buber: The Life of Dialogue*, p. 7.
2. *Ibid.*
3. Quoted by Roy Oliver in *The Wanderer and the Way*, p. 8.
4. *Israel and the World*, pp. 176–77.
5. *Ibid.*, p. 177.
6. *Ibid.*, p. 181.
7. *The Wanderer and the Way*, p. 9.
8. *Pointing the Way*, p. 232.
9. *Ibid.*
10. *Ibid.*, pp. 232–33.
11. *Ibid.*, p. 233.
12. *Ibid.*
13. *Ibid.*
14. *Ibid.*
15. *Ibid.*, p. 234.
16. *Ibid.*
17. *Ibid.*
18. *Ibid.*
19. *Ibid.*
20. *I and Thou*, p. 15.
21. *New York Times*, June 5, 1962.

The Teacher

1. *Between Man and Man*, p. 105.
2. *Ibid.*, p. 106.
3. *Ibid.*, p. 107.
4. *Ibid.*
5. *Ibid.*, pp. 109–110.
6. *Ibid.*, pp. 112–13.

Buber, Hammarskjöld, and Schweitzer

1. *Pointing the Way*, p. 222.
2. *Ibid.*, pp. 222–23.
3. *Ibid.*, p. 223.
4. *Ibid.*
5. *Ibid.*

6. *Ibid.*, p. 224.
7. *Ibid.*, p. 225.
8. *Ibid.*, p. 224.
9. *Ibid.*, p. 227.
10. *Ibid.*
11. *Ibid.*
12. *Ibid.*
13. *Ibid.*, pp. 227–28.
14. *Ibid.*, p. 228.
15. *Ibid.*, pp. 228–29.
16. Dag Hammarskjöld, *Markings*, translated by Leif Sjoberg (London: Faber & Faber; and New York: Alfred A. Knopf, 1964), p. 85.
17. *A Believing Humanism*, p. 57.
18. *Ibid.*, pp. 57–58.
19. Henry P. van Dusen, *Dag Hammarskjöld: The Statesman and His Faith* (New York: Harper & Row, 1966), p. 187.
20. *A Believing Humanism*, p. 58.
21. Dag Hammarskjöld, *Markings*, p. 23.
22. Henry P. van Dusen, *Dag Hammarskjöld*, p. 187.
23. Quoted by Maurice S. Friedman, *Martin Buber: The Life of Dialogue*, p. 6.
24. *A Believing Humanism*, p. 56.
25. *Ibid.*

Bertrand Russell

1. *Pointing the Way*, p. 161.
2. *New Outlook*, June 1963.

Gandhi and Tagore

1. *Pointing the Way*, pp. ix–x.
2. Quoted by Professor Samuel Hugo Bergman in a letter to *New Outlook*, July 1957.
3. Quoted by Aharon Cohen, "Buber's Zionism and the Arabs," *New Outlook*, September 1966.
4. Letter to *New Outlook*, July 1957.
5. *Ibid.*
6. *Pointing the Way*, p. 127.
7. *Ibid.*, p. 128.
8. *Ibid.*, p. 129.

9. *Ibid.*
10. *Ibid.*, p. 131.
11. *Ibid.*, pp. 136–37.
12. *Ibid.*, p. 138.
13. *Two Letters to Gandhi*, p. 5. Extracts were published in *Israel and the World*, pp. 227–33, and *Pointing the Way*, pp. 139–47.
14. *Two Letters to Gandhi*, pp. 6–7.
15. *Ibid.*, p. 7.
16. *Ibid.*, pp. 7–8.
17. *Ibid.*, pp. 9–10.
18. *Ibid.*, pp. 12–13.
19. *Ibid.*, p. 13.
20. *Ibid.*, pp. 14–15.
21. *Ibid.*, p. 16.
22. *Ibid.*, p. 17.
23. *Ibid.*
24. *Ibid.*, p. 19.
25. *Ibid.*, pp. 19–20.
26. *Ibid.*, p. 21.
27. *Ibid.*

Dialogue with Christians

1. *Maariv*, March 2, 1960.
2. Letter to the author from Roy Oliver, March 11, 1969.
3. *Ibid.*
4. J. H. Oldham, *Real Life is Meeting*, pp. 13–16.
5. *Commentary*, June 1948.
6. John A. T. Robinson, *Exploration into God* (London: SCM Press, 1967), p. 17.
7. "Three Pronged Synthesis," *Christian Century*, November 24, 1960, reprinted, in somewhat revised form, with others, in a series titled *How My Mind Has Changed*, ed. by Martin Marty (New York: World Publishing Co., 1961), Chapter 10. The heresy charges which Bishop Pike refers to caused friction between himself and the Episcopal Church. In April 1969 Pike announced that he was leaving the Church on moral grounds, because it was suffering from a "credibility gap" and affirmed doctrines that people no longer believed.
8. Letter from Professor William Hamilton to the author, May 2, 1967.
9. *Eclipse of God*, pp. 6–9.
10. *Two Types of Faith*, p. 12.
11. *Between Man and Man*, p. 5.
12. Herbert Weiner, *The Wild Goats of Ein Gedi* (New York: Meridian Books, 1963), p. 274.
13. Quoted by Ernst Simon in *Jewish Frontier*, February 1948.
14. *Commentary*, March 1966.

Talking with *Sabras*

1. Aharon Megged, *Fortunes of a Fool* (New York: Random House, 1962).

Buber and the Young Protesters

1. H. E. F. Donohue, *Conversations with Nelson Algren* (New York: Berkeley, 1964), p. 166.
2. "Why Youth Bitterly Rebels Against the System," London *Times*, March 7, 1968.
3. Malcolm Diamond, *Martin Buber: Jewish Existentialist*, p. ix.
4. *Time*, August 16, 1968.
5. *The Knowledge of Man*, p. 99.
6. *Ibid.*, p. 100.
7. *Ibid.*
8. *Ibid.*
9. *Ibid.*

Eighty-five

1. Letter from Professor Norman Bentwich to the author, May 9, 1967.

"The Doors of the Shadow of Death"

1. *A Believing Humanism*, p. 229.
2. Cited by Faubion Bowers in "Asia through Theatre," *Village Voice*, March 21, 1968.
3. *Between Man and Man* (paperback ed., London: Fontana Books, 1961), p. 9.

Bibliography

This short selected bibliography concentrates on books published since 1955, and includes all Buber's works that are now available in English translation.

BOOKS BY BUBER

Am v'Olam (People and World). Jerusalem: Zionist Library, 1961.

At the Turning: Three Addresses on Judaism. New York: Farrar, Straus & Young, 1952.

A Believing Humanism: My Testament 1902–1965. Translated by Maurice Friedman. New York: Simon & Schuster, 1968.

Between Man and Man. Translated by Ronald Gregor Smith. London: Routledge & Kegan Paul, 1947. New York: Macmillan, 1948, 1965 (paper).

Daniel: Dialogues on Realization. Translated by Maurice Friedman. New York: Holt, Rinehart & Winston, 1964; McGraw-Hill paper edition, 1965.

Eclipse of God: Studies in the Relation between Religion and Philosophy. New York: Harper & Brothers, 1952; Harper & Row Torchbook edition, 1957.

For the Sake of Heaven: A Chronicle. Translated by Ludwig Lewisohn. Philadelphia: Jewish Publication Society, 1945. New York: Harper & Brothers, 1953; Atheneum paper edition, 1969.

Good and Evil: Two Interpretations. New York: Charles Scribner's Sons, 1953.

Hasidism. Translated by Greta Hort and others. New York: Philosophical Library, 1948.

Hasidism and Modern Man. Edited and translated by Maurice Friedman. New York: Horizon Press, 1958; Harper & Row Torchbook edition, 1966.

I and Thou. Translated by Ronald Gregor Smith. New York: Charles Scribner's Sons, 1937, 1958.

Israel and Palestine: The History of an Idea. Translated by Stanley Godman. New York: Farrar, Straus & Young, 1952.

Israel and the World: Essays in a Time of Crisis. New York: Schocken Books, 1948; 2nd edition, 1963.

Kingship of God. Translated by Richard Scheimann. New York: Harper & Row, 1967.

The Knowledge of Man. Edited by Maurice Friedman. Translated by Maurice Friedman and Ronald Gregor Smith. London: Allen & Uwin, 1965. New York: Harper & Row, 1966.

The Legend of the Baal-Shem. Translated by Maurice Friedman. New York: Harper & Brothers, 1955.

Mamre: Essays in Religion. Translated by Greta Hort. Melbourne: Melbourne University Press, 1946.

Moses: Revelation and the Covenant. Oxford: East and West Library, 1946. New York: Harper & Row Torchbook edition, 1958.

"My Road to Hasidism," in *Memoirs of My People: Jewish Self-Portraits from the 11th to the 20th Centuries,* edited by Leo W. Schwarz. Philadelphia: Jewish Publication Society, 1943. New York: Schocken Books, 1963.

On Judaism. Edited by Nahum N. Glatzer. New York: Schocken Books, 1967.

On the Bible: Eighteen Studies. Edited by Nahum N. Glatzer. New York: Schocken Books, 1968.

Origin and Meaning of Hasidism. Translated by Maurice Friedman. New York: Horizon Press, 1960; Harper & Row Torchbook edition, 1966.

Paths in Utopia. Translated by R. F. C. Hull. London: Routledge & Kegan Paul, 1949. Boston: Beacon Press, 1958 (paper).

P'gishot (Meetings). Jerusalem: Mosad Bialik, 1965.

Pointing the Way: Collected Essays. Translated by Maurice Friedman. New York: Harper & Brothers, 1957.

The Prophetic Faith. Translated by Carlyle Witton-Davies. New York: Macmillan, 1949; Harper & Row Torchbook edition, 1960.

Tales of the Hasidim: The Early Masters. Translated by Olga Marx. New York: Schocken Books, 1947.

Tales of the Hasidim: The Late Masters. Translated by Olga Marx. New York: Schocken Books, 1948.

Tales of Rabbi Nachman. Translated by Maurice Friedman. Bloomington, Indiana: Indiana University Press, 1962. New York: Horizon Press, 1968.

Ten Rungs: Hasidic Sayings. Translated by Olga Marx. New York: Schocken Books, 1947, 1962.

Two Letters to Gandhi, from Martin Buber and J. L. Magnes. Jerusalem: Rubin Mass, 1939.

Two Types of Faith: The Interpretation of Judaism and Christianity. London: Routledge & Kegan Paul, 1951. New York: Harper & Row Torchbook edition, 1961.

The Way of Man. London: Routledge & Kegan Paul, 1950. Chicago: Wilcox and Follett Co., 1951. New York: Citadel Press, 1966.

The Way of Response. Edited by Nahum N. Glatzer. New York: Schocken Books, 1966.

The Writings of Martin Buber. Selected, edited, and introduced by Will Herberg. New York: Meridian Books, 1956.

BOOKS ABOUT BUBER

Balthasar, Hans Urs von. *Martin Buber and Christianity: A Dialogue between Israel and the Church.* Translated by Alexander Dru. New York: Macmillan, 1962.

Beek, Martinus A., and J. Sperna Weiland. *Martin Buber: Personalist and Prophet.* Paramus, N.J.: Paulist/Newman, 1968.

Cohen, Arthur A. *Martin Buber.* New York: Hillary House, 1957. London: Bowes and Bowes, 1957.

Diamond, Malcolm L. *Martin Buber: Jewish Existentialist.* New York: Harper & Row Torchbook edition, 1968.

Friedman, Maurice S. *Martin Buber: The Life of Dialogue.* Chicago: University of Chicago Press, 1955. New York: Harper & Row Torchbook edition, 1960.

Oliver, Roy. *The Wanderer and the Way: The Hebrew Tradition in the Writings of Martin Buber.* Ithaca, N.Y.: Cornell University Press, 1968.

Schilpp, Paul A., and Maurice Friedman, eds. *Philosophy of Martin Buber.* La Salle, Ill.: Open Court, 1967.

Smith, Ronald Gregor. *Martin Buber.* London: John Knox, 1967.

Index